WE THE PEOPLE

Building A New Democracy in Nigeria
As a Model for Africa

Edited by

Professor Peter U. Nwangwu, M.Sc., Pharm.D., Ph.D.

Foreword by

U.S. Consul General Thomas R. Hutson
Former United States Consul General at the American
Embassy, Lagos, Nigeria.

American
Congressional
Press

WE THE PEOPLE

Building A New Democracy in Nigeria
As a Model for Africa

Professor Peter U. Nwangwu, MSc Pharm.D PhD

Copyright © 2017 American Congressional Press, LLC

A catalogue record for this book is available from the Library of Congress

ISBN 978-0-9979566-0-3

Published by American Congressional Press, LLC
2414 Northtown Court
Midland, Texas 79705
USA
Phone: USA Toll Free: (877) 300-7766
Nigeria: +234 81 7114 7116
Email: info@americancongressionalpress.com
Website: http://www.americancongressionalpress.com

Available from Amazon.com, and other distributors and retail outlets

TABLE OF CONTENTS

WE THE PEOPLE

Alphabetical Listing of Chapter Authors

1. Dr. Chidi Achebe, M.D MPH MBA
   Chairman and CEO
   African Integrated Development Enterprise
   Boston, Massachusetts
   Internal Medicine Specialist, Whittier Street Health Center
   Former Assistant Professor, Tufts University School of Medicine
   Email: chidiinBoston@aol.com

2. Prof. Deborah E. Ajakaiye, PhD FAS FNMGS FGS OON MNI
   Pre-eminent Geophysicist and Geophysical Scientist
   Former Dean, Faculty of Natural Science, Ahmadu Bello University
   Former Dean, Faculty of Natural Science, University of Jos
   First Female Professor of Physics in Black Africa
   Email: drdea7@gmail.com

3. Inam Akrasi
   Executive Director
   International Cooperation Chez African Center for Resource Studies
   Orleans, France
   Email: iakrasi@gmail.com

4. Prof. Okey Ibeanu, PhD
   Professor of Political Science
   Former Dean, Faculty of Social Sciences

University of Nigeria, Nsukka
Email: Oibeanu@yahoo.co.uk

5. Miss Jemila Ibrahim, BSc
   Youth Leader and Mentor
   Acting Executive Director, Bessie's Peace Foundation
   Omaha, Nebraska, USA
   Email: ibrahimjemila1@gmail.com

6. Prof. Uduogie Michael Obi Ivowi, PhD FNTI FNAE
   Renowned Professor of Physics Education
   President Nigerian Academy of Education
   Former President and Fellow, Science Teachers
   Association of Nigeria
   Former Executive Secretary, Nigerian Educational
   Research & Development Council
   Email: umivowi@gmail.com

7. Dr. Gary Maxey, PhD D. Miss
   Founder and Development Director
   West African Theological Seminary
   Lagos, Nigeria
   Email: drgarymaxey@gmail.com

8. Prof. Aminu S. Mikailu, BSc MSc PhD
   Professor of Accountancy, Usmanu Danfodiyo
   University
   Former Vice Chancellor, Usmanu Danfodiyo
   University
   Former Vice Chancellor, Kaduna State University
   Email: aminumikailu2001@gmail.com

9. Prof. Peter U. Nwangwu, MSc Pharm.D PhD FACCP
   FASCP
   Professor of Pharmacology, Toxicology and Clinical
   Pharmacy

Senior Vice President for Africa
Global Edison Corporation
Irving, Texas
Email: punwangwu@gmail.com

10. Gabriel Nwanze, BSc FMNES ACE
Author, Publisher, and Youth Leader
Lagos, Nigeria
Email: nwanzegabriel@gmail.com

11. Lewis Obi
Editorial Consultant, Sun Publishing, Ltd.
Former Managing Director and Editor-in-Chief,
African Concord Newspapers
Lagos, Nigeria
Email: lewisobi66@gmail.com

12. Prof. Grace C. Offorma, BA.Ed. M.Ed PhD FCON
Professor of Curriculum Studies
Former Dean, Faculty of Education
University of Nigeria, Nsukka
President, World Council for Curriculum and
Instruction (Nigerian Chapter)
Email: gofforma@gmail.com

13. Prof. Elewechi Okike, PhD MPhil MSc BSc FHEA
FRSA MNIM
Former Head of Accounting, University of Sunderland
Visiting Professor, Qassim University, Saudi Arabia
Chief Executive, Academy for Excellence in Education
Director, International Center for Research in
Accountability and Governance, Washington, UK
Founder and Chair, Book Aid for Africa
Email: elewechi.okike@afexed.com,
elewechi.okike@centrag.org

14. Prof. Damian Opata, MA (English) MA (Philosophy)
    Professor of African Literature
    Former Dean, Faculty of Arts
    University of Nigeria, Nsukka
    Email: damian.opata@unn.edu.ng

15. Dr. Abimbola Oyindamola Odumosu, BSc PhD DSE
    Founder, RRHM and Accountability Movement
    Senior Water and Sanitation Engineer (WASH)
    WASH Consultant to UNICEF, WHO, and other
    United Nation Agencies
    Email: abi@odumosu.info

16. Dr. John Tor-Agbidye, DVM MSc PhD
    President/CEO and Neurotoxicologist
    Jatco Network International, Inc.
    Abuja, Nigeria
    Email: ceo@jatconetwork.com,
    jtoragbidye@gmail.com

17. Dr. Obinna Ubani-Ebere, PhD RFG CABCS CACM
    CFS CICA
    International Corruption Risk Mitigation Specialist
    Flashpoints Risk Management, LLC
    Stockbridge, Georgia
    Email: oubaniebere@flashpoints.consulting,
    oubaniebere@gmail.com

18. Okwuagbala Uzochukwu Mike, B.Sc.
    Metallurgical and Materials Engineer
    Founder, SmartConnect Website Designing Company
    Anambra State, Nigeria
    Email: pmicheal2013@gmail.com

DEDICATION

This book is dedicated to my friend and brother, the late Professor Chinua Achebe, a great lover of, and advocate for, WE THE PEOPLE. All his adult life, he protested the abuse and mistreatment of WE THE PEOPLE of the Federal Republic of Nigeria by undemocratic rulers, through his spoken and written words, and by total rejection of often prostituted national honors offered to him by several Nigerian presidents.

WE THE PEOPLE will always remember Chinua Achebe's courage and unequivocal challenge of the glaring and reckless abuse of WE THE PEOPLE through decades of undemocratic and mindless governance by Nigerian leaders.

Prof. Peter U. Nwangwu, Pharm.D. Ph.D

ACKNOWLEDGEMENTS

I want to express my abiding gratitude to my distinguished chapter authors who contributed immensely to the development of the book, WE THE PEOPLE. Listing them alphabetically, they include: Dr. Chidi Achebe, son of the world famous writer, my friend, the late Prof. Chinua Achebe; Prof. Deborah Ajakaiye, Inam and Ann Elizabeth Akrasi, Prof. Okechukwu Ibeanu, Miss Jemila Ibrahim, Prof. Uduogie Ivowi, Dr. Gary Maxey, Prof. Aminu Mikailu, Mr. Gabriel Nwanze, Mr. Lewis Obi, Prof. Grace Offorma, Prof. Elewechi Okike, Prof. Damian Opata, Dr. John Tor-Adigbye, Dr. Obinna Ubani-Ebere, Dr. Abimbola Odumosu, and Mr. Okwuagbala Uzochukwu Mike.

Prof Elewechi Okike provided invaluable supervision with the book publication process, and my son, Sidney Nnamdi Nwangwu, was excellent with patiently typing manuscripts for many chapters. We give photo credit to Vanguard Newspapers Nigeria for the photo on the book cover and WE THE PEOPLE emblem, adapted from 'Occupy Nigeria' protests, which commenced on January 2, 2012 against fuel price increase. I thank Rebecca for helping to format the book, Stephanie for developing the WE THE PEOPLE logo, Kira Gale for guidance and Steve for the book cover design. Our publisher, American Congressional Press, LLC is the very best. I thank you all.

Prof. Peter U. Nwangwu, MSc Pharm.D PhD FACCP FASCP.

FOREWORD

WE THE PEOPLE
Thomas R. Hutson
U.S. Consul General

Seldom in the history of man were more profound words written or spoken.

Just as they propelled the new continent of America two and a half centuries ago into the most powerful and freest nation in the world, so shall the profound words in the book, WE THE PEOPLE, propel Nigeria – and, indeed all of Africa -- into a new, vibrant and incomparable force for good. The book, WE THE PEOPLE, is the kind of document that will resonate throughout history—not unlike the American Declaration of Independence, or The Federalist Papers.

As a career diplomat I am very much a latter-day "Africa hand," starting in 1983 when I accepted an assignment in Lagos – then the capital of Nigeria – as Deputy Consul General and Regional Consular Officer for a dozen West African countries. That was the beginning of my love affair with Nigeria – and Africa.

"A Man Called Peter"
It also led me to my friendship with Peter U. Nwangwu, who is inarguably the most remarkable man I have met in more than a half century of travel in all parts of the world, in my 77 years of existence on planet earth.

This man called Peter, or "Prof" by his students, chose to come to my *alma mater,* the University of Nebraska in January 1972 because of the utter corruption and scourge of examination malpractices (expo) in the flawed educational system in Nigeria. Through a connection of "old boys" he was recommended to me by a dear, retired colleague Herman Bailey, with whom I served at the U.S embassy in Lagos, and whose brilliant and courageous daughter Juanita became one of my beloved late daughter's best friends while on school holidays in Nigeria.

As detailed elsewhere in this book, Professor Peter U. Nwangwu has unmatched academic and professional credentials. At the University of Nebraska, he completed a bachelor's, master's, and two doctorates with unparalleled speed. He set two records at the University of Nebraska in over 100 years' history of the university: he was the first student to earn a bachelor's degree in Chemistry on honor roll only after two years of university education, after secondary school; he was also the first student in the history of the University allowed to work on two terminal doctorate degrees, the Pharm.D., and Ph.D., simultaneously, which he completed in record time. To celebrate and honor his international stature and achievements, he was decorated in 2008 with the prestigious, "Outstanding International Alumnus of the University of Nebraska". Only one person in the world is selected for this award to celebrate their global stature and international contributions. Professor Nwangwu was the second person to receive the award since it was established at the University of Nebraska. He might have been chosen as President of the four-campus University of Nebraska system had I not unwisely arranged well-placed newspaper articles bruiting Peter's candidacy, with the result that my friend Peter -- and the former Governor of Nebraska whose candidacy also became public-- were both excluded from the interview round of the confidential global executive search process that is as inviolable as selecting a pope.

"Cleaning Corruption from Bottom to Top"
When leaving Lagos in 2014, after a brief visit to Nigeria, my friend Peter and I were traveling to Turkey on business. We stayed at a very comfortable small hotel at Ikeja, not too far from Murtala Muhammed International Airport. However, on the day of our flight, heavy traffic was all over Lagos – despite having a police escort -- and we arrived ten minutes

late for checking in. Peter courteously, steadfastly, and diplomatically searched for a solution to boarding our flight which was still more than an hour away from closing the doors. When that failed, he went back behind the office counter of Turkish airlines to pursue the matter. In the process, we were asked to bring a "dash" of U.S. $300. Even though I was suggesting that I would be willing to pay that, my friend Peter would have nothing to do with a bribe, so we returned to the hotel. The next morning, we visited the airline managing director at his office in Ikoyi, where Peter documented names, having kept a virtual transcript. This took the better part of four hours, but reflected Peter Nwangwu's total commitment against bribery and corruption.

"Corruption at the Top"
Dr. Nwangwu is a scientist in the fullest sense of that word. With his Pharm.D in pharmacy and Ph.D. in pharmacology, he saw the opportunity to bring pharmaceutical manufacturing to Nigeria rather than acquiesce to foreign production for sale in the country. One plan was to build a pharmaceutical factory in Jos. He pursued this with the legendary vigor for which he has become famous. He built the factory, was awarded a five years' contract by the Nigerian defense ministry to manufacture and supply drugs to Nigerian Army, Navy, and Air force. In the process of implementing and servicing a contract that was signed by the minister of defense in consultation with the minister of health, without any demand for bribery, it was made clear to Peter that demand for bribery by senior staff of the ministry of defense was ubiquitous, led by the then permanent secretary. Characteristically, Peter refused – and walked away from the 5-year contract.

Make no mistake, Peter Nwangwu sees corruption as a curse that must be excised at all levels in Nigeria. This will become a mantra for the movement which he is prepared to lead throughout his native land. We the people need a person at the top who personifies honesty, integrity, and absolute intolerance for corruption—Peter Nwangwu is that person. I served as U.S Consul General in several countries including Russia, Canada, Taiwan, and Nigeria. I will simply say that in my more than half century of work abroad and in America, I have yet to encounter any other person of such knowledge, integrity, humility, and honesty.

The Difference of Nations
From a Nigerian base, this kind of leadership will find resonance and renascence among youth, among women, and especially among the educated. For these people, they can look to places like Singapore and Malaysia which have less natural resources than Nigeria, but have achieved far greater results. What should be seen is the difference of how principled leadership brings vast opportunities for we the people. We the people demand an incorruptible leader.

The future of Nigeria and Africa are intertwined with a leader who cares not about his personal fate, but about the destiny of his country and continent. WE THE PEOPLE book and movement is the clarion call for Nigeria and all of Africa to cast off the desultory past and embrace a thunderous revolutionary future.

ABOUT THE BOOK

Before releasing to the public, the book, "WE THE PEOPLE: Building a New Democracy in Nigeria as a Model for Africa," the authors decided to first seek the comments and analysis of eminent intellectuals of high integrity about the book. Distinguished Nigerians from all major parts of Nigeria, and non-Nigerians who live outside Nigeria, were given the opportunity to read the book and issue a written review of the book.

The wide range of professionals who expressed their opinion on the book include a University Vice Chancellor (President), representing the academic community; top level religious leaders at the highest level, representing various segments of religious institutions inside and outside Nigeria, including Catholic, Anglican, Presbyterian, Pentecostal and Muslim groups; a seasoned political leader of integrity who served as President of the Nigerian Senate; and a veteran Washington, D.C. lobbyist, who understands democratic institutions from her experience as a White House and Washington, D.C. lobbyist. The comments of each person about the book is preceded by a brief biography on each reviewer.

Prof. Peter U. Nwangwu, M.Sc., Pharm.D., Ph.D., FACCP., FASCP.

On behalf of all the authors

Francis Cardinal Arinze

His Eminence Francis Arinze is a distinguished Nigerian Cardinal of the Roman Catholic Church. He is Prefect Emeritus of the Congregation for Divine Worship and the Discipline of the Sacraments, having served as Prefect from 2002 to 2008. He earned his doctorate degree in Sacred Theology summa cum laude from Pontifical Urban University in Rome; he was ordained to the priesthood in Rome in 1958. He became the youngest Roman Catholic Bishop in the world on August 29, 1965 at the age of 32 and was consecrated Archbishop of Onitsha on June 26, 1967.

He is the current Cardinal Bishop of Velletri-Segni, succeeding Cardinal Joseph Ratzinger, who became Pope Benedict XVI. Arinze was one of the senior advisors to Pope John Paul II, and was eligible for election as Pope and considered strongly palpable before the 2005 Papal Conclave which elected Pope Benedict XVI. A devout and humble servant of God, his energy, warm personality and vivacious laughter are uplifting and contagious.

Our Ref: 96/17/910

Nigeria is a country blessed with many people who are highly qualified in matters scientific, medical, legal, academic, commercial, agricultural and otherwise. God has given Nigeria petrol and other minerals and rich agricultural land. Earthquakes and tsunamis are not recorded in Nigeria.

And yet millions of people in Nigeria suffer from poverty, irregular supply of electricity, poor water supply, rough roads, unemployment, insecurity and deprivation of many of their rights. Many very capable Nigerians have run overseas to the USA, Great Britain, Canada, Germany and other countries.

That is why I welcome the present book: *"We the People: Building a New Democracy in Nigeria"*. The writers argue in favour of Nigerians who accept and honour basic principles of justice and honesty, who reject corruption in all its forms, who cannot be bought with money, who do not allow tribal or religious sentiments to elbow out justice and fair play, and who do not look on politics as a way to enrich themselves. They also advise the older political leaders to allow younger people to take over leadership because fresh and bold ideas are easier for the young to absorb and carry out.

These transformations will not be possible without a change of heart and genuine religion from Nigerians in places high and low. I appeal to all Nigerians to read this book, to practise and share its ideals, and to contribute, each person in his or her own way to a cleaner and happier Nigeria. God bless Nigeria.

 Francis Cardinal Arinze

6 January 2017

Largo del Colonnato, 3 - 00120 Vatican City (Europe) - Tel. +39 06 698 85513 - Fax +39 06 698 81378

Senator Ken Nnamani, GCON

Dr. Ken Nnamani is a Nigerian politician who served as President of the Senate of the Federal Republic of Nigeria from 2005 to 2007. He earned both BBA and MBA degrees from Ohio University in Athens, Ohio, USA. He is a businessman and industrial consultant who worked for Du Pont De Nemous International and Nova Chemicals International as Marketing Executive. He also served as Principal Consultant for Moredec Limited. He founded the Ken Nnamani Center for Leadership and Development in Abuja on May 6, 2008, for facilitating qualitative and transformative leadership and development in Africa. As Senate President, one of his major accomplishments was stopping the 3rd term presidential ambition of former Nigerian President, Olusegun Obasanjo, because it was a violation of the Nigerian Constitution. He is a recipient of the second highest Nigerian national honor, The Grand Commander of the Niger (GCON).

"Whenever you find yourself on the side of the majority, it is time to pause and reflect."—Mark Twain.

Nigeria as a nation has suffered terrible setbacks in its national development agenda. When compared with several nations that 60 years ago were at par with Nigeria, such as Malaysia and Singapore, Nigeria has not performed as well in its national development, even though Nigeria is endowed with more natural and economic resources than these other nations.

It is easy and traditional to blame bad leadership in Nigeria for this misfortune and poor developmental strides.

While it is clear that bad leadership and unbridled corruption are major factors in the unacceptable state of the current Nigerian economy and the poor condition of living for the average Nigerian, no one has properly evaluated the contribution of the Nigerian grassroots, the followership, to the developmental problems of Nigeria.

The classic and compelling book, "WE THE PEOPLE: Building a New Democracy in Nigeria as a model for Africa," ascribes the hardships in Nigeria, and the failures of the nation in their development agenda to WE THE PEOPLE of Nigeria. It is we the people of Nigeria who elect bad leaders by voting along tribal and religious lines, or on the basis of who gave us the most incentive. WE THE PEOPLE of Nigeria are mostly corrupt, lawless, unpatriotic, and prejudiced along tribal and religious lines. Corruption and lack of accountability in our daily lives as a people, is the routine lifestyle because majority of the grassroots live that way. But, sometimes, in the words of Mark Twain, "Whenever you find yourself on the side of the majority, it is time to pause and reflect."

The book systematically documents those failures of WE THE PEOPLE of Nigeria, and logically argues that the only hope for Nigeria is the growth of a new breed of patriotic WE THE PEOPLE of Nigeria through a non-violent nationwide movement that will use the book and the media to change the mindset of Nigerians towards a lifestyle of accountability and patriotism. The premise of the movement is that only a clean bottom can create a clean top in Nigeria. By first growing a clean bottom of at least 50 million new breed of decent WE THE PEOPLE of Nigeria, from every tribe and religion, who are bonded and united, then cleaning the top of Nigeria, the leadership, will be inevitable and enduring.

This book is quite timely and a compelling read for all Nigerians both at home and in the diaspora. I recommend the book and support the movement and its purpose. May God bless and greatly prosper the divine work of the WE

THE PEOPLE MOVEMENT, and use this work to totally transform Nigeria.

S_en K_en Nnamani, GCON

Senator Ken Nnamani, *GCON*
Former President of the Senate of Nigeria

Archbishop Foley Beach

The Most Reverend Foley T. Beach is an American Archbishop who serves as the Primate and Archbishop of the Anglican Church in North America (ACNA). The Anglican Church in North America includes over 1,000 Anglican churches in the United States, Canada, Mexico and Cuba. The Anglican Church in North America defines Christian marriage as a lifelong union between a man and a woman, and consequently condemns homosexual relationships as sinful. The congregations hold a pro-life position on abortion and euthanasia. Archbishop Foley Beach is a dynamic servant of God who has brought growth and expansion in the ministries and social outreach of the Anglican Church in North America.

Anglican Church in North America

Provincial Office
800 Maplewood Avenue
Ambridge, PA 15003

Office of the Archbishop
367 Athens Highway
Judah Crossing – Building 650
Loganville, GA 30052

Ph (724) 266-9400 • Fax (724) 266-1129

The Most Rev. Dr. Foley Beach, Archbishop and Primate

Endorsement of WE THE PEOPLE

9 February 2017

"You are the salt of the earth, but if salt has lost its taste, how shall its saltiness be restored? It is no longer good for anything except to be thrown out and trampled under people's feet. "You are the light of the world. A city set on a hill cannot be hidden. Nor do people light a lamp and put it under a basket, but on a stand, and it gives light to all in the house. In the same way, let your light shine before others,

so that they may see your good works and give glory to your Father who is in heaven" - Jesus in Matthew 5:13-16 (ESV)

The plan of Jesus Christ was that His disciples everywhere would be the salt of the earth and the light of the world, through their exemplary life of honesty, justice and accountability in their communities. They are to add flavor like salt, and give light to everyone in the community, and the community will see their good and exemplary deeds and praise God.

What happened to us as the Church being salt in the world? How did we lose our saltiness? Where is the light of Christ that should drive out the darkness in our communities?

The compelling book, ***"WE THE PEOPLE: Building a New Democracy in Nigeria as a Model for Africa,"*** is a clarion call for a nationwide movement to change the mindset of Nigerians towards a lifestyle of shining the Light of Jesus Christ and accountability to one another.

It is my hope and prayer that the Church of Jesus Christ would take on its calling in restoring the Gospel Light in Nigeria and restore the taste of salt in Nigeria.

Faithfully in Christ,

+ Foy 7. Beach

The Most Rev. Dr. Foley Beach
Archbishop and Primate
Anglican Church in North America

~ Reaching North America with the Transforming Love of Jesus Christ ~

The Most Rev. Prof. E. M. Uka

The Most Rev. Prof. Emele Mba Uka was elected at the 19th General Assembly of the Presbyterian Church of Nigeria as Prelate and Moderator, in which capacity he has served as the head of all Presbyterian churches in Nigeria. The Presbyterian Church in Nigeria has over 2,000 churches, 7,000 ministers and about 5 million members. He attended Princeton Theological Seminary in Princeton, New Jersey, USA and holds four degrees, including a Ph.D. Before his election as Prelate and Moderator, he taught at the University of Calabar and held several administrative positions for 28 years.

Book Review: by Rev. Prof. E.M. Uka, Former Moderator, The Presbyterian Church of Nigeria.

Publication Credentials:

Title of the Book: We the people – Building a New Democracy in Nigeria as a model for Africa.
Editor   –   Prof. Peter U. Nwangwu (MSC. Pharm. D., Ph. D.)
Publisher   –   American Congressional Press
Date   -   2017
Pagination   -   387 pages with 18 Chapters

Introduction

As a concerned Nigerian Intellectual and clergy, born 75 years ago and trained in Nigeria and in the US, UK, Canada and Israel, with over thirty years of University teaching experience in Nigeria, at the University of Calabar, I consider this volume highly thought provoking, extremely challenging and inspiring. Each chapter spoke to my concerns about the gargantuan corruption and lawlessness killing our country, and offered strategies for salvaging a sick country before it slips permanently into irreversible coma.

The task of cleaning up the stench of corruption in Nigeria is monumental, not unlike the challenge of Hercules cleaning the Augean stables. Hercules was a mythical king of one of the Greek islands – Augean of Elis – and was endowed with super human powers. His challenge was to clean out stables where for 30 years the dung of about 30,000 horses had led to a pile so vast that it could be done only by the diversion of the waters of two large rivers through the stables. Unlike Hercules in the Augean challenge, the dung of the bad behaviour of over 100 million humans that has accumulated in Nigeria in over 50 years of misrule, corruption, and lawlessness in Nigeria will require more than the diversion of the waters of the two great rivers to cleanse the stench in Nigeria. Bioden recently pointed out that, "In the real world of human beings and human communities, to successfully overcome 'Augean' challenges require not the super heroism of one man, but the careful, determined, civic–minded and collective action of many members of the community". (Bioden Jeyifo, "Cleansing the Augean Stables," *The Nation Newspapers*, Sunday 27 Nov 2016).

The 18 authors of the book under review are concerned and committed Nigerian intellectuals and professionals at home and in diaspora, men and women, from all six geo-political zones of Nigeria who are bent on cleaning the mountain of stench from accumulated years of corrupt practices and lawlessness that has destroyed the land from top to bottom, and has stopped us as a nation from making meaningful progress and growth. Their belief is that with the collective effort of a new breed of **WE THE PEOPLE OF NIGERIA,** men and women from every tribe and religion united by one purpose, the task of healing Nigeria, of transforming it into a low–crime, low-corruption and prosperous law–abiding nation, where there is justice, and a level-playing field for all citizens will be achieved.

STRATEGIES FOR TACKLING CORRUPTION AND LAWLESSNESS IN NIGERIA:

To tackle this assignment, the strategies encouraged by the authors may at first appear to be idealistic, intellectualistic, metaphysical, and even utopian, but a more careful reflection and analysis reveals that their approach is well-thought-out, deliberate, pragmatic, and perhaps represents the only hope for a new Nigeria. The authors begin by presenting the Constitution of Nigeria, and a comprehensive analysis of the Constitution in chapter two of the book. Nigeria has a Constitution for promoting good governance and welfare of all persons in Nigeria on the principles of freedom, equality and justice, and for consolidating the unity of our country. When the government of any nation violates the Constitution by violation of the fundamental rights of WE THE PEOPLE, such government sets up WE THE PEOPLE for bad behaviour, corruption, and lawlessness. Furthermore, when a government neglects a tribe or region of the country, they breed and create unrest and uprising that may eventually break that country apart.

A Peep Into The Consequences Of Ethnic /Religious uprising from lack of inclusion.

A peep into the outcome of ethnic unrest clearly shows that if unchecked by equity and inclusive governance, the unrest could lead to the unintended consequences of the breakup of a onetime united nation. For example, **India** broke up into three: India, Pakistan and Bangladesh. **Czechoslovakia** broke up into two: Czech Republic and Slovakia Republic. **Yugoslavia** after President Tito broke up into five: Croatia, Macedonia, Bosnia and Herzegovina, Slovenia, Serbia and Montenegro. **The Soviet Union** broke up into 15 separate ethnic nationalities: Armenia, Azerbaijan, Belarus, Estonia, Georgia, Kazakhtan, Kyrgystan, Latvia, Lithuania, Moldova, Russia, Tajikistan, Turkmenistan, Ukraine and Uzbekistan.

Even some Federations put together by the British, like the **East Africa Federation** has since dissolved into Kenya, Uganda and Tanzania. **The Federation of Rhodesia and Nyasaland** dissolved into Zambia, Malawi and Zimbabwe. **The Federation of Malaysia and Singapore** split into Malay, Singapore and North Borneo. **Only the Federation**

of Nigeria is still standing and the British are encouraging us to stay together as a regional power.

Nigeria - A Country In Search Of Nationhood.

Considering our collective commitment to the survival of Nigeria, let us remind ourselves that as Nigerians, we dwell in the same country, eat the same kind of food, drink the same water, breath the same air, wear similar dresses, trade in the same market and use the same currency, travel on the same planes, cars and buses. Our children attend the same schools, write the same examinations and obtain the same certificates. We intermarry across tribes and ethnicities as well as religions. All these form a strong bond that ought to unite us much more than the abstract ones which often threaten to separate us. In a situation where the factors of life that unite us grossly surpass those that divide us, will it not be stupid to sacrifice unity and cooperation on the altar of conflict and competition?

Growing A New Breed of WE THE PEOPLE in Nigeria.

The purpose of the book is to use it to change the mindset of many Nigerians. The authors present in each of the 18 chapters well-articulated arguments calling for new thinking and accountability for Nigerians. Nigeria badly needs some new accountable clean grassroots who can unite together and clean Nigeria from bottom to top. The book argues that only a clean bottom can produce a clean top in Nigeria.

The Grassroots Association for a Corruption-free Nigeria. A non-governmental organization has been formed by the authors of the book as the vehicle under whose umbrella the new breed of WE THE PEOPLE of Nigeria will lead and execute the nationwide movement to clean up

Nigeria from bottom to top. It is the hope of the authors that this association of united Nigerians from every tribe and religion will grow to a numerical strength of 50 million people or more. The association will enter partnerships with Churches, Mosques, Educational institutions, and the Youths nationwide to mobilize members who want to see and live in a new Nigeria. They will present the truths in the 18 chapters of the book to change the mindset of Nigerian grassroots. This united association of new breed of WE THE PEOPLE will work together through the power of their votes to also clean up the top by electing only clean men and women of integrity as leaders and legislatures everywhere in Nigeria

Conclusion: As an overall summary of this review it could be said that all the contributors to the book have made brilliant and scholarly arguments of the critical problems of corruption, lawlessness, and bad governance facing the Nigerian people. The book offers a new and intriguing proposal on cleaning up Nigeria from bottom to top as the only hope and solution for the problems of Nigeria, through the synergy and voting power of a united new breed of WE THE PEOPLE of Nigeria. Since politicians of every political party have continued to fail Nigeria, the authors offer a new platform under which WE THE PEOPLE will take back and save their nation from the stench and decay. These 18 authors from every geopolitical zone of Nigeria, men and women, including three Nigerian youths, speak clearly with one voice for WE THE PEOPLE of Nigeria. This book is a must read for every Nigerian both at home and in the diaspora. May God save and bless Nigeria through the new breed of WE THE PEOPLE of Nigeria, as prescribed and engineered in the book by the authors.

Professor Is-haq Oloyede, Ph.D., OFR, FNAL

Professor Is-haq Olanrewaju Oloyede is a renowned Professor of Islamic Jurisprudence. He served meritoriously as Vice Chancellor (President) of the University of Ilorin. He also served until January 2011 as the President of the Association of African Universities (AAU). In addition, he served on the boards of Association of Commonwealth Universities (ACU), and International Association of Universities (IAU). Prof. Oloyede is a fellow of the Islamic Academy of Cambridge, United Kingdom. Currently, he is the Secretary General of the Nigerian Supreme Council of Islamic Affairs, and co-secretary of the Nigeria Inter Religious Council. He was appointed by Nigerian President Buhari as the Registrar of the Joint Admission and Matriculation Board (JAMB). He is the recipient of the Nigeran national award of Order of the Federal Republic (OFR).

BRIEF REVIEW OF THE BOOK TITLED "WE THE PEOPLE: BUILDING A NEW DEMOCRACY IN NIGERIA AS A MODEL FOR AFRICA"
BY
PROFESSOR PETER U. NWANGWU, M.Sc., PHARM.D., PH.D.

REVIEWED BY PROF. IS-HAQ OLOYEDE, Ph.D., OFR, FNAL

This book has emerged at a time Nigeria is at a crossroad in regard to its destiny. It has been published at a time Nigerians have been told that the future of the nation demands that all the citizens embrace the anti-corruption agenda of the present administration as a precondition for national rebirth. Edited by unarguably one of the most prominent citizens of this country, Professor Peter Nwangwu, this volume engages with urgent questions of national importance not from the perspective of the outsider but from the vantage point of the insider who breathes and experiences the malaise against which the book is fashioned.

Appropriately titled "We the People: Building a New Democracy in Nigeria as a Model for Africa", the book contains eighteen (18) chapters and covers 387 pages. The chapters were contributed by Nigerians of very diverse background and orientation. But they all have the same desire and share the same passion - the necessity for national socio-political, cultural and economic regeneration. In other words, the politics behind this publication is the search for new approaches to the idea of the nation in a way that would effectuate development and accentuate the promotion of the welfare of Nigerian citizens.

In order to achieve the above objectives, two major trajectories, as far as the methodological framework of this book is concerned, has been adopted by the editor. The first relates to the exploration of the systemic challenges and problems confronting the Nigerian nation while the second features the proposition of possible solutions to them. Thus this book becomes an enigma of some sort; like the sanitary inspector, it looks for the problem and, like the horticulturist, it offers perspectival and insightful analyses of the solution. Like a beautiful mansion, its 'rooms', for in that manner its chapters may be described, can be divided into five main sections. These include the section on constitutionalism in Nigeria (Chapters 1 and 2), the section on problems of national consciousness/development and partisan politics in Nigeria (chapters 3 and 4), the section on corruption (chapters 5, 6, 7 and 8), the section on intersectional dialectics in the history of the French revolution and the Nigerian experience of nationhood (chapter 10) and last but of no less importance, the section which is prescriptive of the gravitas that Nigeria and Nigerians of tomorrow, creatively referred to by the editor as "WE THE PEOPLE', must possess in order for the nation to fully realize its potentials (chapters 9, 11, 12, 13, 14, 15, 16, 17 & 18).

In addition to its lucidly crafted arguments and the beauty of its discourse – should we expect something less in a text written by a group of highly tested intellectuals, scholars and technocrats of international repute- the entries in this volume are backed with adequate data and relevant statistics. Nigerians in the diaspora who have made successes of their different careers would not be keen to come home until, Professors Okike and Mikailu argue, there is good governance, security and transparent and honest leadership all around the country (p. 216-217).

I commend the editor, Professor Nwangwu for this timely and wonderful effort and I recommend, without any prevarication, the book to all Nigerians for in this volume there are 'tools' with which we can make some sense of the inanities in aspects of our national life.

Prof Is-haq Oloyede OFR, FNAL
Former Vice Chancellor, University of Ilorin
Registrar, Joint Admission and Matriculation Board (JAMB)
Professor of Islamic Jurisprudence, and
Secretary General, Nigeria Supreme Council of Islamic Affairs

ABUJA 19th of February 2017

The Rev. Dr. Fredrick Odutola

The Rev. Dr. Fred Odutola was elected in 2000 as the General Secretary and Chief Executive Officer of the Bible Society of Nigeria. During his tenure, the Bible Society of Nigeria became the leader of the other 40 Bible Societies in Africa and also the largest distributor of the English Bible in the world. Dr. Odutola is a lawyer and principal partner in his law firm with a base in Lagos, and liaison offices in London and New York. Currently, he serves as the Director General of Congress on Christian Ethics in Nigeria (COCEN) and is the Vice Chairman of the Governing Council of West Africa Theological Seminary. Dr. Odutola is a transparent man of integrity who lives according to his Christian ethics and beliefs.

WE, THE PEOPLE

And having thus chosen our course, without guile, and with pure purpose, let us renew our trust in God, and go forward without fear, and with many hearts.
Abraham Lincoln. July 4, 1861 Message to Congress.

I thank God for the people of timber and caliber who prayerfully put these writings together. I have been blessed by the content and the expectation herein expressed is in tandem with the thematic preoccupation of the Congress on Christian Ethics in Nigeria (COCEN) which I represent.

Most of the times we are looking for solution from without when the solution is available from within. All Jesus needed to start His ministry were twelve (12) workers who learnt from him for three years and then graduated to expand the ministry and thus Christianity was born and spread throughout the world. Jesus described us as the salt of the earth and the light of the world. Salt does not have to be plenty before it makes the soup sweet. A ray of light in darkness gives illumination. This simply means that if those of us who claim to be Christians are truly Christians and we live out our Christian ethics in our families, with our neighbours, in our churches, in the marketplace, in our offices, in government, in politics, and in all our ways, Nigeria will be a paradise on earth.

Many Nigerians are eagerly looking for the saviour from abroad, whereas, such help comes from above through means deposited in "We the People" of Nigeria. The "Doi Moi" principle used by China and India's recipe were home grown panacea for success and we today can see how both India and China are excelling, having come out of the doldrums.

The positive Change we expect to bring Nigeria back to its lost glory and beyond is embedded in "We, The People" who have stakes in this nation called Nigeria. In the words of Mahatma Gandhi, the father of modern India, "BE THE CHANGE YOU WANT TO SEE". Let that change start from me, let it start from you and let it continue with "We, The People"

Yes we are tempted but we should remember that we are in the world and not of the world. I still vividly remember when The Bible Society was going to buy a property that now became the 42-bedroom Guest House, Bible Depot and Halls in Wuse Zone 5 in January, 2010. The property was listed for four hundred and twenty-five million naira (N425m). I prayerfully negotiated until two hundred and fifty million naira (N250m) was accepted. At the point of payment, the seller asked me how much I wanted him to write in the receipt. I asked him to write the amount I paid him. He looked at me and said, "I am so surprised. What is in it for you? Even Pastors when they want to buy property for their church, they add their own". I told him that those are Pastors who don't know the essence of Philippians 4:19 – "But my God shall supply all your need according to his riches in glory by Christ Jesus". Maybe I could have been fifty million naira richer but "Wealth gotten by vanity shall be diminished; but he that gathereth by labour shall increase" Proverbs 13:11. I did not also forget that it was only Achan who offended but his whole family was stoned to death.

William Wilberforce, a Christian in government then stood up for abolition of slave trade. He met with stiff opposition but stood his ground until eventually the house voted in his favour to abolish slave trade. Sometimes, true to the words of Abraham Lincoln, "Lonely is the man who understands", it becomes a lonely journey when you are surrounded by mean of easy virtues. Stand for the truth.

I therefore on behalf of COCEN, recommend that we do not only read this book, let us purchase copies to distribute to our friends so that they will see that the expected Change to take Nigeria to level of progress and prosperity, with the fear of God is within, when everyone of us is doing the right thing. YES, WE CAN.

Dr. Fred. B. Odutola
Director General, Congress on Christian Ethics in Nigeria (COCEN)
Vice Chairman, Governing Council, West Africa Theological Seminary
Immediate Past CEO, The Bible Society of Nigeria
Immediate Past Chairman, United Bible Societies, Africa Area Board.

Sandra R. Fowler, Washington, D.C., USA

Sandra Fowler is a Commercial Development and Construction Consultant, an oil and gas executive and a White House and Washington D.C. lobbyist and liaison. She_earned her_university degree in Architecture. Ms. Fowler has over 33 years of experience in business, management, commercial real estate, and the construction industry and has been responsible for a variety of building projects. Most recently, Ms. Fowler served as Vice President of Asset Management and Construction for the National Capital Revitalization Corporation, a public-private corporation in Washington, D.C., where she was responsible for over $2 Billion in assets, and over $3.5 billion in construction projects. She serves as Executive Vice President and Washington D.C. liaison for Global Edison Corporation, an energy, oil and gas, and power plants construction company with global experience in building large power plants. Sandra's earlier career in working closely with the late Senator Strom Thurmond, the powerful chairman of the Armed Services Committee, launched Sandra as a potent White House and Washington, D.C. lobbyist and liaison.

BOOK REVIEW: "WE THE PEOPLE"
BY SANDRA R. FOWLER
WASHINGTON, D.C., USA.

WE THE PEOPLE is more than a book, it is the start of a great national non-violent movement: It is an in-depth road map for the people of Nigeria to build a political structure for all the people from the bottom to the top. My favorite line in the book is a quote in the Preface by a student "Sir, I beg to disagree. Nigeria has tsunamis, very big tsunamis. The tsunamis in Nigeria are our leaders". It is impossible to overstate the importance of Nigeria shutting down the corruption as well as the image of corruption; this book describes the why and how.

WE THE PEOPLE takes you on a journey: walking you through the Constitution of Nigeria which gives the reader a road map of how the people who are committing corruption are violating the laws of Nigeria, through actual examples of the scale and gravity of political and systematic corruption which allows you to feel and understand the devastation of greed. I love how the authors describe solutions to each area of corruption and how the people can take back their Country.

WE THE PEOPLE is riveting, it will make you angry, it is a book that you will not be able to put down once you start reading it. The book is a must read for all Nigerians, all lovers of Nigeria and the African continent; men, women, and governments worldwide who care about integrity in governance in the continent of Africa. I endorse the book wholeheartedly with great enthusiasm.

Professor Nuhu O. Yaqub, OFR

Prof. Nuhu Yaqub serves currently as the Vice Chancellor (President) of Sokoto State University. Previously, he also served as Vice Chancellor (President) of the University of Abuja from June 2004 to May 2009. He was a Fulbright Scholar-in-Residence at Wake Forest University, USA. He is a founding member and former Executive Director of the Center for Research and Development (CRD), Kano. He is a Professor of Political Science who is widely published in the area of Comparative Politics, Political Economy of Industrialization, Military Politics, African Government and Politics, and Labor Politics. He earned his doctorate degree from the University of Sussex, UK, and is a recipient of the Nigerian national honor, Order of the Federal Republic (OFR).

A REVIEW OF THE BOOK,
"WE THE PEOPLE: BUILDING A NEW DEMOCRACY IN NIGERIA AS A MODEL FOR AFRICA"

EDITED BY
PROFESSOR PETER U. NWANGWU, M.Sc., PHARM.D, Ph.D.

REVIEWER: Prof. NUHU YAQUB, OFR

The book contains 18 chapters, which have been written by scholars from diverse backgrounds; and the chapters are spread over 388 pages. As an advocacy enterprise, the book has one string that links all the chapters together; it is a clarion call to the reader to embrace changing the entire

Nigerian landscape, whether it is in politics, economics, education, science and technology, or the other social dynamics of the country. The language used by each author is simple, straightforward English that is easily digestible by the reader.

THE CENTRAL AND CRITICAL ISSUES OF <u>WE THE PEOPLE: BUILDING A NEW DEMOCRACY IN NIGERIA AS A MODEL FOR AFRICA</u>

The main objective of the book is encapsulated in the following:

> "The book, WE THE PEOPLE, is an educational tool designed to convey the truths about the Nigerian condition and to **change** the mindset of individual Nigerians, one person at a time; **we must have a new breed of clean WE THE PEOPLE at the bottom, the grassroots, to enable us clean the top**. We are eager to build a strong united force of at least 50 million new breed of WE THE PEOPLE of the Federal Republic of Nigeria, from every tribe, religion, and political party; men and women of every age, economic class and from every ward of every local government in every state and the Federal Capital Territory.... (p.385.)

The book is among the increasing volumes of writing that seek to x-ray the "problems of Nigeria", eloquently spoken in the book. The various chapters demonstrate the extent to which the Nigerian state and people should begin to embrace cathartic solutions to the numerous problems afflicting the nation and the Nigerian grassroots.

In the case of the book WE THE PEOPLE, the solutions to the myriad problems that have been suggested, among others, include a change of attitude; moral suasion by appeal or by conviction; and through the creation of a critical mass of members (from the grassroots) that will vote out those corrupt politicians at the top echelon of society (who presumably are the ones that have brought the country to her knees and odiousness). This would be carried out through a democratic process aimed at building a new society that WE THE PEOPLE shall be proud to call their home.

In Chapter 11 by Inam Akrasi, (pp.245-246), he argued that:

"Our cup of frustration, like that of the French population in 1789, is full. The French took up arms against the Monarchy and the established Old Regime in a very violent and bloody Revolution...the Revolution resulted in the total transformation of France, putting in place new political, governmental and social order that remain till today. We the People will transform Nigeria totally, but not through blood shed. The French revolution resulted in powerful change and transformation because of the united will of the people mobilized in a popular Movement, under strong leadership. The current situation in Nigeria is as bad as it was in France in 1789: "Our cup of frustration...is full". The authors further argued as follows:

"Through education and dialogue, we want to raise a new breed of honest and corrupt-free Nigerians who will convince their fellow Nigerians, one person at a time, to commit to doing the right thing in their personal lives to bring about a new and clean Nigeria. As we mobilize this force of clean Nigerians, the new WE THE PEOPLE, our movement will clean Nigeria from the bottom to top. It is a clean bottom that will produce a clean top. Our goal is to raise a critical mass of over 50 million clean Nigerians in this movement, which will transform Nigeria irrevocably. From this 50 million new Nigerians of every tribe and religion, from every ward of every local government in Nigeria, we will find men and women of integrity who will run for elected office, and be voted for by the new breed of WE THE PEOPLE in a powerful movement to use the power of the ballot to put only men and women of integrity into positions of leadership everywhere in Nigeria, for a clean and law-abiding Nigeria."

CONCLUDING REMARKS

To conclude this review, I would like to reiterate that WE THE PEOPLE is a good piece of scholarly work that has filled some missing gaps in our various unsuccessful attempts at developing a country in which everybody shall be free, in which there shall be democracy, development, national integration and the sharing of love as well as empathy. The bastardization of these universal values by crooked politicians is what has led us to be everything but noble. Our country is the butt of the global community.

I thank most profoundly the editor and other contributors to this patriotic exercise. Current generations and those yet unborn shall be proud and grateful for this initiative. I recommend the book as a must read for all Nigerians, and support the WE THE PEOPLE movement with great passion and enthusiasm.

PREFACE

During the administration of Professor Chinedu Nebo as Vice-Chancellor at the University of Nigeria, I served as Executive Assistant to the Vice-Chancellor, Professor of Pharmacology, Toxicology, and Clinical Pharmacy, and also concurrently as the Chief Development Officer of the University of Nigeria, and President/CEO of the University of Nigeria Research and Economic Development (UNRED) Foundation, Inc. One of my favorite leisure activities was to spend time with groups of several dozen students who wanted me to be their mentor and role model. We discussed several issues about life, education, and Nigeria.

In one of those discussion sessions, I talked to them about how much God has graciously blessed the country of Nigeria. I told them that apart from various economic resources Nigeria was blessed with, Nigerians are very fortunate because the country was not subject to several natural disasters such as earthquakes, tornadoes, hurricanes, and tsunamis. One of the students raised his hand, and when I recognized him to speak, he said: "Sir, I beg to disagree. Nigeria has tsunamis, very big tsunamis. The tsunamis in Nigeria are our leaders." The entire group laughed, but agreed with him.

When a nation is devastated by natural disasters, such as was the case in Japan a few years ago, the whole world would intervene and mobilize resources and funds to help the citizens of that nation. Unfortunately, when human tsunamis called the leaders of a nation recklessly abuse and traumatize the citizens of that nation such as Nigeria, the world would not intervene because they do not want to meddle with the internal affairs of a sovereign state. The citizens are thereby forced to endure their deprivation and devastation in silence.

The book, WE THE PEOPLE, begins by presenting and examining the Constitution of the Federal Republic of Nigeria, and asks important questions about reckless and undemocratic behavior by Nigerian leaders. It also asks important questions about the unfortunate culture of suffering in silence by WE THE PEOPLE of Nigeria, when a small number of selfish and reckless individuals turn into tsunamis that wreak havoc with impunity on WE THE PEOPLE and the Nigerian nation.

The Webster's Dictionary defines the Constitution as, "the system of fundamental principles according to which a nation, state, corporation, or the like, is governed". It is a binding legal document, which must not be violated by leaders of a nation. In fact, all leaders are required to swear an oath to uphold the dictates and requirements of the Constitution. One of the most important jobs of the leader of a nation is to uphold and enforce the Constitution. If a leader violates or fails to uphold and enforce the content and requirements of the Constitution, he is impeached and removed from office immediately. He has no defense or excuse whatsoever under the law. Such a leader is reckless, irresponsible, and lawless, by failing to uphold the Constitution, which he swore an oath to uphold and defend.

Who makes the Constitution of a nation, and why is it such a powerful document? When two or more people who are not blood relatives own a property, business or any entity together, it is a wise and common practice to make a written agreement on how to own and operate that entity. Usually each co-owner will make their own contribution on how that entity should exist and operate. Their combined wishes are collated and documented as a binding agreement. If they hire a manager to operate that business or entity, that manager must abide by that written agreement, which documents the wishes and demands of the owners of that entity. Should that manager discard the written agreement of the owners, and recklessly operate the business or entity the way s/he wants, the owners have the responsibility to terminate the appointment of that reckless, lawless manager. In the same way, in a country of more than 150 million people, from different tribes, it is necessary for the 150

41

million people to have a written agreement on how they will live together and be governed in the entity they own together. Since 150 million people cannot come together in one location to speak their mind, carefully selected representatives of the people are assembled together to speak the mind of the people they came to represent.

This very time consuming and very expensive process document the wishes of the people on how things must be done in the country. At the end of the elaborate discussions and deliberations, an important document of the agreement of WE THE PEOPLE is produced, called the Constitution. This document of the wish of the people on how they must be governed becomes law, the highest law of the land. All other laws everywhere in the country become subservient to the Constitution, the collective wish of WE THE PEOPLE. It is the supreme law of the land. All Nigerian presidents, all governors, every lawmaker, every judge, all swear an oath to uphold, defend and enforce the constitution, the wish of WE THE PEOPLE. The constitution spells out very clearly the rights of WE THE PEOPLE, and how they must be treated and governed in the country they own. Sovereignty belongs to WE THE PEOPLE. If any president or leader violates the constitution or right of WE THE PEOPLE, that president or leader must be impeached and removed from office. The constitution is far bigger than the ruling political party, or any political party in the land. It must be obeyed and upheld by the ruling political party in all their conduct, and actions. All political parties in Nigeria put together, all politicians in Nigeria put together, including the Nigerian president are all by far smaller than the Constitution; without the Constitution, the President has no power or authority.

In chapter one of this book following the introduction, the Constitution of the Federal Republic of Nigeria is presented as raw data. To a scientist, raw data is information, valuable information. It is from carefully examining the information offered from raw data that a scientist comes to certain decisions and conclusions after proper reflection. This preface will not make any decisions and conclusions for you the reader, without giving you the benefit of first reading the Constitution yourself and deliberating on the supreme law of the land, which spells out the rights of the people and how WE THE PEOPLE must be governed. For the purposes of our discussions in this book, it is sufficient to read only chapter 2 of the Constitution titled, "Fundamental Objectives and Directive Principals of State Policy".

In chapter two of the book, following a presentation of the constitution in chapter one, we conduct a systematic analysis of the demands of the constitution, including important questions about failures and abuses in respecting and upholding the Constitution by our leaders.

For a new Nigeria to emerge however, we do not only need a new breed of honest and credible leaders who will respect the people and Constitution of Nigeria, we must first begin with a new breed of honest and responsible Nigerian grassroots. Nigeria badly needs a credible WE THE PEOPLE, who will do the right thing and compel Nigerian leaders to do the right thing consistently. Present day WE THE PEOPLE are nearly all corrupt, tribalistic, greedy, impatient, and dishonest, with no sense of national pride or integrity. Most present day Nigerians hardly believe in any cause they can die for because of principle and integrity. They take and receive bribes, cannot be trusted or relied upon to dedicate themselves unfailingly to a duty, moral or national cause or movement. They are mostly selfish and self-centered, and can be rude and insensitive to their fellow Nigerians. This is especially obvious and glaring among Nigerian drivers and road users; many are rude, impatient, inconsiderate and reckless. Most present day Nigerians are prejudiced along tribal and religious lines, and would support or vote for a candidate based on the person's tribe or religion. Some lack the ability to debate or take a stand on issues based on the facts, rather than tribal or religious sentiments.

Many present day Nigerians join political parties or vote for candidates based on the party or candidate that will give them more money for their personal pocket. Yet such politicians quickly forget those voters and focus on stealing the people's money for themselves without providing needed services or benefits for the people. Those politicians feel they have already paid the people to get their votes; therefore, they must concentrate on amassing wealth for themselves to recover the money they spent during the campaign. In the final analysis, it is WE THE PEOPLE that will suffer and be deprived, because they were too greedy and selfish by voting on the basis of who gave them money, instead of who has the required honesty and integrity to serve the people.

Nigeria badly needs a new breed of WE THE PEOPLE, Nigerians who believe in something they can die for. The massive revolution that gave birth to a new Tunisia happened because one Tunisian citizen whose personal rights were abused by a police woman set himself on fire to protest the violation of his rights by the police woman. The nationwide protests that followed the man's death forced the President of Tunisia out of office. How many Nigerians will set themselves on fire because a police woman violated their personal right? Nigeria badly needs a new breed of WE THE PEOPLE who are willing to die for the cause of doing the right thing. Begin with dedicating yourself to the cause of building a new Nigeria where there is decency and integrity. Refuse corruption in all shapes and sizes. Never give anyone even one penny in bribe, and refuse to take any form of bribe from anyone. These are the basic requirements of the new WE THE PEOPLE movement. As we unite at the grassroots level to devote ourselves to a new corruption-free Nigeria, this movement will clean Nigeria from bottom to top.

Our message will be clearly and widely articulated by both print and electronic media; bloggers and various social media specialists will make our message go viral as we mobilize serious Nigerians who are sick and tired of the decadence in Nigeria. We will give Nigerians an alternative platform under which WE THE PEOPLE can take back their nation and save Nigeria from dirty politicians and political parties. In the process, decent men and women will emerge as leaders in Nigeria, and shall clean Nigeria from top to bottom to merge with the bottom to top grassroots movements of the new breed of WE THE PEOPLE of Nigeria, at every ward of every local government in every state in Nigeria. Only a clean group of WE THE PEOPLE can save Nigeria from eventual collapse. Existing political parties in Nigeria do not have the ability or even genuine commitment to save and transform Nigeria into a clean corruption-free nation where there is justice and equal opportunity for all.

Politics in Nigeria today is a business, a dirty business. Political parties sometimes led by a group of mafia often use money, intimidation and other evil devices including rigging to force themselves into office at every level of government. Their goal is not to serve the people, but to embezzle funds from the government treasury. Ministerial and all other appointments are exclusively for the party members to reward them for their party loyalty. Often these party members donated incredible amounts of money to the party as an investment, which is rewarded by political appointments. Often, these political appointees see their appointment as pay back for their investment, and so they steal the resources of the nation with impunity, knowing that the party will not question their theft. Very important matters such as service and justice for the people, growing a vibrant economy, creating a level-playing field where who-you-know is a non-issue in job offers. Often in Nigeria, commitment to good governance with integrity is not in the agenda of the ruling political parties, or their members appointed to various offices. In the process, the rights and privileges of the grassroots, WE THE PEOPLE, are trampled upon and violated with impunity.

Our purpose in writing this book is to educate WE THE

PEOPLE, and show us that a lot of the suffering, deprivation and abuses faced by WE THE PEOPLE has been brought upon us by the bad decisions and bad behavior of WE THE PEOPLE. Therefore, if we want the suffering of the poor, and abuses by bad leaders to stop, then WE THE PEOPLE must first change from our bad decisions and bad behaviors that gave the bad leaders the power to abuse and violate us. Do not vote based on your political party, your tribe, your religion, or the candidate that gives you money. Political parties in Nigeria at present have no moral compass, have no passion for the good of the common man, or passion for building a new clean, just and prosperous Nigeria. Political parties in present day Nigeria are mere vehicles for irresponsible politicians to rob and embezzle the wealth of the nation. Politicians move from one party to another so easily depending on which vehicle offers them the most advantage, not because they are driven by any political ideology that will save the country. If these politicians can switch parties overnight depending on the party that serves as the best vehicle for them to get into office so they can rob WE THE PEOPLE, why should WE THE PEOPLE feel any obligation to any particular party? Therefore, when you vote based merely on your political party, your tribe, your religion, or the candidate that gives you money, you become part of the problem and you help propagate bad leadership and lawlessness in Nigeria.

I have observed the many bad consequences of electing bad greedy leaders to govern Nigeria. The reason bad Nigerian leaders depend on crude oil for the economy of the nation is that the other sectors such as agriculture take too long to yield their proceeds. They want the money right now, and since crude oil will yield the money right now, they focus on crude oil so they can raise and steal the money right now. This propensity for quick, easy money has corrupted the civil service and every sector in Nigeria. Those who get quick, easy money throw it around in grand style in society. People in society no longer respect citizens for their integrity, but by what they have and how much money they throw around. How they got the money they throw around is not a serious issue anymore. Many people in society have become infected by this craze for quick, easy money, regardless of how it comes. In the process, we have lost the dignity for labor, as only the minority in society want to work hard to earn money. We have also lost respect for hard earned money, since quick, easy money makes hard earned money look laughably small. So the price for simple labor or service has become so very high, with no respect for the value of money.

This unfortunate trend has turned Nigeria into a society of desperate hustlers for money. There are no moral codes or compass anymore. Corruption is everywhere. Integrity and honesty in public and private lives are nearly totally extinct. Everywhere in society, people are impatient and in a mad rush. People use their intellect to devise all sorts of ways to cheat or steal from their fellow humans, all in pursuit of quick easy money, a tone set by bad politicians who were elected by us, WE THE PEOPLE, merely on the basis of political party, tribe, religion, or the candidate that gives you money. WE THE PEOPLE, are therefore largely responsible for all the problems and crimes in the Nigerian society.

Man-made evils in our society have caused Nigeria to be classified as a failed state in some circles. There are too many evils, injustices, and reckless abuse of the law in all segments of our society. A few bad politicians who arrogate to themselves the right to decide what happens in the country have held Nigeria hostage. As a result of the disjointed crime-ridden society and the primitive life, most Nigerians who have the opportunity to run away from Nigeria have done so. Millions of Nigerians are scattered all over the world, in many cases, against their will and desire. Many have raised children in foreign lands who have never even visited Nigeria as a result of their fear of the many evils in the country. Generations of Nigerians have been lost permanently in foreign lands; they have never visited Nigeria and may never visit Nigeria. How can WE THE PEOPLE allow a few arrogant bad Nigerian politicians to drive away and scatter millions of Nigerians in foreign lands against their will? Why did WE THE PEOPLE elect the bad politicians that created the hostile and crime-ridden Nigeria that caused many decent Nigerians to run away from their own country? How long will this continue?

In the meantime, most of these Nigerians that were forced to flee to foreign lands have become the best medical doctors, pharmacists, professors, nurses, engineers, etc in America, England, Germany, France, Russia and every nation where they ran to. We can either continue to chase our own people to foreign lands against their will, or WE THE PEOPLE can take a strong stand and pay the price to confront and fight against evil politicians and the evil culture they have enthroned in society. Nigeria can be cleaned up. Nigeria must be cleaned up, for the benefit of our children, their children, and the many millions of Nigerians who have been scattered in many foreign lands against their will. We can bring back millions of intelligent Nigerians to give Nigeria their expert skills enjoyed by Americans, Germans, Russians and citizens of other countries.

WE THE PEOPLE of the Federal Republic of Nigeria, the grassroots, the common man have the capacity and power to change Nigeria into a new nation based on the principles of democracy and social justice; a safe, decent, corruption-free, law-abiding nation where there is a level playing field for all citizens. Sovereignty belongs to the people of Nigeria, from whom government through the constitution derives all its powers and authority, solely for the benefit and blessings of WE THE PEOPLE.

Do I really believe that Nigeria can be changed and transformed into a low-crime, low-corruption, prosperous, law-abiding nation where there is justice and a level-playing field for all citizens? Yes, I do. The key is with WE THE

48

PEOPLE. No present-day political party can achieve it, because none is equipped to do so. Permanent change in Nigeria must come from WE THE PEOPLE, the grassroots of Nigeria. It is only a genuine massive bottom to top change in Nigeria that can transform Nigeria. Invariably, a changed bottom must also change the top, permanently. I believe that Nigeria can be changed and is ready for change, because many people in society are tired of the mess and decadence. They want change, but they do not know how to make it happen.

Education and dissemination of the facts is an important step in the process of change. When you confront people with the facts, the truth in those facts can change them, one person at a time. This book has been written to educate WE THE PEOPLE. We will know the truth, and the truth shall set us free, one person at a time, in this important nationwide and worldwide movement among Nigerians for a new breed of WE THE PEOPLE. One way or another, this book will get into the hands of Nigerians everywhere as hardcopy or electronic version. Bloggers, twitters, radio and television talk shows and even schools, churches and mosques will spread the central truths in this book, in search of a new breed of WE THE PEOPLE. In the course of time we shall attain the critical mass required to explode as an unstoppable mass movement for a new and clean Nigeria. We have devoted a chapter in the book on the qualities, character, and commitments required of this new breed of WE THE PEOPLE. They will not fail Nigeria.

We have recently incorporated an educational foundation in America, FOUNDATION for INTEGRITY in GOVERNANCE in AFRICA (FIGA) Inc., which among other things will support the development of the new breed of WE THE PEOPLE through education of Nigerians everywhere. The Foundation for Integrity in Governance in Africa (FIGA), Inc., is a non-profit 501(c)3 foundation chartered to promote and cause integrity in governance in Africa. Membership of the foundation is open to persons, groups, and corporations from anywhere in the world who are committed to integrity and justice in governance in Africa. Activities of the foundation include dissemination of information and facts regarding the compelling need for integrity, justice, sensitivity for the voiceless poor of the continent, and wiping out corruption and impunity in the governments of the nations of Africa, for the benefit of the common man who need fair-ness, level-playing field for all, and a society free from corruption, as a lifestyle at all levels. The grassroots, and all classes of people in the communities, in Africa, as well as those in diaspora, will be mobilized and educated on their civil rights and their collective rights to self-determination, through discussions and dialogue, published books and literature, and the social media. Eventually, a proper platform will be created to allow people with integrity to be selected for good governance through the mandate of the new breed of WE THE PEOPLE, the grassroots. The foundation is supported financially by the tax-free and free will donation and gifts of men and women from all over the world who want to enthrone integrity, justice and good governance in Africa, starting from Nigeria which is home to 25 percent of the people in Africa.

Prof. Peter U. Nwangwu, Pharm.D PhD
Abuja, Nigeria

ABOUT THE EDITOR

Professor Peter U. Nwangwu, M.Sc Pharm.D Ph.D FACCP FASCP

Every medical scientist who uses the murine model of human cardiomyopathy for studies in cardiovascular disease worldwide today has benefited from the invention of Dr. Peter U. Nwangwu who documented and published the first in-vivo murine ventricular tachycardia in a single surface electrocardiogram lead. Renowned scientists such as professors at Harvard medical school who currently use this model quote Dr. Nwangwu in their research publications as the medical scientist who first documented and published murine ventricular tachycardia.

Nwangwu has invented and published two new techniques in pharmacology used worldwide, including a new technique for identification of time of myocardial infarction employing Tc-99 pyrophosphate, and a new reliable and precise technique for screening antiarrhythmic drugs, which received worldwide acceptance and became popular worldwide. Nwangwu also developed and characterized seven new antiarrhythmic drugs, which are protected by U.S patents. In a recent article by scientists in a peer reviewed European journal, *Turkish Journal of politics*, vol.2, No.2, p.81, winter 2011, the scientists cited Nwangwu as, "a world renowned clinical pharmacologist who ranks among the top ten pharmacologists in the world."

Nwangwu is a transformational leader with preeminent abilities to craft and implement new methods of doing things better, a strategic thinker practiced in compelling visions, creative initiatives, and energetic implementation of those visions. Nwangwu is an exceptional individual with distinguished educational and intellectual capacity and achievements. He thrives in a complex, high-performing environment, and is excellent with multi-tasking. Nwangwu has a leadership philosophy that stimulates and celebrates teamwork, and empowers others to productivity and great accomplishments through motivation, encouragement, and personal example.

After completion of his Pharm.D., Ph.D. degrees at University of Nebraska, Nwangwu accepted a position as Director of Clinical Research & Assistant Professor of Pharmacology and Toxicology at Florida A & M University in 1979. In 1981 he was appointed Associate Professor of Pharmacology and Toxicology at St. John's University New York. He served on the editorial board of four international pharmaceutical journals, and is a fellow of American College of Clinical Pharmacology (FACCP), and fellow of American Society of Consultant pharmacists (FASCP). He is licensed to practice pharmacy in the states of Nebraska and Texas, and is certified by the American Pharmacy Association as APHA-certified immunization clinical pharmacist.

In 1983 he joined the world headquarters of the drug company, Ayerst Laboratories, a division of American Home Products, in Manhattan New York as Clinical Research Administrator. His textbook on Clinical trials and new drug development, *Concepts and Strategies in New Drug Development*, was ranked by the publisher, Praeger, New York, as their best seller in the United States, Canada and Europe.

He started the first US Food and Drug Administration registered and inspected drug-manufacturing company owned by a black man in America, and served for 15 years as President/CEO of pharmaceutical manufacturing companies in corporate America. He served on the scientific, technical and drug regulatory committee of the National Pharmaceutical Alliance, Washington, D.C., and still currently serves as member, "The Council of Healthcare and Biotechnology Advisors", Gerson Lehrman Group, New York, which is a select group of distinguished scientific and technical professionals carefully assembled by the Wall Street New York firm, Gerson Lehrman Group, to provide paid healthcare and biotechnology market research, industry recommendations, and consulting services worldwide.

As university administrator he served as Executive Assistant to the President (Vice-Chancellor) at the University of Nigeria and Professor of Pharmacology, Toxicology, and Clinical Pharmacy. He was key member of the President's cabinet at that premier research university of over 50,000 students. He served also as Chief Development Officer of the University of Nigeria (Vice President for University development), and as President of University of Nigeria Research & Economic Development (UNRED) Foundation, Inc.

Nwangwu has received many awards & honors, including being listed in more than 24 reference books, such as *Men of Achievement* 1981; *Who's Who in Frontier Science and Technology*, 1984/85; *World Book of Honor*, "*Who's Who in the World*", 7th edition, 1984/85; *The International Who's Who of Contemporary Achievement*, "*Personalities of America*", 1981-1982; *Two Thousand Notable Americans*, Ist Edition, *International Who's Who of Intellectuals*, 1981; *5,000 Personalities of the World*, Edition One, *International Book of Honor, 1st World Edition; Community Leaders of America*, 12th Edition, 1981, *The Directory of Distinguished Americans*, 1981 Edition, etc. In 2006, he was honored in the U.S as the recipient of "The 2006 Congressional Medal of Distinction". In 2005, he was decorated with 3 meritorious awards: "The 2005 President Ronald Reagan Republican Gold Medal"; "Man of the Year 2005"; and "Businessman of the Year 2005". In 2008, his Alma mater selected him as "The 2008 Outstanding International Alumnus of University of Nebraska". He was selected unanimously by a national political party (ADC) to run for President of Nigeria in the 2011 presidential elections.

Nwangwu is a gifted and proactive entrepreneur who has

engineered significant successful new projects in a variety of industrial sectors, including Education, Oil & Energy, and the pharmaceutical & medical device industries.

INTRODUCTION

The book, WE THE PEOPLE, is the product of a fine team of 18 distinguished authors who live in four different countries of the world; Nigeria, the United States of America, Britain and France. Nigerians at home and in the diaspora, women and men, young and old, Christians and Muslims, from many professional backgrounds and every geo-political zone in Nigeria, participated in writing this book; therefore, the central message and truths documented in this book is not the opinion of one man, but is the collective wisdom and opinion of WE THE PEOPLE of Nigeria.

Nigeria has suffered enough setbacks and abuse as a nation from bad leaders. Nigerians as a people have suffered enough deprivation, social injustice, government-induced poverty, insecurity, lawlessness and disrespect through bad and corrupt leadership. Nigerians are tired of the decadence and cannot continue on the current path of deprivation and destruction. The government and people of Nigeria have a Constitution, for the purpose of promoting the good governance and welfare of all persons in our country, on the principles of freedom, equality and justice, and for the purpose of consolidating the unity of our people. Every Nigerian president swears an oath to uphold, defend and implement the Constitution of Nigeria, the highest law in the Federal Republic of Nigeria.

In Chapter One of this book, we present the constitution of Nigeria in its entirety as raw data for review and reflection. Chapter two of the Nigerian Constitution, "Fundamental Objectives and Directive Principles of State Policy" is a fine summary of the entire constitution. It directs the government on their duties and responsibility to WE THE PEOPLE, and also directs WE THE PEOPLE on their responsibilities as citizens of Nigeria. For the purposes of our discussion and deliberation on the Nigerian Constitution in this book, it is sufficient to read only Chapter 2 of the Nigerian Constitution.

In Chapter two of this book, "WE THE PEOPLE," we

present an analysis of the demands of the Nigerian Constitution. By the time you complete reading chapter two of this book, you will most probably come to the conclusion that the Nigerian nation is in such a big mess today because the government has failed woefully in obeying the demands and directives of the Constitution on how the government should treat WE THE PEOPLE, and also because WE THE PEOPLE have failed in the demands and directives of the Constitution on how to treat their fellow citizens. How can government violate and disobey the highest law of the Federal Republic of Nigeria? In civilized countries of the world, if a president violates the Constitution, he is impeached and removed from office immediately. It is the duty of the national assembly to impeach the president and remove him from office for violating the Constitution, including abusing the rights and privileges of WE THE PEOPLE as provided for in the Constitution. When a national assembly is woefully corrupt, blinded by their insatiable appetite to accumulate wealth, they will do nothing to a president who violates the Constitution, and WE THE PEOPLE will continue to suffer deprivation and abuse from the government.

In Chapter 3 of this book: "Destruction of the National Fabrics and Foundation: Evils of Pervasive Lawlessness, and Role of Personal Accountability," we examine the condition of the Nigerian state; discussing the near-total breakdown of the national fabrics and foundation, how lawlessness and woeful lack of law enforcement negatively impacts every sector of human endeavor in Nigeria, and the role of personal accountability in restoring the fallen dignity of man in Nigeria.

In Chapter 4, we reflect on Nigerian political parties; how they operate without ideology, and the lack of discipline among party members because of the absence of political party ideology. In the absence of shared common commitments to an ideology, there a high level of indiscipline, conflict and disarray in political parties in Nigeria. This is why politicians in Nigeria move from one party to another with such ease and frequency, without any guilt, discomfort or sense of obligation. Nigerian political parties are characterized by excessive focus on capturing power, excessive individualism, opportunism, abject neglect for WE THE PEOPLE, and total disregard for the welfare, rights and the good of the common citizen. There is a high level of disrespect for rules and the Constitution on the democratic processes by Nigerian political parties. Nigerian political parties do not have the will or desire to serve WE THE PEOPLE. Since Nigerian political parties as we know them today are characterized by indiscipline, excessive opportunism and disregard for the welfare, rights and the good of the common Nigerian citizen, WE THE PEOPLE have a duty to craft a structure that will allow WE THE PEOPLE to use their votes to take back their country from the ideology-bankrupt political parties who have not produced disciplined responsible and accountable leadership in Nigeria since independence. A cardinal symptom of the disease of lack of leadership in Nigeria is massive corruption in all aspects of national life in Nigeria. Corruption keeps Nigeria underdeveloped and hurts WE THE PEOPLE very badly.

In Chapter 5, we present the first in a series of discussions on corruption in Nigeria. This first chapter on corruption is an overview, examining the causes, effects, and suggested solution to corruption. Some specific cases were cited to convey the scope of corruption in Nigeria, and the widespread presence of corruption in both public and private establishments in Nigeria is discussed.

In Chapter 6, we focus our discussions of corruption to the National Assembly. The Nigerian National Assembly, the two houses of lawmakers in Nigeria, is perhaps the most disturbing house of law breakers in Nigeria, based on the lawless acts of many members, and the size and depth of corruption in the National Assembly. Abuses in budget approvals through budget padding, abuses in confirmation hearings, oversight duties, and constituency projects portray both houses of lawmakers as the biggest liability to Nigeria in the matter of bribery, corruption and inordinate pursuit for illegal wealth. WE THE PEOPLE have a duty to intervene by flushing out all the bad eggs and replacing them with decent legislators with integrity through our votes.

In Chapter 7 we examine how corruption keeps Nigeria underdeveloped, from the testimony of Prof. Peter Nwangwu who narrates his personal experience with confronting bribery and corruption in Nigeria. Finally, in our series of discussions on corruption, we examine in Chapter 8, the roots and foundations of corruption in Nigeria, presenting corrective tools for mitigation of corruption in Nigeria.

One of the sad consequences of the massive corruption in Nigeria and the lawless insecurity and primitive environment in Nigeria, is the massive exit of many Nigerians to foreign lands. Many Nigerians in Diaspora would rather return to their homeland; many live and die in foreign lands, against their will. Therefore, in Chapter 9, we present a detailed and well-articulated discussion on "The benefits of Building a New Nigeria that will Bring Back Most Nigerians in the Diaspora." Many Nigerian intellectuals and fine professionals live and contribute to the development and economy of foreign nations, when they can be in Nigeria contributing greatly to the development of Nigeria in every professional and economic sector.

Several developing countries of the world, including Singapore, Malaysia, Dubai, South Korea have crafted successful home-grown development agenda that emancipated them from primitive behavior and set them on a high pedestal of civilization. In Chapter 10, "Towards a Holistic Development Trajectory for Nigeria," we tried to paint a broad picture of components of homegrown development agenda that can set Nigeria on the right path to successful nationhood.

In Chapter 11, we examine the French revolution as an example from the history of other nations and peoples where WE THE PEOPLE decided to take back power from a corrupt and oppressive government who lacked just and proper consideration for the grassroots. Power belongs to the people. In the French revolution, the people took back power from corrupt leaders in a nationwide movement that totally transformed France for good, permanently.

True transformation of a nation does not happen in a vacuum. Only a new breed of transformed WE THE PEOPLE of Nigeria can transform Nigeria in a bottom-to-top cleanup of Nigeria, one person at a time. In Chapter 12, we review the character and commitments required in the new breed of WE THE PEOPLE to build a new democratic and prosperous Nigeria.

In Chapter 13, we offer an interesting and well-articulated discussion on building towards corruption-free Nigeria from bottom-to-top. The argument is clearly presented that winning a corruption-free war from top is impossible; we can only win the corruption-free war by fighting it from bottom-to-top. Only a clean corruption-free bottom can lead to a clean corruption-free top.

In Chapter 14, we examine the role of the youth in building a new Nigeria through WE THE PEOPLE movement. The Nigerian youth are vulnerable, and are disproportionately affected by bad leadership in Nigeria. Increasingly poor educational systems, unemployment, unlevel playing field, lack of social justice and poor economic environment for entrepreneurial initiatives and development constitute severe stumbling blocks for the youth of Nigeria. Several remedies and coping mechanisms are offered, including the potent role the Nigerian youth can play through the WE THE PEOPLE movement to produce a new, corrupt-free, prosperous and safe Nigeria.

In Chapter 15, "The New Breed of We the People: Cultivating the Spirit and Mindset of Excellence in the Nigerian Youth/Grassroots," we examine the elements and tools required to build the spirit and mindset of excellence in the new breed of Nigerian Youth/Grassroots. The practical counsel offered would help grow a new breed of Nigerian Youths and grassroots that will empower the transformation process in Nigeria.

The educational system in Nigeria has degenerated badly at all levels. In Chapter 16, we examine the many man-made problems with Nigeria's Educational System, suggesting ways of transforming the Nigerian educational system for a more prosperous and progressive Nigeria. The student is not in the center of the educational process in Nigeria today. In many classrooms, the entire education experience is focused on the teacher, and the class is designed for listening to the teacher, rather than engaging the student in learning. The chapter clearly articulates the difference between schooling and education, and shows what we should do as a nation to engage in education, instead of schooling, for proper development of our youths for the benefit of the Nigerian society.

In chapter 17, we examine the important and robust subject of "Intellectuals as Nation Builders". Cerebral intellectuals with integrity who have blessed their respective nations by their intellectual prowess and preparations have led most civilized and progressive nations of the world. Nigeria has produced many intellectuals, but Nigeria has not been fortunate to have a cerebral intellectual with integrity as leader of Nigeria since independence. Cerebral intellectuals with integrity have shied away from leadership aspirations in Nigeria because the political process in Nigeria is mostly a very dirty game. Furthermore, the amount of money required to engage in the political campaign process in Nigeria is intimidating, unreasonable, and a great discouragement to the intellectual class who will not vainly waste such amount of money, even if they had it. Nigeria badly needs to give cerebral intellectuals with integrity the opportunity to transform Nigeria for good permanently by serving in many leadership positions including President, state governors, and legislatures. An important part of the WE THE PEOPLE movement is to recruit such Nigerian intellectuals at home and in the diaspora, support them, and facilitate the process of putting them in positions of leadership nationwide to save the Nigerian nation and be a blessing to WE THE PEOPLE through good governance.

We conclude the book with a discussion in chapter 18 on the A, B, C of how to transform Nigeria permanently. This discussion outlines 8 problems, in alphabetical order, that we must confront and solve to create a new Nigeria, including: Agriculture and Food Security; Bribery, Corruption, and Rule of Law; Crime and Insecurity;

Democracy and National Development; Economy and Unemployment; (in)Frastructural Development and Residency Rights; Good Education (not schooling) and Youth Development; Healthcare and Protection of Life. We discuss the needs of Nigeria with these problems, but also offer workable solutions to the problems in a manner that will transform the Nigeria nation. Nigeria needs a qualified cerebral intellectual President, with character, integrity, and a strong and unyielding will to do the right thing for the nation, and for WE THE PEOPLE, consistently without fear or favour. Nigeria can be a great, clean, safe, and corrupt-free nation that will be celebrated and respected everywhere in the world.

In the Postface of this book following the last chapter, we discuss the WE THE PEOPLE movement. The movement seeks to grow a new breed of WE THE PEOPLE of Nigeria that cuts across tribal, religious, and political inclinations; men and women of all ages and economic status who will commit to doing the right things in their daily lives, free from corrupt tendencies; men and women who will join in a nationwide movement to clean-up Nigeria, one person at a time, in a bottom-to-top transformation of Nigeria. Eventually, a clean bottom will lead to a clean top, as WE THE PEOPLE use the power of our votes to select clean men and women of integrity for leadership positions nationwide, as we take back our country from corrupt politicians and leaders who abuse WE THE PEOPLE. Additional details are provided in the Postface, including how to become a member of the WE THE PEOPLE movement. We have registered a non-governmental organization (NGO), "THE PEOPLE'S GRASSROOTS ASSOCIATION FOR A CORRUPTION-FREE NIGERIA". This NGO is the nationwide movement of WE THE PEOPLE. Our goal is to raise at least 50 million united Nigerians of every tribe and religion, men and women, young and old, from every ward, every local government, every state, every geo-political zone of Nigeria; we want to raise this united force of a new-breed of Nigerians within the next two years, for a corruption-free Nigeria through a potent nationwide movement that will include proper and careful exercise of our voting rights to elect honest, decent, intellectuals with integrity as leaders and legislatures for a new and transformed Nigeria of our dreams.

Following the Postface, we present the WE THE PEOPLE PLEDGE. This pledge is a one-page solemn document, which the new breed of WE THE PEOPLE must embrace and practice in their daily lives. To participate in the WE THE PEOPLE movement and join the NGO, "THE PEOPLE'S GRASSROOTS ASSOCIATION FOR A CORRUPTION-FREE NIGERIA, each member must embrace and commit to the WE THE PEOPLE PLEDGE. The pledge binds us together, and binds us as a group to the new corruption-free Nigeria of our deepest dreams.

Finally, we present the aims and objectives of our registered non-governmental organization, "THE PEOPLE'S GRASSROOTS ASSOCIATION FOR A CORRUPTION-FREE NIGERIA". This NGO is the official registered name of the WE THE PEOPLE movement. Membership is open to all Nigerians of every tribe and religion throughout Nigeria and in the Diaspora. Interested non-Nigerians are welcome to join the association as associate members with full rights and benefits in the movement for a corruption-free Nigeria.

Prof. Peter U. Nwangwu, MSc Pharm.D PhD FACCP FASCP

FOR, AND ON BEHALF OF ALL THE AUTHORS

CHAPTER 1

Constitution of the Federal Republic of Nigeria 1999

We the people of the Federal Republic of Nigeria

Having firmly and solemnly resolve, to live in unity and harmony as one indivisible and indissoluble sovereign nation under God, dedicated to the promotion of inter-African solidarity, world peace, international co-operation and understanding

And to provide for a Constitution for the purpose of promoting the good government and welfare of all persons in our country, on the principles of freedom, equality and justice, and for the purpose of consolidating the unity of our people

Do hereby make, enact and give to ourselves the following Constitution:-

Chapter II

Fundamental Objectives and Directive Principles of State Policy

13. It shall be the duty and responsibility of all organs of government, and of all authorities and persons, exercising legislative, executive or judicial powers, to conform to, observe and apply the provisions of this Chapter of this Constitution.

14. (1) The Federal Republic of Nigeria shall be a State based on the principles of democracy and social justice.

(2) It is hereby, accordingly, declared that:

(a) sovereignty belongs to the people of Nigeria from whom government through this Constitution derives all its powers and authority;

(b) the security and welfare of the people shall be the primary purpose of government: and

(c) the participation by the people in their government shall be ensured in accordance with the provisions of this Constitution.

(3) The composition of the Government of the Federation or any of its agencies and the conduct of its affairs shall be carried out in such a manner as to reflect the federal character of Nigeria and the need to promote national unity, and also to command national loyalty, thereby ensuring that there shall be no predominance of persons from a few State or from a few ethnic or other sectional groups in that

Government or in any of its agencies.

(4)   The composition of the Government of a State, a local government council, or any of the agencies of such Government or council, and the conduct of the affairs of the Government or council or such agencies shall be carried out in such manner as to recognise the diversity of the people within its area of authority and the need to promote a sense of belonging and loyalty among all the people of the Federation.

15.   (1) The motto of the Federal Republic of Nigeria shall be Unity and Faith, Peace and Progress.

(2)   Accordingly, national integration shall be actively encouraged, whilst discrimination on the grounds of place of origin, sex, religion, status, ethnic or linguistic association or ties shall be prohibited.

(3)   For the purpose of promoting national integration, it shall be the duty of the State to:

(a)   provide adequate facilities for and encourage free mobility of people, goods and services throughout the Federation.

(b)   secure full residence rights for every citizen in all parts of the Federation.

(c)   encourage inter-marriage among persons from different places of origin, or of different religious, ethnic or linguistic association or ties; and

(d)   promote or encourage the formation of associations that cut across ethnic, linguistic, religious and or other sectional barriers.

(4)   The State shall foster a feeling of belonging and of

involvement among the various people of the Federation, to the end that loyalty to the nation shall override sectional loyalties.

(5)   The State shall abolish all corrupt practices and abuse of power.

16.   (1) The State shall, within the context of the ideals and objectives for which provisions are made in this Constitution.

(a)   harness the resources of the nation and promote national prosperity and an efficient, a dynamic and selfreliant economy;

(b)   control the national economy in such manner as to secure the maximum welfare, freedom and happiness of every citizen on the basis of social justice and equality of status and opportunity;

(c)   without prejudice to its right to operate or participate in areas of the economy, other than the major sectors of the economy, manage and operate the major sectors of the economy;

(d)   without prejudice to the right of any person to participate in areas of the economy within the major sector of the economy, protect the right of every citizen to engage in any economic activities outside the major sectors of the economy.

(2)   The State shall direct its policy towards ensuring:

(a)   the promotion of a planned and balanced economic development;

(b)   that the material resources of the nation are harnessed and distributed as
best as possible to serve the common good;

(c)   that the economic system is not operated in such a manner as to permit the concentration of wealth or the means of production and exchange in the hands of few individuals or of a group; and

(d)   that suitable and adequate shelter, suitable and adequate food, reasonable national minimum living wage, old age care and pensions, and unemployment, sick benefits and welfare of the disabled are provided for all citizens.

(3)   A body shall be set up by an Act of the National Assembly which shall have power;

(a)   to review, from time to time, the ownership and control of business enterprises operating in Nigeria and make recommendations to the President on same; and

(b)   to administer any law for the regulation of the ownership and control of such enterprises.

(4)   For the purposes of subsection (1) of this section -

(a)   the reference to the "major sectors of the economy" shall be construed as a reference to such economic activities as may, from time to time, be declared by a resolution of each House of the National Assembly to be managed and operated exclusively by the Government of the Federation, and until a resolution to the contrary is made by the National Assembly, economic activities being operated exclusively by the Government of the Federation on the date immediately preceding the day when this section comes into force, whether directly or through the agencies of a

statutory or other corporation or company, shall be deemed to be major sectors of the economy;

(b)   "economic activities" includes activities directly concerned with the production, distribution and exchange of whether or of goods and services; and

(c)   "participate" includes the rendering of services and supplying of goods.

17. (1) The State social order is founded on ideals of Freedom, Equality and Justice.

(2) In furtherance of the social order-

(a)   every citizen shall have equality of rights, obligations and opportunities before the law;

(b)   the sanctity of the human person shall be recognised and human dignity shall be maintained and enhanced;

(c)   governmental actions shall be humane;

(d)   exploitation of human or natural resources in any form whatsoever for reasons, other than the good of the community, shall be prevented; and

(e)   the independence, impartiality and integrity of courts of law, and easy accessibility thereto shall be secured and maintained.

(3) The State shall direct its policy towards ensuring that-

(a)   all citizens, without discrimination on any group whatsoever, have the opportunity for securing adequate means of livelihood as well as adequate opportunity to secure suitable employment;

(b)   conditions of work are just and humane, and that there are adequate facilities for leisure and for social, religious and cultural life;

(c)   the health, safety and welfare of all persons in employment are safeguarded and not endangered or abused;

(d)   there are adequate medical and health facilities for all persons:

(e)   there is equal pay for equal work without discrimination on account of sex, or on any other ground whatsoever;

(f)   children, young persons and the aged are protected against any exploitation whatsoever, and against moral and material neglect;

(g)   provision is made for public assistance in deserving cases or other conditions of need; and (h) the evolution and promotion of family life is encouraged.

18.   (1) Government shall direct its policy towards ensuring that there are equal and adequate educational opportunities at all levels.

(2)   Government shall promote science and technology

(3)   Government shall strive to eradicate illiteracy; and to this end Government shall as and when practicable provide

(a)   free, compulsory and universal primary education;

(b)   free secondary education;

(c)   free university education; and

(d)   free adult literacy programme.

19.   The foreign policy objectives shall be -

(a)   promotion and protection of the national interest;

(b)   promotion of African integration and support for African unity;

(c)   promotion of international co-operation for the consolidation of universal peace and mutual respect among all nations and elimination of discrimination in all its manifestations;

(d)   respect for international law and treaty obligations as well as the seeking of settlement of international disputes by negotiation, mediation, conciliation, arbitration and adjudication; and

(e)   promotion of a just world economic order.

20.   The State shall protect and improve the environment and safeguard the water, air and land, forest and wild life of Nigeria.

21.   The State shall -

(a)   protect, preserve and promote the Nigerian cultures which enhance human dignity and are consistent with the fundamental objectives as provided in this Chapter; and

(b)   encourage development of technological and scientific studies which enhance cultural values.

22.   The press, radio, television and other agencies of the mass media shall at all times be free to uphold the fundamental objectives contained in this Chapter and uphold the responsibility and accountability of the Government to the people.

23.   The national ethics shall be Discipline, Integrity, Dignity of Labour, Social, Justice, Religious Tolerance, Self-reliance and Patriotism.

24.   It shall be the duty of every citizen to -

(a)   abide by this Constitution, respect its ideals and its institutions, the National Flag, the National Anthem, the National Pledge, and legitimate authorities;

(b)   help to enhance the power, prestige and good name of Nigeria, defend Nigeria and render such national service as may be required;

(c)   respect the dignity of other citizens and the rights and legitimate interests of others and live in unity and harmony and in the spirit of common brotherhood;

(d)   make positive and useful contribution to the advancement, progress and well-being of the community where he resides;

(e)   render assistance to appropriate and lawful agencies in the maintenance of law and order; and

(f)   declare his income honestly to appropriate and lawful agencies and pay his tax promptly.

Chapter IV
Fundamental Rights

33.   (1) Every person has a right to life, and no one shall be deprived intentionally of his life, save in execution of the sentence of a court in respect of a criminal offence of which he has been found guilty in Nigeria.

(2)   A person shall not be regarded as having been deprived of his life in contravention of this section, if he dies as a result of the use, to such extent and in such circumstances as are permitted by law, of such force as is reasonably necessary -

(a)   for the defence of any person from unlawful violence or for the defence of property:

(b)   in order to effect a lawful arrest or to prevent the escape of a person lawfully detained; or

(c)   for the purpose of suppressing a riot, insurrection or mutiny.

34.   (1) Every individual is entitled to respect for the dignity of his person, and accordingly -

(a)   no person shall be subject to torture or to inhuman or degrading treatment;

(b)   no person shall he held in slavery or servitude; and

(c)   no person shall be required to perform forced of compulsory labour.

(2)   for the purposes of subsection (1) (c) of this section, "forced or
compulsory labour" does not include -

(a)   any labour required in consequence of the sentence or order of a court;

(b)   any labour required of members of the armed forces of the Federation or the Nigeria Police Force in pursuance of their duties as such;

(c)   in the case of persons who have conscientious objections to service in the armed forces of the Federation, any labour required instead of such service;

(d)   any labour required which is reasonably necessary in the event of any emergency or calamity threatening the life or wellbeing of the community; or

(e)   any labour or service that forms part of
-

(i)   normal communal or other civic obligations of the well-being of the community.

(ii)   such compulsory national service in the armed forces of the Federation as may be prescribed by an Act of the National Assembly, or

(iii)   such compulsory national service which forms part of the education and training of citizens of Nigeria as may be prescribed by an Act of the National Assembly.

35.   (1) Every person shall be entitled to his personal liberty and no person shall be deprived of such liberty save in the following cases and in accordance with a procedure permitted by law -

(a)   in execution of the sentence or order of a court in respect of a criminal offence of which he has been found guilty;

(b)   by reason of his failure to comply with the order of a court or in order to secure the fulfilment of any obligation imposed upon him by law;

(c)   for the purpose of bringing him before a court in execution of the order of a court or upon reasonable suspicion of his having committed a criminal offence, or to such extent as may be reasonably necessary to prevent his committing a criminal offence;

(d)   in the case of a person who has not attained the age of eighteen years for the purpose of his education or welfare;

(e)   in the case of persons suffering from infectious or contagious disease, persons of unsound mind, persons addicted to drugs or alcohol or vagrants, for the purpose of their care or treatment or the protection of the community; or

(f)   for the purpose of preventing the unlawful entry of any person into Nigeria or of effecting the expulsion, extradition or other lawful removal from Nigeria of any person or the taking of proceedings relating thereto:

Provided that a person who is charged with an offence and who has been detained in lawful custody awaiting trial shall not continue to be kept in such detention for a period longer than the maximum period of imprisonment prescribed for the offence.

(2)   Any person who is arrested or detained shall have the right to remain silent or avoid answering any question until after consultation with a legal practitioner or any other person of his own choice.

(3)   Any person who is arrested or detained shall be informed in writing within twenty-four hours (and in a language that he understands) of the facts and grounds for his arrest or detention.

(4)   Any person who is arrested or detained in accordance with subsection (1) (c) of this section shall be brought before a court of law within a reasonable time, and if he is not tried within a period of -

(a)   two months from the date of his arrest or detention in the case of a person who is in custody or is not entitled to bail; or

(b)   three months from the date of his arrest or detention in the case of a person who has been released on bail, he shall (without prejudice to any further proceedings that may be brought against him) be released either unconditionally or upon such conditions as are reasonably necessary to ensure that he appears for trial at a later date.

(5)   In subsection (4) of this section, the expression "a

reasonable time" means -

(a) in the case of an arrest or detention in any place where there is a court of competent jurisdiction within a radius of forty kilometres, a period of one day; and

(b) in any other case, a period of two days or such longer period as in the circumstances may be considered by the court to be reasonable.

(6) Any person who is unlawfully arrested or detained shall be entitled to compensation and public apology from the appropriate authority or person; and in this subsection, "the appropriate authority or person" means an authority or person specified by law.

(7) Nothing in this section shall be construed -

(a) in relation to subsection (4) of this section, as applying in the case of a person arrested or detained upon reasonable suspicion of having committed a capital offence; and

(b) as invalidating any law by reason only that it authorises the detention for a period not exceeding three months of a member of the armed forces of the federation or a member of the Nigeria Police Force in execution of a sentence imposed by an officer of the armed forces of the Federation or of the Nigeria police force, in respect of an offence punishable by such detention of which he has been found guilty.

36. (1) In the determination of his civil rights and obligations, including any question or determination by or against any government or authority, a person shall be entitled to a fair hearing within a reasonable time by a court or other tribunal established by law and constituted in such manner as to secure its independence and impartiality.

(2) Without prejudice to the foregoing provisions of this section, a law shall not be invalidated by reason only that it confers on any government or authority power to determine questions arising in the administration of a law that affects or may affect the civil rights and obligations of any person if such law -

(a)   provides for an opportunity for the persons whose rights and obligations may be affected to make representations to the administering authority before that authority makes the decision affecting that person; and

(b)   contains no provision making the determination of the administering authority final and conclusive.

(3)   The proceedings of a court or the proceedings of any tribunal relating to the matters mentioned in subsection (1) of this section (including the announcement of the decisions of the court or tribunal) shall be held in public.

(4)   Whenever any person is charged with a criminal offence, he shall, unless the charge is withdrawn, be entitled to a fair hearing in public within a reasonable time by a court or tribunal:

Provided that -

(a)   a court or such a tribunal may exclude from its proceedings persons other than the parties thereto or their legal practitioners in the interest of defence, public safety, public order, public morality, the welfare of persons who have not attained the age of eighteen years, the protection of the private lives of the parties or to such extent as it may consider necessary by reason of special circumstances in which publicity would be contrary to the interests of justice;

(b)   if in any proceedings before a court or such a tribunal, a Minister of the Government of the Federation or a commissioner of the government of a State satisfies the court or tribunal that it would not be in the public interest for any matter to be publicly disclosed, the court or tribunal shall make arrangements for evidence relating to that matter to be heard in private and shall take such other action as may be necessary or expedient to prevent the disclosure of the matter.

(5)   Every person who is charged with a criminal offence shall be presumed to be innocent until he is proved guilty;

Provided that nothing in this section shall invalidate any law by reason only that the law imposes upon any such person the burden of proving particular facts.

(6)   Every person who is charged with a criminal offence shall be entitled to -

(a)   be informed promptly in the language that he understands and in detail of the nature of the offence;

(b)   be given adequate time and facilities for the preparation of his defence;

(c)   defend himself in person or by legal practitioners of his own choice;

(d)   examine, in person or by his legal practitioners, the witnesses called by the prosecution before any court or tribunal and obtain the attendance and carry out the examination of witnesses to testify on his behalf before the court or tribunal on the same conditions as those applying to the witnesses called by the prosecution; and

(e)   have, without payment, the assistance of an interpreter if he cannot understand the language used at the trial of the offence.

(7)   When any person is tried for any criminal offence, the court or tribunal shall keep a record of the proceedings and the accused person or any persons authorised by him in that behalf shall be entitled to obtain copies of the judgement in the case within seven days of the conclusion of the case.

(8)   No person shall be held to be guilty of a criminal offence on account of any act or omission that did not, at the time it took place, constitute such an offence, and no penalty shall be imposed for any criminal offence heavier than the penalty in force at the time the offence was committed

(9)   No person who shows that he has been tried by any court of competent jurisdiction or tribunal for a criminal offence and either convicted or acquitted shall again be tried for that offence or for a criminal offence having the same ingredients as that offence save upon the order of a superior court.

(10)   No person who shows that he has been pardoned for a criminal offence shall again be tried for that offence.

(11)   No person who is tried for a criminal offence shall be compelled to give evidence at the trial.

(12)   Subject as otherwise provided by this Constitution, a person shall not be convicted of a criminal offence unless that offence is defined and the penalty therefor is prescribed in a written law, and in this subsection, a written law refers to an Act of the National Assembly or a Law of a State, any subsidiary legislation or instrument under the provisions of a law.

37.   The privacy of citizens, their homes, correspondence, telephone conversations and telegraphic communications is hereby guaranteed and protected.

38.   (1) Every person shall be entitled to freedom of

thought, conscience and religion, including freedom to change his religion or belief, and freedom (either alone or in community with others, and in public or in private) to manifest and propagate his religion or belief in worship, teaching, practice and observance.

(2)   No person attending any place of education shall be required to receive religious instruction or to take part in or attend any religious ceremony or observance if such instruction ceremony or observance relates to a religion other than his own, or religion not approved by his parent or guardian.

(3)   No religious community or denomination shall be prevented from providing religious instruction for pupils of that community or denomination in any place of education maintained wholly by that community or denomination.

(4)   Nothing in this section shall entitle any person to form, take part in the activity or be a member of a secret society.

39.   (1) Every person shall be entitled to freedom of expression, including freedom to hold opinions and to receive and impart ideas and information without interference.

(2)   Without prejudice to the generality of subsection (1) of this section, every person shall be entitled to own, establish and operate any medium for the dissemination of information, ideas and opinions:

Provided that no person, other than the Government of the Federation or of a State or any other person or body authorised by the President on the fulfilment of conditions laid down by an Act of the National Assembly, shall own, establish or operate a television or wireless broadcasting station for, any purpose whatsoever.

(3)   Nothing in this section shall invalidate any law that is reasonably justifiable in a democratic society -

(a) for the purpose of preventing the disclosure of information received in confidence, maintaining the authority and independence of courts or regulating telephony, wireless broadcasting, television or the exhibition of cinematograph films; or (b) imposing restrictions upon persons holding office under the Government of the Federation or of a State, members of the armed forces of the Federation or members of the Nigeria Police Force or other Government security services or agencies established by law.

40.   Every person shall be entitled to assemble freely and associate with other persons, and in particular he may form or belong to any political party, trade union or any other association for the protection of his interests:

Provided that the provisions of this section shall not derogate from the powers conferred by this Constitution on the Independent National Electoral Commission with respect to political parties to which that Commission does not accord recognition.

41.   (1) Every citizen of Nigeria is entitled to move freely throughout Nigeria and to reside in any part thereof, and no citizen of Nigeria shall be expelled from Nigeria or refused entry thereby or exit therefrom.

(2) Nothing in subsection (1) of this section shall invalidate any law that is reasonably justifiable in a democratic society -

(a)   imposing restrictions on the residence or movement of any person who has committed or is reasonably suspected to have committed a criminal offence in order to prevent him from leaving Nigeria; or

(b)   providing for the removal of any person from Nigeria to any other country to:-

(i)   be tried outside Nigeria for any criminal offence, or

(ii)   undergo imprisonment outside Nigeria in execution of the sentence of a court of law in respect of a criminal offence of which he has been found guilty:

Provided that there is reciprocal agreement between Nigeria and such other country in relation to such matter.

42.   (1) A citizen of Nigeria of a particular community, ethnic group, place of origin, sex, religion or political opinion shall not, by reason only that he is such a person:-

(a)   be subjected either expressly by, or in the practical application of, any law in force in Nigeria or any executive or administrative action of the government, to disabilities or restrictions to which citizens of Nigeria of other communities, ethnic groups, places of origin, sex, religions or political opinions are not made subject; or

(b)   be accorded either expressly by, or in the practical application of, any law in force in Nigeria or any such executive or administrative action, any privilege or advantage that is not accorded to citizens of Nigeria of other communities, ethnic groups, places of origin, sex, religions or political opinions.

(2)   No citizen of Nigeria shall be subjected to any disability or deprivation merely by reason of the circumstances of his birth.

(3)   Nothing in subsection (1) of this section shall invalidate any law by reason only that the law imposes restrictions with respect to the appointment of any person to any office under the State or as a member of the armed

forces of the Federation or member of the Nigeria Police Forces or to an office in the service of a body, corporate established directly by any law in force in Nigeria.

43. Subject to the provisions of this Constitution, every citizen of Nigeria shall have the right to acquire and own immovable property anywhere in Nigeria.

44. (1) No moveable property or any interest in an immovable property shall be taken possession of compulsorily and no right over or interest in any such property shall be acquired compulsorily in any part of Nigeria except in the manner and for the purposes prescribed by a law that, among other things -

(a) requires the prompt payment of compensation therefore and

(b) gives to any person claiming such compensation a right of access for the determination of his interest in the property and the amount of compensation to a court of law or tribunal or body having jurisdiction in that part of Nigeria.

(2) Nothing in subsection (1) of this section shall be construed as affecting any general law.

(a) for the imposition or enforcement of any tax, rate or duty;

(b) for the imposition of penalties or forfeiture for breach of any law, whether under civil process or after conviction for an offence;

(c) relating to leases, tenancies, mortgages, charges, bills of sale or any other rights or obligations arising out of contracts.

(d) relating to the vesting and administration of property

of persons adjudged or otherwise declared bankrupt or insolvent, of persons of unsound mind or deceased persons, and of corporate or unincorporate bodies in the course of being wound-up;

(e)   relating to the execution of judgements or orders of court;

(f)   providing for the taking of possession of property that is in a dangerous state or is injurious to the health of human beings, plants or animals;

(g)   relating to enemy property;

(h)   relating to trusts and trustees;

(i)   relating to limitation of actions;

(j)   relating to property vested in bodies corporate directly established by any law in force in Nigeria;

(k)   relating to the temporary taking of possession of property for the purpose of any examination, investigation or enquiry;

(l)   providing for the carrying out of work on land for the purpose of soil-conservation; or

(m)   subject to prompt payment of compensation for damage to buildings, economic trees or crops, providing for any authority or person to enter, survey or dig any land, or to lay, install or erect poles, cables, wires, pipes, or other conductors or structures on any land, in order to provide or maintain the supply or distribution of energy, fuel, water, sewage, telecommunication services or other public facilities or public utilities.

(3) Notwithstanding the foregoing provisions of this section,

the entire property in and control of all minerals, mineral oils and natural gas in under or upon any land in Nigeria or in, under or upon the territorial waters and the Exclusive Economic Zone of Nigeria shall vest in the Government of the Federation and shall be managed in such manner as may be prescribed by the National Assembly.

45. (1) Nothing in sections 37, 38, 39, 40 and 41 of this Constitution shall invalidate any law that is reasonably justifiable in a democratic society

(a) in the interest of defence, public safety, public order, public morality or public health; or

(b) for the purpose of protecting the rights and freedom or other persons

(2) An act of the National Assembly shall not be invalidated by reason only that it provides for the taking, during periods of emergency, of measures that derogate from the provisions of section 33 or 35 of this Constitution; but no such measures shall be taken in pursuance of any such act during any period of emergency save to the extent that those measures are reasonably justifiable for the purpose of dealing with the situation that exists during that period of emergency:

Provided that nothing in this section shall authorise any derogation from the provisions of section 33 of this Constitution, except in respect of death resulting from acts of war or authorise any derogation from the provisions of section 36(8) of this Constitution.

(3) In this section, a " period of emergency" means any period during which there is in force a Proclamation of a state of emergency declared by the President in exercise of the powers conferred on him under section 305 of this Constitution.

46.　　(1) Any person who alleges that any of the provisions of this Chapter has been, is being or likely to be contravened in any State in relation to him may apply to a High Court in that State for redress.

(2)　　Subject to the provisions of this Constitution, a High Court shall have original jurisdiction to hear and determine any application made to it in pursuance of this section and may make such orders, issue such writs and give such directions as it may consider appropriate for the purpose of enforcement or securing the enforcing within that State of any right to which the person who makes the application may be entitled under this Chapter.

(3)　　The Chief Justice of Nigeria may make rules with respect to the practice and procedure of a High Court for the purposes of this section.

(4)　　The National Assembly -

(a) may confer upon a High Court such powers in addition to those conferred by this section as may appear to the National Assembly to be necessary or desirable for the purpose of enabling the court more effectively to exercise the jurisdiction conferred upon it by this section; and (b) shall make provisions-

(i)　　for the rendering of financial assistance to any indigent citizen of Nigeria where his right under this Chapter has been infringed or with a view to enabling him to engage the services of a legal practitioner to prosecute his claim, and

(ii)　　for ensuring that allegations of infringement of such rights are substantial and the requirement or need for financial or legal aid is real.

CHAPTER 2

Analysis of the Content and Demands of the Constitution of Nigeria:

How Nigerian Leaders have Failed
WE THE PEOPLE

Prof. Peter U. Nwangwu, M.Sc. Pharm.D PhD FACCP FASCP

Prof. Deborah E. Ajakaiye Ph.D FAS FNMGS FGS OON MNI

Dr. John Tor-Adigbye DVM MSc PhD

"And to provide for a Constitution for the purpose of promoting the good government and welfare of all persons in our country, on the principles of freedom, equality and justice, and for the purpose of consolidating the union of our people."

The Purpose of the Constitution:

The Constitution, the highest law of the land, is a documentation of the collective will and wisdom of the people of Nigeria, for the purpose of directing the actions of government towards achieving the good welfare of all persons in our country, "WE THE PEOPLE," on the principles of freedom, equality and justice; and for the purpose of consolidating the unity of our people. Note that an important requirement for the unity of our people, as outlined in the Constitution, is a consistent and deliberate act of government towards achieving the good welfare of all persons in our country, on the principles of freedom, equality and justice. A government that does not have the will to act consistently towards achieving the good welfare of all persons in our country, on the principles of freedom, equality and justice, is a government that has no interest whatsoever in consolidating the unity of our people. Merely chanting the slogan, "to Keep Nigeria One is a task that must be achieved," is naïve and ignorant. The slogan alone cannot keep Nigeria one. Actions speak louder than words. The Nigerian Constitution demands that the government must focus on the welfare of all persons in our country, on the principles of freedom, equality and justice, as the only method of consolidating the unity of our people.

The Contents and Demands of the Constitution

For our purposes in discussing the contents and demands of the Nigerian Constitution, we shall focus only on Chapter 2 of the Constitution, titled: "Fundamental Objectives and Directive Principles of State Policy." The sections of this important fundamental chapter will be quoted and analyzed, to see how well Nigerian leaders have done in upholding the demands and directives of the highest law of the land, which they swore an oath to uphold and enforce.

<u>Section 13</u>: It shall be the duty and responsibility of all organs of government, and of all authorities and persons exercising legislative, executive, or judicial powers to conform to, observe and apply the provisions of this chapter of this constitution.

Analysis: Section 13 of Chapter 2 of the Constitution demands that all authorities and persons in government exercising legislative, executive, or judicial powers, both at the federal and state level, must conform to, observe and apply the provisions of Chapter 2 of the Constitution – as a duty and responsibility.

<u>Section 14 (1)</u>: The Federal Republic of Nigeria shall be a State based on the principles of democracy and social justice.

Analysis: Democracy and Social Justice? Democracy is not

a status that is invoked, chanted or wished into existence; it is an experience and way of life that gives freedom and liberty to the people. In a democratic society citizens are able to develop their full capacities in an atmosphere of freedom and individual respect created and advanced by the government. A sense of equality, social justice and equity can only resonate in the hearts and minds of the citizens based on clear and just government policies. In a democratic society all citizens respect the rights of others, and the rule of law is a way of life.

So where is democracy and social justice in Nigeria? If the Constitution demands that it is the duty and responsibility of all authorities and persons exercising legislative, executive and judicial powers to conform to, observe and apply the directive that the Federal Republic of Nigeria shall be a state based on the principles of democracy and social justice, why do we live in such a wild jungle in Nigeria? Where are the government, and all authorities and persons exercising legislative, executive and judicial powers? When will there be democracy and social justice in Nigeria, as demanded by WE THE PEOPLE in the Constitution?

Section 14(2): **It is hereby, accordingly, declared that:**

> **(a)Sovereignty belongs to the people of Nigeria from whom government through this Constitution derives all its power and authority:**
> **(b)   The security and welfare of the people shall be the primary purpose of government, and**
> **(c) The participation by the people in their government shall be ensured in accordance with the provisions of this constitution.**

Analysis: Sovereignty belongs to the people of Nigeria. It is the people of Nigeria, WE THE PEOPLE, that own Nigeria, and all the wealth and power of Nigeria. The government derives its powers from WE THE PEOPLE through the Constitution. Government has no power, absolutely no power whatsoever, without WE THE PEOPLE through the Constitution. So why does the government abuse and neglect WE THE PEOPLE, the only source of its power? Why does the government use the power it borrowed from WE THE PEOPLE to badly abuse WE THE PEOPLE repeatedly? And why do WE THE PEOPLE allow this abuse to continue?

The Constitution states: "the security and welfare of the people shall be the primary purpose of government." That statement is not a suggestion, it is law, the highest law in Nigeria, which every leader in Nigeria has sworn to uphold and enforce: that the primary purpose of government is the security and welfare of the people.

The Constitution also demands that, "the participation by the people in their government shall be ensured in accordance with the provisions of the Constitution. WE THE PEOPLE own Nigeria. And the Constitution demands that WE THE PEOPLE must have a clear voice in the government and how we are governed. Recently in Great Britain, there was an important question on whether Britain should remain a part of the European Union or not. The then Prime Minister, David Cameron, passionately wanted Britain to remain in the European Union. As Prime Minister he preached vehemently on the benefits of Britain remaining in the European Union and appealed strongly to the citizens to stay in the European Union. Many world leaders including Obama, the President of the United States of America, urged Britain to stay in the European Union. However, as required in a true democracy, the Prime Minister of Great Britain allowed the people of Britain to have a voice in their government by allowing a referendum where the people spoke their minds on the matter through a vote. When the votes were counted, the majority of the people of Britain voted to exit the European Union. That became the final decision, and the Prime Minister of Britain resigned immediately because the majority of the people voted against his wish on the matter. When was the last time a Nigerian President allowed the participation by the people in their government by allowing the people of Nigeria to vote in a referendum on an important national issue affecting the lives of the people? The Constitution of Nigeria which all the Presidents swore an oath to uphold and enforce demands that WE THE PEOPLE of Nigeria must have a voice in their government.

Section 14(3): The composition of the Government of the Federation or any of its agencies and the conduct of its affairs shall be carried out in such a manner as to reflect the federal character of Nigeria and the need to promote national unity, and also to command national loyalty, thereby ensuring that there shall be no predominance of personas from a few State or from a few ethnic or other sectional groups in that Government or in any of it agencies.

Analysis: The highest law of Nigeria demands that the composition of the government of the Federation or any of its agencies, and the conduct of its affairs (the way business is done or carried out) shall be done in such a manner as to reflect the federal character of Nigeria, and the need to promote national unity, and also to command loyalty. The way to promote national unity and command national loyalty is through proper inclusiveness and social justice. The Constitution directs and demands it. Why do Nigerian Presidents willfully violate the law on this matter? Why would any president ask for national unity if they violate the law of proper inclusiveness and social justice?

Section 14 (4): The composition of the Government of a State, a local government council, or any of the agencies of such a Government or council, and the conduct of the affairs of the Government or council or such agencies shall be carried out in such manner

as to recognize the diversity of the people within its area of authority and the need to promote a sense of belonging and loyalty among all the people of the Federation.

Analysis: As with the Federal Government, the Constitution demands that at the state or local government level, the composition of the government should be carried out in such a manner as to recognize the diversity of the people of the Federation. This directive of the Constitution includes the demand that in a place like Lagos State which is a core Yoruba land, for example, since there is a very strong Igbo and Hausa presence, Igbos and Hausas should be included in the government of Lagos state, to recognize the diversity of the people within its area of authority, and the need to promote a sense of belonging and loyalty among all the people of the Federation. This is the demand of the highest law of the land. It must be obeyed.

Section 15(1): The motto of the Federal Republic of Nigeria shall be Unity and Faith, Peace and Progress

(2) Accordingly, national integration shall be actively encouraged, whilst discrimination on the grounds of place of origin, sex, religion, status, ethnic or linguistic association or ties shall be prohibited.

(3) For the purpose of promoting national integration, it shall be the duty of the State to:

> (a) Provide adequate facilities for and encourage free mobility of people, goods and services throughout the Federation.
> (b) Secure full residence rights for every citizen in all parts of the Federation.

(c) Encourage inter-marriage among persons from different places of origin, or of different religious, ethnic or linguistic associations or ties; and

(d) Promote or encourage the formation of associations that cut across ethnic, linguistic, religious and or other sectional barriers.

(4) The State shall foster a feeling of belonging and of involvement among the various people of the Federation, to the end that loyalty to the national shall override sectional loyalties.

Analysis: The Constitution of Nigeria, the supreme law of the land, directs that national integration shall be actively encouraged and discrimination on the grounds of place of origin, sex, religion, status, ethnic or linguistic association or ties shall be prohibited.

1. The government has the duty to facilitate and encourage free mobility of people, goods and services throughout the federation.

2. The government has a duty to secure full residence rights for every citizen in all parts of the Federation.

3. The government has a duty to foster a feeling of belonging and of involvement among the various peoples of the Federation, to the end that loyalty to the nation shall override sectional loyalties. Unfortunately, the government has failed in its obligation and duties as directed by the Constitution, the will of the people, the highest law of the land. Consider a simple government

progamme such as the national youth service corps (NYSC). Every year, thousands of Igbo university graduates are posted to northern Nigeria as corpers, most of them to teach at secondary schools in northern Nigeria. Most of these secondary schools are in dire need of teachers because of very acute shortages of teachers. These corpers devote themselves to their duties. Many of them receive awards in recognition of their devotion and dedication to service. However, at the end of their service year, 99.5% of these corpers are sent away because their state of origin is not the state where they served. However, where they served is their state of residence. Most of them are willing to stay and continue to work there, but are denied employment because of their state of origin. The highest law of the land demands that the government should secure full residence rights for every citizen in all parts of the Federation. Such residence rights should guarantee employment for any corper wherever they serve regardless of their state of origin. The "use and throw away" syndrome in the national youth service corps is a national evil that violates the constitution of Nigeria. If we have any government at all, such violations of the demands of the Constitution must cease. The Constitution also demands that the government shall foster a feeling of belonging and of involvement among the various people of the Federation, to the end that loyalty to the nation shall override sectional loyalties. This simple and clear demand of the Constitution is the way to keep Nigeria One. Anything else is mere chasing the wind.

Section 15(5): **The State shall abolish all corrupt practices and abuses of power.**

Analysis: The Constitution of Nigeria, the highest law of the land, demands that the government shall abolish all corrupt practices and abuse of power. This directive is very clear. It demands that the government shall abolish, not some corrupt practices but, ALL corrupt practices and abuses of power. What part of this law is difficult for any president or leader in Nigeria to understand? If the demand of this law is clear, why is Nigeria still counted as one of the most corrupt nations in the world, or perhaps the most corrupt nation in the world, given all that happened recently in the Goodluck Jonathan administration? The Prime Minister of Britain called Nigeria "fantastically corrupt." Corruption is a potent cancer that has mercilessly eaten Nigeria to a state of stupor. Why have Nigerian leaders who swore an oath to uphold the demands of the Nigerian Constitution violated the Constitution by allowing this evil of corruption to render Nigeria comatose?

Section 16(1): **The State shall, within the context of the ideals and objectives for which provisions are made in this Constitution;**

(a)harness the resources of the nation and promote national prosperity and an efficient, dynamic and self-reliant economy

(b) control the national economy in such manner as to secure the maximum welfare, freedom and happiness of every citizen on the basis of social justice and equality of status and opportunity.

(c) Without prejudice to its right to operate or participate in areas of the economy, other than the major sectors of the economy, manage and operate the major sectors of the economy

(d) Without prejudice to the right of any person to participate in areas of the economy within the major sector of the economy, protect the right of every citizen to engage in any economic activities outside the major sectors of the economy.

Analysis: The Constitution of Nigeria demands that the government has a duty to:

1. Harness all the natural resources of the nation, and promote national prosperity and an efficient, dynamic and self-reliant economy.

Unfortunately, our leaders have not harnessed all the natural resources of the nation but focused on crude oil to the great detriment of Nigeria and the people of Nigeria.

2. The Constitution also demands that the government has a duty to control the national economy in such manner as to secure the maximum welfare, freedom

and happiness of every citizen on the basis of social justice and equality of status and opportunity. This is a directive of WE THE PEOPLE, through the Constitution, to the government. Has the government controlled the national economy in such a manner as to secure the maximum welfare, freedom and happiness of every citizen on the basis of social justice and equality of status and opportunity? Clearly the answer is NO.

Section 16(2): The State shall direct its policy towards ensuring:

> **(a) The promotion of a planned and balanced economic development.**
> **(b) That the material resources of the nation are harnessed and distributed as best as possible to serve the common good;**
> **(c) That the economic system is not operated in such a manner as to permit the concentration of wealth or the means**

of production and exchange in the hands of a few individuals or of a group; and

(d)   That suitable and adequate shelter, suitable and adequate food, reasonable national minimum living wage, old age care and pensions and unemployment, sick benefits and welfare of the disabled are provided for all citizens.

Analysis: The Constitution of Nigeria directs the government to promote a planned and balanced economic development. Unfortunately, successive Nigerian presidents who swore an oath to uphold and obey the constitution focused primarily on the sale of crude oil as the sole and singular economic development for Nigeria. Where is the planned and balanced economic development demanded by the Constitution? The Constitution also demands that the material resources of the nation are harnessed and distributed as best as possible to serve the common good; that the economic system is not operated in such a manner as to permit the concentration of wealth or the means of production and exchange in the hands of few individuals or of a group. Unfortunately, Nigerian Presidents and leaders have failed woefully in upholding this demand of the Constitution, which they swore an oath to uphold.

The Constitution of Nigeria also directs that suitable and

adequate shelter, suitable and adequate food, reasonable minimum living wage, old age care and pensions and unemployment sick benefits and welfare of the disabled are provided for all citizens. Nigerian leaders have also failed in upholding this demand of the Constitution of Nigeria.

Section 16(3): **A body shall be set up by an Act of the National Assembly which shall have power;**

> **(a)To review, from time to time, the ownership and control of business enterprises operating in Nigeria and make recommendations to the President on same; and**
> **(b)   To administer any law for regulation of the ownership and control of such enterprises.**

(4) For the purposes of subsection (1) of this section –

(a) the reference to the "major sectors of the economy" shall be construed as a reference to such economic activities as may, from time to time, be declared by a resolution of each House of the National Assembly to be managed and operated exclusively by the Government of the Federation,

and until a resolution to the contrary is made by the National Assembly, economic activities being operated exclusively by the Government of the Federation on the date immediately preceding the day when this section comes into force, whether directly or through the agencies of a statutory or other corporation or company, shall be deemed to be major sectors of the economy;

(b) "economic activities" includes activities directly concerned with the production, distribution and exchange of whether or of goods and services; and

(c) "participate" includes the rendering of services and supplying of goods.

Analysis: Three things come to mind in regards to the directive of the Constitution in this section:

(1) The agreement between Nigeria and International Oil Companies operating in Nigeria should be carefully reviewed and re-visited. These international oil companies take away a very significant portion of the profits from crude oil development in Nigeria, in some cases as much as 40 percent of the income. Are these international oil companies such as Shell, Mobile, etc. still needed in Nigeria? What do they do that trained Nigerians cannot do? If Nigerians can do it under

99

the umbrella of a Nigerian National Oil Company, why should Nigeria continue to give away 40 percent of our oil development income? We can solve a lot of our infrastructural needs and transform Nigeria through that additional 40 percent income from proceeds of oil development in Nigeria.

(2) Until just recently, the US had a law in the books that America will never export even one cup of crude oil. America probably had the largest oil reserve in the world, but rather than sell crude oil, the law required America to refine the crude oil in America and sell the various refined petroleum products at much higher prices to the world. So rather than sell their crude oil, they will keep their crude oil reserves and import crude oil from gullible and blind countries like Nigeria and Saudi Arabia, refine the imported crude oil and sell the finished refined products back to Nigeria, Saudi Arabia and other countries of the world at several times the price of the crude oil. So why are we short-sighted in Nigeria? Why should we sell crude oil to America, and then buy the finished refined products from America at much higher prices? Why do we not refine the crude in Nigeria and export the finished refined products at prices much higher than the crude oil we sell off in a hurry? Besides, a strong local refining industry will create several jobs and impact the Nigerian economy in several ways. But the sad story now is that America will longer buy Nigerian crude oil because they have discovered so much more crude oil in America. America now wants to begin exporting their massive excessive crude oil. Nigerian government should embark on massive local crude oil refining in Nigeria. The refined

products can be exported for more money; massive local refining will also bring down the price of petroleum products for the benefit of the people of Nigeria, and will at the same time create jobs, and impact the Nigerian economy positively in several ways.

(3) There is law currently in Nigeria that if crude oil is discovered in someone's personal land or property, the federal government will take over that property. The reason is so the government can develop that oil asset and distribute the income uniformly to all parts of Nigeria. Understandably, even if oil is discovered in your backyard in America that oil becomes your personal property. But why is it that after the Nigerian government seizes this oil asset from the original Nigerian who owns that land, the government then gives it to another Nigerian to own and make money from? In most cases the Nigerians that get the oil assets from the government because of their connections in government live several hundreds of miles away from where the oil assets reside. This is not social justice, and the policy must be reviewed and resolved. The government must recover all those oil assets, have an agency of government that can carefully and properly develop the assets to generate significant revenues that will benefit all Nigerians uniformly. Government should also compensate original owners of the oil asset fairly, including rehabilitation of any ecological damage to the ecosystem in the community. Government must also find a way to pay their compensation directly to the community, rather than through selfish community leaders who pocket the money and leave the community hanging.

Section 17(1): **(1) The State social order is founded on ideals of Freedom, Equality and Justice.**

(2) In furtherance of the social order–

(a) every citizen shall have equality of rights, obligations and opportunities before the law

(b) the sanctity of the human person shall be recognized and human dignity shall be maintained and enhanced.

(c) government actions shall be humane;

(d) exploitation of human or natural resources in any form whatsoever for reasons other than the good of the community shall be prevented; and

(e) the independence, impartiality and integrity of courts of law, and easy accessibility thereto shall be secured and maintained.

Analysis: The Nigerian Constitution which every Nigerian president swears an oath to uphold demands that every citizen shall have equality of rights, obligations and opportunities before the law. It upholds the sanctity of human life, and demands impartiality and integrity of courts of law, and easy accessibility to the court of law. Unfortunately, Nigeria is not a level-playing field for all citizens, very far from that. Who you know is much more superior to what you know. Less qualified people are given jobs in place of excellent candidates, because of the unjust evil phenomenon of who you know; which is against the highest law of the land, the Constitution. Impartiality and integrity of the courts of law is like a very bad dream in Nigeria, because innocent citizens are denied justice by several corrupt judges.

Section 17(3): The State shall direct its policy towards ensuring that-

(a) All citizens, without discrimination on any group whatsoever, have the opportunity for securing adequate means of livelihood as well as adequate opportunity to secure suitable employment;

(b) Conditions of work are just and humane, and that there are adequate facilities for leisure and for social, religious and cultural life;

(c) The health, safety and welfare of all persons in employment are safeguarded and not endangered or abused;

(d) There are adequate medical and health facilities for all persons

(e) There is equal pay for equal work without discrimination on account of sex or on any other ground whatsoever;

(f) Children, young persons and the aged are protected against exploitation whatsoever, and against moral and material neglect;

(g) Provision is made for public assistance in deserving cases or other conditions of need; and

(h) The evolution and promotion of family life is encouraged.

Analysis: The Constitution of Nigeria, the highest law in the land which every president of Nigeria swears an oath to enforce, states that all citizens, without discrimination on any group whatsoever, should have equal opportunity for securing adequate means of livelihood as well as adequate opportunity to secure suitable employment. The Constitution states that it is the duty of the government to ensure that. Unfortunately, the government of Nigeria which has the duty to ensure this has consistently practiced abject and overt discrimination in employment. Widespread nepotism, unacceptable favoritism and discrimination based on religion, tribe, state of origin, who you know, and the social status of your parents pervades employment practices even by government agencies in Nigeria. Recently, it was reported that the Central Bank of Nigeria embarked on a secret widespread recruitment involving several hundreds of only children of the top political class, including a relative of the President of Nigeria, as alleged. More recently, the Federal Inland Revenue Service engaged in a secret recruitment for the children of high and mighty Nigerians as the only beneficiaries. Following that, the Nigerian Prisons Service also conducted its own secret massive recruitment of only selected Nigerians, children of the political class and wealthy Nigerians. For all this to happen in the administration of President Buhari who is fighting corrupt practices in Nigeria is painful and disheartening.

The Constitution of Nigeria also directs the government to ensure that there are adequate medical and health facilities for all persons. Unfortunately, the problems of both accessibility and affordability of adequate health care in Nigeria are dire emergencies that cause many unnecessary deaths daily in Nigeria.

The Constitution demands that the government should provide public assistance in deserving cases or other conditions of need. The streets of Nigeria are littered with needy beggars. Rather than provide assistance for these needy beggars, the government sometimes treats them as outlaws, as in the case of the Lagos government who will load these beggars in trucks and dump them at faraway places, many hundreds of miles away from their home.

Section 18 (1): Government shall direct its policy towards ensuring that there are equal and adequate educational opportunities at all levels:

> **(2) Government shall promote science and technology**
>
> **(3) Government shall strive to eradicate illiteracy; and to this end Government shall as and when practicable provide**
>
> > **(a) free, compulsory and universal primary education**
> >
> > **(b) free secondary education**
> >
> > **(c) free university education**
> >
> > **(d) free adult literacy programme**

Analysis: The Constitution of Nigeria, which every president has sworn to uphold demands that the government shall direct its policy towards ensuring that there are equal and adequate educational opportunities for everyone at all levels. The Constitution further directs that government shall strive to eradicate illiteracy: and to this end government shall as and when practicable provide free compulsory and universal primary education, free secondary education, free university education, and free adult literacy programme.

Educated citizens are the most valuable assets of any nation. Education breeds creative initiatives, patriotism, respect for the law, tolerance, proper sensitivity and respect for differences in religious, tribal, political and cultural beliefs. Education encourages civilized and considerate behavior. Illiteracy is destroying Nigeria as a nation. National unity is impossible among illiterates; therefore, the Nigerian Constitution demands that the Nigerian government shall strive to eradicate illiteracy.

In America, primary and secondary education is free and compulsory. If your child misses school any day, the school will call the parents or guardian of the child to alert them. If it persists a summons will be issued by the court for the parents to come and explain to the judge in a court why their child is not in school. If it continues, you the parent can be put in jail. That is what free and compulsory education means under the law. Unfortunately, in Nigeria, many parents are the ones who deprive their children of education by sending them to hawk various products on the streets to make money for the family. The government sees these child-hawkers and laborers on the streets and does nothing about it. After many years of working on the streets, these children are lost permanently to illiteracy; it becomes impossible for them to go back to school after a certain age. They add to the illiteracy burden of the nation.

On University education in America, the government has directed its policy towards ensuring that there are equal and adequate opportunities for student loans to cover the costs of university education for every American citizen who wants to attend university in America. The government has given full guarantees to all banks in America for all educational loans given to students to attend university, covering all expenses. The loans are very easy to get; your only qualification is that you are a student at any university or institution of higher learning. You are entitled to the loan each year until you graduate. No interest is charged on the loan while you are in school and the loan is not due for repayment to the bank until you graduate from the university and start working. The annual interest charged after you graduate is very low, such as 2 percent, and your monthly repayment is deliberately low to make it easy for you to make the payments. This makes it easy for American citizens who want to attend university to do so without depending on their parents. In the very rare case where a student refuses to repay the loan to the bank after graduation, the bank has nothing to worry about because the American government will pay the bank for the loan. In the meantime, the American government did not really lose anything because the benefits of educating that American citizen is worth far more than the amount of that loan they repaid the bank. Patriotism and civilized behavior is high in America because America has invested highly in the education of her citizens.

Section 19: **The foreign policy objectives shall be-**

(a) Promotion and protection of the national interest

(b)   Promotion of African integration and support for African unity

(c) Promotion of international co-operation for the consolidation of universal peace and mutual respect among all nations and elimination of discrimination in all its manifestations

(d)   Respect for international law and treaty obligations as well as the seeking of settlement of international disputes by negotiation, meditation, conciliation, arbitration and adjudication; and

(e) Promotion of a just world economic order

Analysis: The foreign policy objectives of Nigeria as directed by the Constitution are clear and simple. Unfortunately, Nigeria does not have a good image among the nations of the world. Part of the disrespect comes from the level of corruption and primitive behavior at home in Nigeria by the government and people of Nigeria: the other part comes from the lawlessness and criminal behavior of some Nigerians in diaspora in their quest to acquire wealth to support a life of ostentation back home in Nigeria.

Section 20 and 21: **20 – The State shall protect and improve the environment and safeguard the water, air and land, forests and wild life in Nigeria**

21 – The State shall-

(a)Protect, preserve and promote the Nigerian culture which enhance human dignity and are consistent with the fundamental objectives as provided in this Chapter; and

(b) Encourage development of technological and scientific studies which enhance cultural values.

Analysis: The Constitution directs that the government shall protect and improve the environment including proper safeguard of water, air and land. The air we breathe and the water we drink should be pure and safe. Unfortunately, several Nigerians die often from drinking contaminated water and breathing polluted air.

Section 22: **The press, radio, television and other agencies of the mass media shall at all times be free to uphold the fundamental objectives contained in this Chapter and uphold the responsibility and**

accountability of the Government to the people.

Analysis: The Constitution demands that the press, radio, television and other agencies of the mass media shall at all times be free to uphold the fundamental objectives contained in Chapter 2 of the Nigerian Constitution, and to uphold the responsibility and accountability of the government to the people.

Here are some very important questions worth pondering over:

1. How many journalists and staff of the press, radio, television and other agencies of the mass media have read the Constitution of Nigeria, especially Chapter 2 of the Constitution – "Fundamental Objectives and Directive Principles of State Policy"? The figure is likely to be less than 0.01% of all people who work in the Nigerian media. If they have not read the Constitution, how will they know the "Fundamental Objectives and Directive Principles of State (Government) Policy"?

2. The Constitution directs that the press, radio, television and other agencies of the mass media shall at all times uphold the fundamental objectives contained in Chapter 2 of the Constitution. If most of our media people are totally ignorant of the content of the Constitution, especially Chapter 2, which they are required to uphold, how can they live up to that duty and the responsibility of upholding the Constitution?

3. The Constitution demands that the press, radio, television and other agencies of mass media shall at all times uphold the

responsibility and accountability of the Government to the people. In other words, the media should hold the Government, beginning with the President, responsible and accountable to WE THE PEOPLE of Nigeria. If the media does not know the rights of the people and the duties of the government to the people as directed in the Constitution, which the President swore an oath to uphold, how can the media hold the president and government accountable to WE THE PEOPLE for those duties?

4. How many Nigerian Presidents have read the Constitution of Nigeria, especially Chapter 2, "Fundamental Objectives and Directive Principles of State Policy"? Each president has sworn an oath to uphold it, but did they read it? The content and demands of the Constitution on the rights and privileges of the people of Nigeria, WE THE PEOPLE, are clearly defined in Chapter 2 of the Constitution. Did any Nigerian president understand the rights and privileges of the people which they swore to uphold? Why has no Nigerian president kept to the oath they swore; why has every Nigerian president violated the rights and privileges of WE THE PEOPLE as clearly outlined in Chapter 2 of the Nigerian Constitution?

Section 23: The national ethics shall be Discipline, Integrity, Dignity of Labour, Social Justice, Religious Tolerance, Self-reliance and Patriotism.

Analysis: The directive of the Nigerian Constitution, the collective will and wisdom of WE THE PEOPLE, the highest law in Nigeria, is that the national ethics shall be Discipline, Integrity, Dignity of Labour, Social Justice, Religious Tolerance, Self-reliance and Patriotism. The Constitution directs that the normal life-style of all Nigerians, our day-to-day way of life, should be characterized by Discipline, Integrity, Dignity of Labour, Social Justice, Religious Tolerance, Self-reliance and Patriotism. We have missed the way as a nation. We are lost in the wilderness and need to find our way back to the national ethics enshrined in the Constitution.

Section 24: **It shall be the duty of every citizen to –**

(a) Abide by this Constitution, respect its ideals and its institutions, the National Flag, the National Anthem, the National Pledge, and legitimate authorities;

(b) Help to enhance the power, prestige and good name of Nigeria, defend Nigeria and render such national service as may be required;

(c) Respect the dignity of other citizens and the rights and legitimate interests of others and live in unity and harmony and in the spirit of common brotherhood;

(d) Make positive and useful contribution to the advancement, progress and well-being of the

**community where he
resides;**

**(e) Render assistance to
appropriate and lawful
agencies in the
maintenance of law and
order; and**

**(f) Declare his income
honestly to appropriate
and lawful agencies and
pay his tax promptly.**

Analysis: The Nigerian Constitution did not only direct the government on their duty and responsibility to the people of Nigeria; in section 24 of Chapter 2, the Constitution specifically directs the citizens, WE THE PEOPLE, on their duties and responsibility to the nation and fellow Nigerian citizens.

(1) It shall be the duty of every citizen to abide by this Constitution, respect its ideals and its institutions, the National Flag, the National Anthem, the National Pledge, and legitimate authorities. How many Nigerians have read the Nigerian Constitution? How many are even capable of doing so? Perhaps one in every 100,000 of the 170 million people that live in Nigeria? Perhaps more likely the number is one in every 300,000, or even much less. If Nigerian citizens have not read their Constitution, how can they abide by a Constitution they have not read, or hold their leaders accountable to the demands of the Constitution?

(2) It shall be the duty of every citizen to help enhance the power, prestige and good name of Nigeria, defend Nigeria and render such national service as may be required. Anyone involved in bribery and corruption, or any dishonest gain or activity, of

any type at any level has failed in their duty to enhance the power, prestige and good name of Nigeria.

(3) It shall be the duty of every citizen to respect the dignity of other citizens and the rights and legitimate interests of others, and live in unity and harmony and in the spirit of common brotherhood. Religious and tribal sentiments and conflicts of any type is a violation of the Nigerian Constitution. We must respect the dignity of other citizens, live in unity and harmony and in the spirit of common brotherhood. This is the law of the land, which every citizen must obeyed.

(4) It shall be the duty of every citizen to make positive and useful contribution to the advancement, progress and well-being of the community where they reside. Brighten the corner where you are. If every Nigerian citizen brightens the corner where s/he is, Nigeria will be a beautiful and wonderful nation to live in. There will be no Nigerians in diaspora anywhere in the world.

(5) It shall be the duty of every citizen to render assistance to appropriate and lawful agencies in the maintenance of law and order. Nigeria is a very lawless nation. Refuse to be part of lawlessness, instead help to fight every type or size of lawlessness wherever you are.

(6) It shall be the duty of every citizen to declare his or her income honestly to appropriate and lawful agencies and pay his or her tax promptly. Most Nigerians evade tax routinely. People live in N800 million naira mansions in Abuja, own multiple cars and homes in various places, throw lavish parties to display their wealth and ostentation, but pay very little or nothing in tax to the nation. They have constitutional obligations to pay taxes

promptly to the nation. Any president of Nigeria who understands the demands of the Constitution, would make every citizen who flaunts their wealth to show how much they paid in taxes to the nation; if they did not pay enough, the state will seize and liquidate some of their property to pay their due and appropriate tax. There will be no exception.

Citizens also have a duty to the nation to reject and fight corruption wherever they encounter it. The current Nigerian president is waging a war on corruption. However, corruption is so endemic and widespread in Nigeria that the president cannot fight the war alone. It is the duty of every responsible Nigerian to reject and fight corruption wherever they encounter it. The president cannot be everywhere, and in every situation to fight corruption in every part of Nigeria. When one encounters lawless and corrupt policemen along the road extracting money from drivers on the road, one must ask, "how can Buhari be here to stop this corruption?" We must refuse to give the greedy policemen on the road even one penny, and reject their unconstitutional behavior.

Recently, a group of lawless men led by a corrupt individual who extorts money from people and invades people's lands to steal and sell them came to mess with Professor Nwangwu's ten plots of land at Ogidiani in Idemili North local government of Anambra State. He filed a petition against them to the Commissioner of Police, Anambra State Command. The Commissioner directed the file to the Deputy Commissioner in charge of the Criminal Investigation Department. The administrative officer there assigned the case to a team led by an Assistant Superintendent of Police (ASP). When Professor Nwangwu met with this young police officer in his office, he told Professor Nwangwu that they need to go and make some arrests on the matter, but that they do not have any vehicle or money to fuel a vehicle. He asked Professor Nwangwu for money for them to hire and fuel a vehicle. Professor Nwangwu knew their corrupt tricks for extracting money from petitioners. He told the ASP that he had a good SUV that sits 8 people comfortably, and that

114

he had his driver with him. "Since you don't have a vehicle, you can use my SUV and my driver", Professor Nwangwu told him. The ASP was totally speechless and disappointed. As he recovered from the shock he said, "we need to type the documents to make the arrests and we need money to type the documents." Professor Nwangwu stood up and walked out of his office. He pleaded for him not to leave, but Professor Nwangwu left and went away. The following morning, Professor Nwangwu returned to the administrative officer at the police headquarters and told him that he had lost total confidence in their ability to handle his petition. He was startled and wanted to know what happened. Professor Nwangwu told him the ASP in charge of the team he assigned his case was corrupt, and that he had lost confidence in their ability to handle the case. After providing him with further details on what transpired, the officer apologized to Professor Nwangwu. He assured Professor Nwangwu that he would withdraw his case from the corrupt team and give it to a different team. Professor Nwangwu accepted his offer to reassign the case to a different team but warned him to educate and talk harshly to the new team about any attempt to extract any money from him. He did. He told the ASP in-charge of the new team that this man was a professor, a former Nigerian presidential candidate; that they could get into big trouble for any corrupt tendencies they displayed. Having being forewarned, the new team tamed their appetite and corrupt tendencies and did their job without trying to extract money from Professor Nwangwu.

Buhari cannot be everywhere to fight corruption. We badly need a new breed of WE THE PEOPLE in Nigeria; clean, responsible, honest citizens committed to the national ethics demanded by the Constitution - Discipline, Integrity, Dignity of Labour, Social Justice, Religious Tolerance, Self-reliance and Patriotism. Only a new breed of WE THE PEOPLE can save Nigeria. Let us commit to a new Nigeria, changing one person at a time, in a nationwide movement of the new Nigerian grassroots. This movement is an association of Nigerians that cut across every ethnic, linguistic, religious, cultural and or other sectional barriers.

As we bond together in a national movement to clean Nigeria from bottom to top, we will attain a critical mass that will use our votes to clean the top from a clean bottom. Only a clean bottom can put in place a clean top. This book provides additional details on how to join this important nationwide movement to change Nigeria for good by WE THE PEOPLE.

CHAPTER 3

Destruction of the National Fabrics and Foundation:

Evils of Pervasive Lawlessness and Role of Individual Accountability

Abimbola O. Odumosu, BSc PhD DSE

The National Fabrics and Foundation

One dictionary definition of fabrics is "a complex underlying structure". Fabric is the structure, framework, or composition of a material or unit of existence. An example is family as the fabric of life, or a good family as fabric of the nation. Foundation is defined by the dictionary as "the basis on which a thing stands". Foundation is the footing, base, substructure and underpinning on which something rests or exists.

UBUNTU is an African philosophy, fabric, and foundation which advocates being fully human through other people's humanity. The word has its origin in the Bantu language in South Africa and commonly means, "I am because you are". It says, "I am not me....... without we". UBUNTU is one word that means so many things—respect, helpfulness, sharing, caring, tolerance, trust, usefulness, community, humanity.

When Nelson Mandela was growing up as a child, it was very common for an elder in the community to spank and punish any child (not just his child, any child in the community) for being lazy or slothful. The reason is because if that child is allowed to grow up as a lazy or slothful man, he will impact negatively on the community because the community will be deprived of his usefulness and contributions to the community. UBUNTU—the fabric and foundation of society, which believes that, "I am because you are". What I do affects not just you, but the entire community, the entire nation.

What has happened to UBUNTU in the contemporary African society? In most African nations, the national fabrics and foundations have been destroyed. The tragedy of this destruction of national fabrics and foundations is especially glaring in Nigeria. The underlying structure and framework, the basis and footing on which respect, helpfulness, sharing, caring, tolerance, trust, usefulness, community, humanity and decency exist in the nation has been destroyed.

Lawlessness:

The dictionary defines lawlessness as, "being without law", "uncontrolled by a law, unbridled, unruly, unrestrained, illegal." In Nigeria, "being without law" is not the issue or problem. Nigeria has adequate laws, but most Nigerians are "uncontrolled by the laws". There is pervasive lawlessness in Nigeria. Most Nigerians are unbridled, unruly, unrestrained, and illegal in their day-to-day life and activities. Most Nigerians are routine law-breakers, making Nigeria a very lawless society. Law enforcement in Nigeria is very primitive. In fact, most law enforcement officers in Nigeria are routine law-breakers. Part of the reason why many Nigerians break laws with impunity is because they are confident that in the very unlikely event a law enforcement officer catches them, they can very easily get out of trouble by bribing the law enforcement officer with very little money. In other cases, many Nigerians feel they are above the law, and so break laws routinely with impunity, feeling that a law enforcement officer cannot mess with them because they have status in the community or nation.

Evils of Pervasive Lawlessness:

All laws are made to create orderliness in the society, and respect the rights of other citizens. Laws protect the safety, security, and wellbeing of all citizens. Breaking any law threatens the safety and security of other citizens. It is a crime to break the law. Anyone who commits a crime by

118

breaking any law is a criminal. Most people who break any law do not understand that they label themselves as criminals. Criminals belong in jail, because they must be put in jail to protect the rest of society from their lawless behavior.

Many citizens of Nigeria suffer serious harm, including death, from lawless criminals who are everywhere in the Nigerian society. Criminal behavior that may cause the death of another citizen is not limited to armed assaults such as armed robbery, but include other lawless behavior such as driving on the wrong side of the street, purchasing your driver's license without completing proper driver education, and many other lawless behaviors that may be taken for granted by some because they are rampant in society. Lawlessness is evil. Pervasive lawlessness is a great evil and curse on the nation. The evils of pervasive lawlessness include insecurity, hardship and suffering of citizens from breakdown of law and order, untimely and unnecessary death of innocent citizens, massive emigration and flight of those citizens who are able to do so to other countries.

The Role of Individual Accountability:

The English Webster's dictionary has defined Accountability as:
   A state of being accountable:
   Answerability.
   Willingness to accept responsibility for one's action.
   Blameworthiness.
   Expectation of giving account.

I learned about an accountable lifestyle as a child. My parents were always on the move, as my father was a medical doctor in the old Western region of Nigeria, and he was transferred from one city to another, from Shagamu to Benin to Ondo etc. To ensure that we his children secured a good education, we lived with our aunties and uncles. Whenever we left home we were told in Yoruba language, 'ranti eniti oje', which means "remember who you are": know who you are, and live a life away from home as who you are? Attending a Catholic school where our Principal used a variety of means to instill in us a high sense of responsibility later strengthened this lifestyle of accountability. She taught us that we must protect other people's property; your friend's book that you borrowed, better than your own. These are my earliest memories of accountability, and it stuck with me all my life, to live a life worthy of my roots, my parents' life values, and God's expectation of me. This virtue also helped me when I became a developmental worker working in all kinds of disaster situations for the United Nations, far away from home, and a call to live my life worthy of my life's virtues, responsibility and in an accountable manner.

As a developmental worker with UNICEF, United Nations, and other agencies, 100 percent of our funds are provided by donors; therefore, accountability became foremost in my life, the need to be accountable to donors and also to our beneficiaries. As such, I lived and talked accountability every waking hour. You can therefore imagine the pains in my heart whenever I visit Nigeria and witness the pervasive lawlessness and lack of accountability in the country, even at the highest level; inappropriate utilization of public funds, disregard of every aspect of the law, such as displayed on our roads, driving on the wrong side of the road and reckless disregard for other road users. I also witnessed the poor display of integrity; everybody wants to get rich quick-- the end justifies the means, just get rich quick. This poor display of accountability is seen in every sphere of Nigerian life; it is encountered on arrival at our airports. Corrupt officials hounded a business friend of my husband at the airport and he had to fly straight back to Italy after he managed to get out of the clutches of the airport staff. Paid airport officials at every step of the departure protocol have become shameless beggars who hound you for money. The fabrics and foundation of good behavior have been destroyed badly everywhere in Nigeria.

Issues of Accountability in Nigeria:

The youth in Nigeria are often self-absorbed because they feel the society has failed them. Before you are accountable, you have to have ownership in your environment and community. When there is a sense of ownership, there will be a sense of responsibility. Accountability is a strange concept in the Nigerian society. It is like a strange language, from our educational institutions to our religious houses nationwide. What types of rules and regulations should be made in Nigeria to help enforce accountability and appropriate behavior? Who will make and enforce such rules? How will offenders be punished, and who will punish them. How will those rules and regulations be different from the many laws we have currently in Nigeria, which most Nigerians break regularly daily? Why are existing laws not properly enforced? Why are law offenders and lawbreakers not punished in Nigeria?

There is a sense that Nigeria is a construct that was given to us for our individual benefit. In Nigeria, we use metaphors like "share of the national cake"; "turn by turn". Most Nigerians feel that they are entitled to a piece of the national cake, the oil wealth of Nigeria for their personal benefit. This concept does not believe in working hard and earning benefits from hard work. Rather, from their sense of entitlement, they are driven to frequently steal the wealth of the nation as their share of the national cake. Those elected to position of leadership feel that it is now their turn to loot the treasury, because looting the treasury is done "turn by turn". These are the prevailing concepts, mind-set and belief that drive how we engage with our country; Nigeria is a commodity to be shared and looted, not groomed and developed.

The national fabrics and foundation has been destroyed in Nigeria. The concept and phenomenon of UBUNTU— "I am because you are", "I am not me......without we", has been totally destroyed. The story was told about how a community responded to a recent water shortage in Lekki, a community at the outskirts of Lagos, Nigeria. For about 2 months in

Lekki, there was acute shortage of water. Inquiries from the water corporation as to the cause of this debilitating water shortage for the community revealed that the former General Manager had stolen all the money, so there was no money to buy chemicals to purify the water. Our bad behavior breeds bad consequences for others, and sometimes, bad consequences for the entire community or nation.

Accountability Movement:

Even in our Churches and Mosques in Nigeria today, professing Christians and Moslems are weak on proper accountability. This is very unfortunate, because our Churches and Mosques should be strong and vibrant on teaching and promoting accountability with vigor and passion. The teachings of Christianity and Islam are very strong on a life of accountability and obeying the law. Why are the priests and Imams so lukewarm about teaching Accountability and Rule of Law to Christians and Moslems? If every professing Christian and Moslem in Nigeria embraces an accountable and corruption-free lifestyle at all costs, Nigeria will become a heavenly paradise on earth.

One NGO, A Non Governmental Organisation, Renewal and Refreshing Hosanna Ministry (RRHM), in November 2015 decided to live up to its divine responsibility by embarking on "Accountability Movement", led by Dr. Abimbola Odumosu.

The vision is to help develop high levels of accountabity in the Nigerian society, and to enlighten the populace on the benefits of being accountable. Various techniques including media adverts and debates will be used to teach accountability. The project recognizes that the most effective way to guarantee a corrupt-free society for the citizens is to embrace the Rule of Law, and work together in living an accountable lifestyle. Through a series of e-newsletters, television and radio programmes, coupled with children's programmes, the accountability movement will provide an opportunity for accountable citizens to rise and lead public offices. This fine example of a movement in accountability initiated by an NGO should be applauded. This is the only hope of a corruption-free and accountable Nigeria where rule of law prevails. It is the only hope of repairing the national fabrics and foundation, which have been badly destroyed.

The Accountability Pathway:

➤ The Desire to Be Accountable Comes from Within: I have decided to be conscious of the effects that my actions will have on other people in my home, at work and my community at large. No one else can do this for me. It is my responsibility and I have decided to carry it out.

➤ The Marks of Truth and Trustworthiness: I will strive to live an exemplary life. My words and my actions will be transparent and in sync with each other. I will leave no room for contradiction.

➤ Respect for The Law: I will be a law-abiding citizen, never allowing myself live above the laws of the land irrespective of my position or status in the society, realizing that anyone who breaks any law commits a crime, and therefore is a criminal. Since I do not want to wear the label CRIMINAL, I will discharge all my civic duties in accordance with the law, and will go the extra mile in order to maintain the laws of the land.

➤ Commitment to Society: I will always consider the needs of my society. UBUNTU: "I am because you are"; "I am not me.........without we". I will strive to work for the common good, and knowing that what affects me affects the people I live with, I will be mindful of all my actions. I will not hesitate to contribute to the growth and progress of my society to the best of my capacities in all areas possible.

> Support Positive Change: I will support all moves towards positive change in the society, irrespective of my personal inclinations and ambitions.
> Be My Brother's Keeper: I will not abuse whatever power I have or position I occupy in the society, but will use it to protect and help those who are powerless, socially and economically disadvantaged.
> Integrity is it! I will not involve myself with any forms of exploitation, abuse, or corrupt practices.
> Lifestyle of Accountability: I will be accountable to my family, peers, colleagues, community, and country.
> Respectfulness: I will treat others with dignity and respect, regardless of gender, age, race, religion, or in whatever ways we may be different.

Elements that Build and Engineer Accountability

1. Commitment:

The first step in the accountability walk **is COMMITMENT** from within.

Legitimate reasons for commitment to accountability and rule of law include:

> I like being seen as a person that keeps her word. Whatever I say I will do, I will endeavor to do it. It helps me to be authentic.
> It promotes growth in every area; it helps to grow all relationships, father and son, mothers and daughters, husband and wife, boss and employee relationship, and to build a great team.
> It is a quality that is required from good leaders; leaders must deliver on their words.

> It promotes kindness, and kindness is a great act of humanity

> As a child of God, I know that one day I must give an account of my life to God, so why not start now?

> A life of accountability helps me to be **truly who I am, and want to be.**

2. It All Starts with You:

Here is an interesting series of thoughts on the role of individual responsibility and accountability to the current state of the Nigerian nation:

"Thinking about Nigeria, Nigerians and the subject of change:

- *Why do we expect one man to change the course of the country when individually we continue to destroy it? Yes, I'm talking to you the Nigerian citizen.*
- *When last did you bribe to get out of doing the right thing? That policeman, that customs agent, the Local Government Authority staff, when was the last time you refused bribery?*
- *When last did you take the wrong side of the road because no one could see you? Or drive through a red light because no one was watching?*
- *Do you still defy traffic laws because the road management authorities or police officers are not around, or bypass the PHCN pole and meter to reduce your bill and steal from discos who are suffering because of citizens like you who don't pay at all or refuse to pay for the right amount used?*
- *Let's talk about taxes! How many business owners pay the right amount of taxes? Don't you prefer to bribe the taxman to write lower taxes for you than to pay your full amount?*
- *Do you still throw trash on the road from your cars,*

in front of your children and wards who then
continue the cycle of destruction?

3. Respect for The Law:

What is respect for the law, and how can we enforce it in our country, Nigeria?

Here are two real life stories, based on personal experiences:

Sometime in July 2013, I was in Houston, Texas, with my family and we were on our way back from church. We came to a major crossroad, which had its traffic lights non-functional.

Now, that seems like a perfect opportunity for chaos, but lo and behold, drivers were taking their turns to cross – everyone was being patient and orderly. My family and I from Nigeria were all dazed and felt like we were watching a movie. It occurred to one of us later that we ought to have recorded it.

Fast-forward to January 2016 and a different location – Lagos, Nigeria. I was stuck in a terrible jam as we were trying to cross over from one major road to another. Even with the presence of traffic control officers, it was utter chaos. Cars had doubled up the lanes, and thus, traffic flow had ceased. It took a great deal of shouting, car bashing, and aggressiveness before order could be restored and traffic moving again.

These two contrasting scenarios demonstrate graphically what we mean by respect for the law. In the Houston scenario there was natural order from discipline and accountability, whilst in the Lagos scenario there was utter disregard for law and order.

It is unfortunate to say that it appears as if Nigerians, and perhaps Africans as a whole, intrinsically have no respect for the laws of the land, whereas in other continents, there is a natural inclination that the law must be respected (of course there are law breakers in every part of the world, and not just Africa). Part of the difference is with law enforcement. When there is strong and severe law enforcement that will punish every offender, the citizens learn to respect the law.

Here are other ways we break the law routinely in Nigeria while driving:

- o **Use of Cell Phones:** It is illegal to talk on your phone, send or read text messages without a hands-free device while you are driving. In fact, it's a primary offense with a fine attached to it. According to statistics from the Federal Road Safety Corps (FRSC), 15 percent of accidents in the major cities of Nigeria are caused by use of cell phone. There have been several videos on the Internet showing the damage caused by use of cell phones while driving. Most of us at some point or the other have been guilty of this offense. This is a poor accountability practice, which we must stop as those who are accountable citizens.
- o **Driving on the wrong side of the road**: This is a common occurrence especially in big cities in Nigeria. The usual perpetrators are commercial bus drivers, and sadly even educated citizens, and elite members of the society join them. I will like to strongly appeal to those engaged in such practices to desist from such lawless acts a major priority so that we can be more orderly.
- o **Lack of respect for pedestrians and road signs**: It is disappointing to see how drivers speed on past Zebra Crossings, even when they see people waiting to cross; they park in places where a No-Parking sign is clearly visible, they turn into roads that have a No-Entry sign, they disregard speed limits, and violate traffic rules with impunity. Nigeria badly needs a new breed of WE THE PEOPLE who will strive to obey traffic rules and signs, and be considerate of other road users, pedestrians and drivers alike.
- o **Drunk Driving:** Drunk driving is a national phenomenon that has led to a lot of accidents and deaths of future leaders. According to the FRSC, drunk driving accounts for 54 percent of road

accidents in Nigeria. There are always reminders on television and radio stations about the ills and consequences of drunk driving. Accountable citizens of Nigeria, must never be caught in this act.

4. Embracing Positive Change:

It is often said that change is the only constant thing in life. Everywhere we look, we see or feel one type of change or another. There is change in climate, people change, the times change, and so on.

How we respond to change defines our capacity to adapt. We can choose to respond the right way, or the wrong way. In essence, when life hands you lemons, do you make lemonade out of the lemon, or simply complain about the bitterness of the lemon?

For example, if a person is diagnosed with cancer, first of all, a change has taken place in the person's health. Now how the person chooses to adapt to that change, will determine the person's state of being, whether he or she will get well, or whether the condition will continue to deteriorate. Some may undergo a change in diet and lifestyle; while some may take the news as a death sentence and live a reckless life, thinking that after all, they are going to die anyway. In Nigeria, a lot of changes have taken place and will continue to take place. Governments have changed, policies have changed, and even people have changed. The question is how have we as individuals adapted to the series of changes that have taken place? Have we responded positively, or negatively?

Embracing positive change means making positive choices. Let us take for example the level of corruption in our country. It has escalated over the years, and even though the present administration is waging a war against corruption, there are many battles to be fought, not just at the government level, but right down to us individuals in our everyday lives. It is up to us, which side of the battlefield we want to stand on.

Will you choose to give a bribe or take one? Or will you stand against it no matter the threats or dangers that might seem to come your way. Will you stand against injustice, even if it means that you will stand alone, or will you cower away and join the crowd? Will you cross the highway on foot just because you want to save time, or will you use the pedestrian bridge? Will you obey the speed limit, or will you drive on as you see fit just because the road is free? Embracing positive changes is all about making the right choices, and even though we all run with the 'I had no choice,' line, in reality, we always have a choice – right or wrong.

5. Keeping Commitment versus African Time:

When we sign a contract, we have made a commitment to abide by the terms of that contract. When we enter into a written or verbal agreement with someone, it is the same thing.

I guess we're all familiar with the term 'African time', which basically is another way to describe being late for something. Even though it is used in jest, it is a reflection of our poor ability to be punctual, be it for meetings, events, or delivery of services. Of course, this habit of 'African time' has several causes (or rather excuses) - bad traffic (Lagos residents can testify to this especially during rush hours), fuel scarcity, bad roads, the weather (those days when almost all roads turn into rivers), and a host of others.

In my case, lately, it has been tough getting our son to school before the 8 o'clock resumption time. Our routine hasn't changed, but the amount of time spent on the way to school has. The fuel queues have increased his travel time from 15 minutes to 30 minutes. It took a few late days before I made the mental decision that the only way he was going to make it on time, was not to hurriedly speed through the morning routine, but to adjust his sleep and wake up times to allow for the extra 15 minutes.

I imagine many other parents experience this challenge, and it would be easy for us to expect the schools to understand, but the commitment to be punctual for school or work or church or a meeting, should never be dependent on traffic or fuel scarcity. If all it takes to keep that commitment

129

is a small adjustment in lifestyle, then why not do it?

It's easier to give an excuse, or apologize, or keep rushing in the mornings, somehow hoping that the outcome would be different, but doing the right thing is not always easy, is it?

If we expect to have a society that is functional, if we expect steady power supply, good roads, and good governance, then it is about time we started living up to expectations and keeping our commitments to be where we say we will be, and when we say we will be there.

A Personal Encounter on being an Accountable Citizen:

If you are a Nigerian living in Nigeria, or even anywhere else in the world, you would probably be familiar with the frustrating process of obtaining a Nigerian passport, especially if you want to go about it the right way – no short cuts, no bribes. I found myself at the point where I needed to renew my passport, and of course, I did not even contemplate using any of the 'short cuts'. Needless to say, the whole process was far from pleasant.

Given the resolve not to take undue advantage of the system or secure the bridging-support of contractor-officers, the form completion and payment to the bank were done on **Monday, 2 November 2015** but finally submitted to the Front Desk Officers the following day **–Tuesday, 3 November 2015.** I was advised to report back for data processing by **Wednesday, 11 November 2015.** Having completed this on the appointed due date, I had imagined that the new Passport would be ready for collection by **Tuesday, 17 November 2015.** Walking casually to the Passport Office to collect the new Passport, I came across a church member who was grumbling that she paid for the same day processing on Monday 16 November 2015, and was requested to pick it up the following day, Tuesday, 17 November 2015. She actually got her Passport that day while mine, which had gone through the due process was not ready. That more than infuriated me and just had to

130

precipitate a crisis. I reported the matter to the Special Assistant to the Chief Passport Officer.

I was wearing my 'Accountability Speaks' lapel pin while I was precipitating the crisis, and this must have created some aura and standing of a Senior Government Official. The swagger and manner of officialdom and discussion with the Passport Office commanding heights, no doubt, fast tracked the processing and delivery of the Passport by midday of **Wednesday, 18 November 2015.**

In another scenario, my daughters had completed new applications for their ePassports, paid all charges since August 2015, but had not been successful. Several phone calls and travels from outside the United States did not also yield any success. Just after the New Year, I accompanied them both to the Nigerian House with the aim of getting to the root of the problem. Adorning my Accountability Speaks lapel pin, I casually strolled in along with them.

From where I was sitting, a gentleman that appeared to be a superior officer in the department went out, and I quickly stepped behind him and complained. Invariably, he also had a similar Green-White-Green Lapel Pin on. In summary, my daughters also got their passports. In both cases we secured our passports without bribing anyone. It is actually possible to achieve our goals without bribing anyone. We may need to plan ahead so we have more time to achieve our purposes without bribing anyone.

How Possible Is to Be Honest and True When No one Is Watching?

Just last year, the Internet and the media were abuzz with the story of Josephine Agwu, a cleaner who was working at the Murtala Mohammed International Airport in Lagos. She had found the sum of N12M and returned it to the security unit of the airport. Agwu's monthly salary was a mere N7, 800. With such a meager salary, Agwu could have walked away with the money and started a new life for herself in another city.

In another incident, Edward Ezekiel Onoriode, an officer of the Nigerian Police Force, discovered a purse, which contained cash in foreign and local currencies, recharge cards, nine ATM cards, and various forms of identification, and a gold necklace. Now, the officers of the Nigerian Police Force do not exactly have the best income or welfare package, so he had the option to quietly keep the purse and perhaps make his life a little better, or even keep the items that were worth something to him, and then return the purse, but he returned everything intact to the owner.

The owner of the purse offered him a monetary reward, but Onoriode refused stating: "It's good to do the right thing, not because of any reward that comes with it, but because it is the right thing to do."

In Abuja, Nigeria, Umeh Usuah, a taxi driver, found the sum of N18M left in his cab by a passenger. After he discovered the money, he returned it to the owner. Usuah did not have to return the money. He could have used the money to start up another business in another part of town, or another state altogether and no one would know.

In all three events, these people could have counted their discoveries as 'blessings' from God to turn their situations around, and with the present economic situation in the country, it would have actually seemed like the 'wise' thing to do; but that is where honesty and integrity come in.

It all boils down to doing what is right, regardless of your circumstances. Doing good is a constant. If everyone could emulate these three people, if our leaders could emulate these traits, would we not have a better society? Knowing that the funds that have been entrusted with them are not to be used for their personal gratification, but used to execute projects that would make the society better.

The WE THE PEOPLE movement.

As was stated in the Preface of this book, God has blessed Nigeria as a nation. The Nigerian nation has suffered badly from two related calamities---bad leaders, and bad followers.

A selfless cerebral intellectual as president has never led Nigeria. First, such a president will select a selfless intellectual cabinet of accountable men and women to run the affairs of the nation, and he must hold his cabinet completely accountable. Rubbish should never happen anywhere in the country under the watch of such a president. He or she must pursue balanced economic development that will stimulate economic growth and prosperity for all Nigerians. Security and properly functional infrastructure will be evident abundantly everywhere in Nigeria.

Most of the present day WE THE PEOPLE of Nigeria, the followers, the grassroots, are reckless law breakers who hustle for money, disrespect their fellow citizens, highly corrupt, and have little or no sense of integrity and accountability. The Nigerian nation has suffered a long endless cycle of bad followers electing bad leaders, who in turn abuse and disrespect the grassroots who blindly put them in office. Often, the bad leaders were elected because they bribed bad followers to vote for them.

This viscous cycle of bad followers electing bad leaders cannot continue. The WE THE PEOPLE project is a national movement of the Nigerian grassroots engineered by responsible Nigerian intellectuals at home and in the diaspora, to train and grow a new breed of WE THE PEOPLE of Nigeria who will first clean up themselves and then clean up Nigeria from bottom to top. Only a clean bottom can put in place a clean top. This book, WE THE PEOPLE, is an educational material that will serve as a potent tool to train and grow a new breed of WE THE PEOPLE of Nigeria. The movement cuts across every religious, tribal, and political boundary in Nigeria. The goal of this movement is to bring together within two years 50 million Nigerian men and women of every tribe, religion, social class and age to bond together in a strong nationwide accountability movement in which this new breed of WE THE PEOPLE of Nigeria will form the critical mass required to completely transform Nigeria from bottom to top. Membership in the WE THE PEOPLE movement is open to all Nigerians of every tribe and religion who will commit to doing the right and accountable things in their lives, and commit to transform Nigeria, one life at a time. More details on how to join the movement is provided in the Postface at the end of the book, but please do not rush to the Postface, we want you to read the whole book.

CHAPTER 4

The Ideological Crisis of Nigerian Political Parties: Some Reflections

Prof. Okechukwu Ibeanu, Ph.D.

Prefatory remarks

There is a widely held position by scholars and other observers that Nigerian political parties operate without ideology and in the absence of ideology, party members lack discipline, making it difficult for the party to enforce its will and supremacy. Two general consequences are then suggested to arise from these deficits, which are supposed to be bad for democratic governance. First is the level of conflict within political parties, which sometimes is even sterner than interparty conflicts. The logic here is that if members of a political party shared common commitments to an ideology and the party whip, which is the ultimate expression of party supremacy, functioned properly, there should not be the level of conflict and disarray that we often find in political parties. The second suggested consequence is the rapidity with which Nigerian politicians move from one party to another or establish new parties. This is what has been variously characterized as "carpet crossing", "vagrancy" and "nomadism" among others.[1] The point canvassed by proponents of this position is that with party ideology and supremacy there will be clear lines of party commitments that politicians would find difficult to cross. The fact that

---

[1] J. Shola Omotola 'Nigerian political parties and political ideology', *Journal of Alternative Perspectives in the Social Sciences*, Vol. 1, No. 3, 2009; Abubakar Momoh 'Party system and democracy in Nigeria, 1999 – 2010' in Obafemi, O., Egwu, S., Ibeanu, O. and Ibrahim, J. (eds.) *Political Parties and Democracy in Nigeria*, Kuru: Nigerian Institute for Policy and Strategic Studies, 2014.

Nigerian politicians can move from one political party to another ad libitum without any "discomfort" signals the absence of party ideology and party supremacy.

There are three important inferences that could be made from these positions, which should not be taken for granted. Consequently, they call for profound interrogation. The first is that Nigerian political parties operate without ideologies. This cannot be taken for granted because we need to know what exactly party ideologies are, particularly whether they are the same with or differ from a national ideology. A second deduction that calls for interrogation is that this perceived absence of party ideology explains the crisis that we observe in political parties. This cannot be taken for granted because for one thing, it could in fact be a very reductionist argument in the sense that everything that is wrong with parties boils down to this presumed lack of ideology. And for another thing, it could in point of fact lead to untidiness in explanation. This is because it is possible that both absence of ideology and crisis in parties are dependent variables to be explained, rather than a cause and effect relationship. The third deduction that should not be treated casually is that there is always a necessary connection between party supremacy and sustenance of democracy. Put in other words, party supremacy is necessarily good for democracy. This cannot be taken for granted, as has been noted by many students of political parties dating all the way back to Bagehot. According to LaPalombara and Anderson, Bagehot's anxiety that constituency government will replace the more virtuous parliamentary government has been echoed by many other scholars, who suggest that "mass-based, disciplined parties are not necessarily healthy for democracy".[2] One may add that disciplined petty bourgeois parties, if they were possible, would even be unhealthier for democracy because it may well be in the internal disarray of these parties that democracy becomes of any value to the

---

[2] J. LaPalombara & J. Anderson (1992). 'Political parties' in M. Hawkesworth & M. Kogan (eds.), *Encyclopedia of Government and Politics*: Vol. 1, London: Routledge, 1992, p. 406.

vast majority of Nigerians.

Absence of Ideology or Ideology in crisis

The first of the three presumptions that I want to interrogate is that Nigerian political parties operate without ideologies. Is this really correct? My simple answer is no. However, Nigerian political parties are in crisis, an aspect of which is ideological. Once we have a proper understanding of this crisis, some of our preconceptions about Nigerian political parties would make better sense. Surely, it is not difficult to see that Nigerian political parties are in turmoil, both within and among themselves. It is widely said in both academic writings and popular discourses about Nigerian political parties that they are always at war within and with themselves, lack internal democracy, have no ideology, disrespect their rules, have been captured by moneybags, lack discipline and have become instruments of national disintegration. The Uwais Committee Report summarizes this widespread concern about Nigerian political party:

> One of the most crucial and yet least developed democratic institutions in the country is the political party system. There are currently 50 registered political parties in the country, most of which are an assemblage of people who share the same level of determination to use the party platform to get to power. As such, it is usually difficult to identify any party programmes or ideologies. The structure of the political parties is such that internal democracy is virtually absent. The political parties are weak and unable to effectively carry out political mobilization, political education and discipline.[3]

---

[3] Federal Republic of Nigeria *Report of the Electoral Reform Committee* (Uwais Committee Report), December 2008, p. 4

The crisis of Nigerian political parties is in fact, composed of three sub-crises namely, a rule crisis, an identity crisis and an ideological crisis. First, on the rule crisis, Nigerian political parties have elaborate rules that supposedly guide their activities. These include the Nigerian constitution, the Electoral Act, party constitutions, and several guidelines developed by Electoral Management Bodies and the political parties themselves on sundry issues, such as nomination, financing, campaigning, among others. The rule crisis manifests as a general tendency in political parties to breach and disobey rules, including their own rules and regulations. This rampant disregard for rules is what appears as lack of "internal party democracy" and accountability.

Second, political parties in Nigeria are undergoing an identity crisis. What are Nigerian political parties? Are they ethnic parties, class parties, popular parties, mass parties, or cadre parties? The crisis of identity also means that these parties are essentially activated during elections and they practically disappear after elections, except for those that go into government. The crisis of identity affects the stability of parties, not only in terms of structure and organization, but also in terms of leadership and membership. Compared to political parties in some other parts of the world, Nigerian political parties lack longevity, and each round of transition and elections have seen the emergence of new political parties. Compared to say the Justicialist Party (Peronists) in Argentina or Institutional Revolutionary Party (PRI) in Mexico, Nigerian political parties do not retain their identities over a long period of time. It is partly this transience of identity that appears as lack of party discipline and "nomadism" among their members.[4]

Thirdly, and most importantly, there is a specific crisis of ideology in political parties. This is what many observers erroneously characterize as absence of party ideology. Nigerian political parties are deeply ideological formations from at least two levels. At the first level, they are steeped generally in market ideology, Nigeria being constitutionally a

---

[4] Momoh, *op cit.* p. 92.

market economy and market democracy. Within this market context, the Nigerian constitution provides the overarching ideological framework for political parties to operate. Section 224 of the 1999 Constitution provides that "the programme as well as the aims and objects of a political party shall conform with the provisions of Chapter II of this Constitution". Chapter II of the Constitution contains the "Fundamental Objectives and Directive Principles of State Policy". The political, economic and social objectives contained in that chapter can be summarized as pursuit of national unity and integration, a corruption-free market economy and a liberal-welfarist society respectively. Given this constitutional directive, Nigerian political parties naturally gravitate to the centre of the political spectrum, being neither left of centre or right of centre, but pursuing essentially identical goals of national unity and market economy. At a second level, Nigerian political parties are steeped in petty bourgeois ideology, which is characterized by excessive focus on capturing power, excessive individualism and opportunism, as well as instability. You could not find a better recipe for turmoil than a combination of market ideology and petty bourgeois ideology.

The ideological crisis of Nigerian political parties therefore manifests in the form of "competition among likes". Nigerian political parties find it difficult to create distinct and recognizable programmatic platforms for elections because essentially the same ideological orientation is already inscribed in their DNA and this fuels the cutthroat competition we find among political parties. My point is that it is not correct that Nigerian political parties operate without ideology. Even less correct is that the existence of ideology necessarily creates value consensus, which in turn reduces conflicts, as a long tradition of functionalist political analysis is wont to believe. To the contrary, it is conceivable that it is the value consensus imposed on Nigerian political parties by both market ideology and petty bourgeois ideology that accounts for conflicts within and between political parties. As Ake correctly argues:

> Commonly shared values may

concentrate demands on the same scarce goods making the competition for them more intense, and exacerbating conflict. One can easily imagine a situation in which value-consensus would lead to a Hobbesian state of war. What would happen to a political system whose members hold the belief that power must be sought at all cost and exercised without restraint?[5]

These apt remarks perfectly capture the character of the petty bourgeoisie and its ideological orientations. As we shall see, this ideology is consistent with the crisis we observe in political parties.

Explaining the crisis of Nigerian political parties

A second presumption about Nigerian political parties that should not be taken for granted is that lack of ideology explains the crisis that is rampant within political parties, including the seeming inability of parties to exercise supremacy over their members. In fact the import of the comment of the Uwais Committee that political parties are a mere assemblage of power seeking individuals is that parties do not exist as such. My argument is that the crisis is not to be sought in the absence of ideology, but rather it is the manifestation of a particular type of ideology – petty bourgeois ideology. Yet, this ideology is only one plank of our explanation of the crisis of political parties. There are four important characteristics of Nigerian political parties in their current phase of development.[6] First, political parties

---

[5] Claude Ake 'Explaining Political Instability in New States' *The Journal of Modern African Studies*, Vol. 11, No. 3 (Sep., 1973), pp. 348.

[6] I have elsewhere identified three broad phases of the development of political parties namely, the Nationalist-Lagosian phase, the Sectional-Segmental phase and the National-Centralized phase. The current crisis is rooted in the third and present phase. See Okechukwu Ibeanu 'Political parties and the electoral process in Nigeria: a conceptual analysis and some

have become increasingly disrespectful of rules and, consequently, more undemocratic internally. Second, they have become more national and centralized. Third, political parties have become more undifferentiated ideologically and programmatically. Fourth and finally, they have become more money-driven in operation. These four characteristics of parties are the critical expressions of the crisis at the National-Centralized phase of the development of political parties. They therefore require explanation.

The explanation is framed by three related explanatory variables namely, the character of the petty bourgeoisie, the impact of military rule and the preponderance of money politics.

1. *Character of the petty bourgeoisie*

The first element in this explanation is to understand the phenomenal rise in the level of disrespect for rules, particularly as it concerns democratic processes within Nigerian parties. This has been widely posed by many observers as the problem of lack of internal party democracy. Unfortunately, this problem is often treated in a very subjectivist manner, suggesting that it is the conscious machination of party leaders that is to blame. This explanation is too voluntaristic to be fundamental. A deeper understanding of this crisis of rules in Nigerian parties would suggest that it has to be located in the character of the petty bourgeoisie, which has been the most important social force in Nigerian politics. As a class, the petty bourgeoisie has developed specificity such that it is no longer simply an auxiliary class that manages the class projects of the bourgeoisie. In other words, in Nigeria the petty bourgeoisie has become a class with "pertinent effects", at the political and ideological levels of structure. According to Poulantzas, pertinent effects mean that:

recent lessons', Lead discussion paper for the roundtable on Political Parties and the Future of Elections in Nigeria organized by the Nigerian Political Science Association, Abuja, Nigeria, 5th April 2016.

the reflection of the place in the process of production on the other levels constitute a new element which cannot be inserted in the typical framework which these levels would present without this element. This element thus transforms the limits of the levels of structures or class struggle at which it is reflected by 'pertinent effects'; and it cannot be inserted in a simple variation of these limits.[7]

Given its pertinent effects, the intrinsic characteristics of the petty bourgeoisie come to the fore and become pervasive, particularly at the political and ideological levels of structure, which are the principal sites of functioning and reproduction of the "new petty-bourgeoisie".[8] These characteristics according to Poulantzas include petty-bourgeois individualism; attraction to the status quo and fear of revolution; the myth of 'social advancement' and aspiration to bourgeois status; belief in the 'neutral state' above classes; political instability and a tendency to support 'strong states' and Bonapartist regimes; as well as revolts taking the form of 'petty-bourgeois' jacqueries.[9]

We can infer the following as the class instincts of the petty bourgeoisie, which have far reaching effects on politics:

i) *State-centrism*
The petty bourgeoisie is a state-oriented class and it is oriented to strong states. Given that it does not have a principal role in capitalist production, being at best petty commodity producers but mainly salaried workers on the margins of capitalism, this class supports state redistribution of income, which puts its members at an advantage over the working people. State-centrism derives from a fetishism of state power rather than fetishism of commodities.

---

[7] Nicos Poulantzas *Political Power and Social Classes*, London: Verso, 1978, p. 79.

[8] Nicos Poulantzas 'On social classes' *New Left Review*, 78, 1973, p. 33.

[9] *Ibid.*

ii).   *Technocratism*

This derives from the orientation of the petty bourgeoisie to the state. Poulantzas' characterization of the class as particularly supportive of Bonapartist regimes is correct. In the Nigerian context, however, this Bonapartist orientation adopts a Janiform character. The Nigerian petty bourgeoisie is oriented to state institutions that are able to act autonomously from other social forces, including capital, but yet interventionist enough to serve the interests of the petty bourgeoisie, the class that directly controls the state. Thus, this Bonapartism is one driven by a state technocracy, which is a major stratum of the petty bourgeoisie. In short, Bonapartist-technocratic regimes guarantee the relative autonomy of state institutions from capital, enabling the "state-nurtured" petty bourgeoisie to pursue its interests using these state institutions.

iii).   *Status quo orientation*

While the petty bourgeoisie as a class dreads proletarianization, its members have a morbid fear for a revolutionary transformation of society. Therefore, they prefer the capitalist status quo, particularly if the state is in a position to dispense patronages.

iv).   *Aspiration to bourgeois status*

The petty bourgeoisie has a strong tendency to use state resources to build an economic base, mainly transforming into a comprador bourgeoisie (contractors, service providers, import-export traders, foreign exchange dealers, etc.).

v).   *Petty bourgeois individualism/opportunism*

Excessive pursuit of narrow individual and sectional interests variously defined along ethnic, religious, professional and even family lines. Though capitalist, the petty bourgeois state is as a result patently unable to perfect the commodity form at the political level.

Consequently, that state is unable to appear as the unity of the collective interests of the people-nation. Instead, it exists as power parceled out to these various individual and sectional interests.

vi).   *Political instability*
In terms of political action, the petty bourgeoisie is a "swing class". It swings easily between the bourgeoisie and the working people. Of particular note in this regard is the intellectual petty bourgeois, which is permanently divided between intellectuals of the bourgeoisie or intellectuals of the working people. Moreover, it is a class given to revolts and opportunism, including revolts against its own class rule. Poulantzas correctly notes its tendency towards "petty bourgeois jacqueries". Above all, given the foregoing characteristics, political institutions tend to be very unstable and are unable to become separated from the specific sectional interests of the petty bourgeoisie.

These general characteristics of the petty bourgeoisie manifest politically in the following:

a) Inordinate competition to control state power. The pervasiveness of the state, even in the flaunted presence of the market, is striking in the petty bourgeois practice of multiparty democracy.
b) Use of state institutions for private and sectional gains. This explains the pervasiveness of corruption in public agencies notwithstanding the presumed capacity of liberal democratic institutions to regulate the behavior of public officials.
c) Parceling out of state agencies and institutions to individual and sectional interests, including ethnic, religious and other primordial ties.
d) An emphasis on power sharing. In the petty bourgeois practice of multiparty democracy, there is no life outside state power. To lose control of state power is

144

akin to a death sentence. Therefore, power sharing in the form of governments of national unity and such contraptions are gaining traction. They are the petty bourgeois version of inclusive politics.

e) Institutional instability, particularly widespread disrespect for rules and a tendency to undermine the operation of democratic institutions.

These characteristics logically find expression in the functioning of political parties as low party discipline, leading to massive disrespect for rules. In the first place, the indirect role of the petty bourgeoisie in production means that the members of this class inherently lack the discipline and sense of purpose that comes with real productive activities, like the bourgeoisie, working class or peasantry. Second, as a class given to instability and vacillation, the petty bourgeoisie tends to be opportunistic. This is contrary to the discipline needed to build and run political parties on a long-term basis. Third, the excessive individualism of members of this class also makes them prone to opportunism and a proclivity to cut corners. Finally, as a class that operates essentially within state and political institutions, they are prone to manipulating them for individual and sectional purposes. All these are definitely not conducive to party discipline, respect for rules and therefore internal party democracy.

2. *Impact of military rule*

Nigerian political parties have become more national and centralized in organization and more undifferentiated ideologically. I have already demonstrated that these two characteristics are rooted in their common ancestry in market ideology and petty bourgeois ideology. However, they have been deepened by the legacy of military rule. When the military first intervened in politics in January 1966, they blamed sectional, ethnic parties, which had dominated politics since middle colonial rule, for the political problems that led to military intervention. Consequently, successive military rulers perceived that political parties must serve a more integrative purpose. To do so, they have to be national in reach, centralized in organization and cut across communal divides. More importantly, they are to be less ideological and more committed to the market economy. The systematic deradicalization of politics in the period preceding the first military handover of power to civilians in 1979 has been well documented and need not delay us here.[10] Indeed, it was clear that the new political parties that will be part of the return to civil rule in 1979 were already predetermined to be neither regional nor radical. In fact, they were expected to be national in organization and centrist in ideology. Thus, two principal conditions for any association to be recognized as a political party under 1979 Constitution was that it had to have offices in two-thirds of the 19 States of the country and adhere to Chapter II of the Constitution, which, like the 1999 Constitution, was liberal-welfarist in orientation.

Essentially then, the military ensured first, that political parties became more national in reach, as an imperative of national integration and unity, since political parties were blamed for the centrifugal tendencies that almost dismembered the country in the 1960s. Second, parties also became more centrist ideologically. While the argument of several observers that Nigerian political parties do not have ideologies may be attractive, it is not exactly correct. What observers perceive as lack of ideology is in fact the hegemony of market ideology, which was imposed on political parties by the military and the Constitutions they established from 1979 onwards. By this imposition, parties are expected to be centrist, moderate and integrative. The logic was partly that to build a national, ethnically inclusive political party, as demanded in the National-Centrist phase, ideological extremes would be unhelpful. As a result of this centrist shift,

---

[10] Richard Joseph, R. (1978). 'Parties and ideology in Nigeria', *Review of African Political Economy, No. 13*, 1978. See also Okechukwu Ibeanu 'Political parties and the electoral process in Nigeria: a conceptual analysis and some recent lessons', op cit.

Nigerian political parties became increasingly indistinguishable based on ideology or even ethnic composition. One effect of this homogeneity is that politicians can easily move from one party to another without committing "ideological suicide". This has deepened the crisis in political parties. Still, while purists would criticize this ideological monotony, it cannot be denied that it has contributed to some of the successful political bargains that have on occasions stabilized the political system.

3. *The rise of money politics*

A hallmark of the first two phases of the development of Nigerian political parties namely, the Nationalist-Legosian phase and Sectional-Segmental phase is the strong bond between the leaders of the party and the populace. Thus, Herbert Macaulay, the doyen of Nigerian nationalism and founder and leader of at least three early political parties in Nigeria, made a name defending the traditional land rights of indigenous peoples of Lagos. That bond between the people and political parties in the nationalist period progressively attenuated as communal affiliations and the personal interests of party leaders increasingly drove party politics. Consequently, as people lost faith in parties, money became the bond that held parties and the public together. However, the situation has only gotten worse in the National-Centralized phase due to the demand on parties to show national presence. Organizing political parties that are effectively national, which among other things entails fielding candidates in 989 State Assembly constituencies, 360 federal constituencies and polling in 120,000 units, requires a lot of money. Therefore, political parties have become more "monetized", to use the common Nigerian parlance. [11] Inevitably, positions in the parties, including

---

[11] On 2nd April 2011 when the Independent National Electoral Commission (INEC) postponed the first set of elections, two leaders of the ruling party at the time gave me a lecture on how important money has become to party politics in Nigeria. Among other things, they were very upset that INEC lost them a lot of money with the postponement and gave the

candidacy to elected positions, go to the highest bidders. Operating in a multiparty environment with over sixty political parties at one point, the role of money is bound to loom large. Unlike the Sectional-Segmental phase when inter-ethnic competition by political parties necessitated building intra-ethnic solidarities down to the grassroots, party financiers rather than party cadres are presently the driving forces behind political parties. The will of the moneybag trumps democratic principles, including the constitution of the party.

Is party supremacy the path to democratic progress?

The third issue that I set out to interrogate is the idea that party supremacy is good for democracy. In the first place, it seems to me that this idea is a carryover of the parliamentary party system, especially its whip system. In that system, especially as practiced in the UK, both the parliamentary party and the constituency party work together to ensure that members subject themselves to the wishes of the party. Political officials retained their position to the extent that the party has confidence in them. This is understandable because the Prime Minister has to have the confidence of parliament to remain in office, especially so because his/her party is usually the majority party. On the other hand, the constituency party determines the faith of members of parliament and, by extension, the faith of the Prime Minister.

The Presidential system is different in the sense that elected officials have more direct connection with the electorate. In other words, parties do not mediate the relations between elected officials and the electorate in the same way they do in the UK. This is even further strengthened where independent candidature is permitted.

---

specific example of the polling agents they sent to the 120,000 polling units across the country. They indicated that each agent was paid 8,000 Naira for that day. I was shocked at what my mental arithmetic was telling me – a whopping 960 million Naira for party agents alone for only one Election Day.

Unlike the Prime Minister, the President does not require the confidence of the legislature as such to remain in office. In fact, it may well be the attempt to over enforce party supremacy in a Presidential system that partly fuels the proliferation of political parties in Nigeria.

The second problem that faces party supremacy in the Nigerian context is the electoral system itself. Single member constituencies based on simple plurality (first-past-the-post) tends to give too much responsibility for getting elected to the candidate, rather than the party. Compare this with various list systems common in proportional representation (PR). In PR, seats are more or less allocated to political parties, which is an incentive to candidates to tow the party line.

Third, because single member constituencies based on simple plurality gives a lot of responsibility to candidates, and given the rise in money politics in Nigeria, individuals who can sponsor their own elections and better still the election of other candidates become very important in political parties. And depending on how impoverished the party is, these individuals could become more important than the party itself. This explains why occupants of executive positions have become very important in party life in Nigeria. They are likely to have the funds to "sponsor" their parties.

My point is that while party supremacy may sound attractive because we feel that it could curb the undisciplined behaviour of individuals in political parties, the reality is that party supremacy could in fact become a fetter on democracy within the parties. For one thing, given the petty bourgeois character of parties and the rise of money politics, party supremacy will simply express the whims and caprices of moneybags in the party, not necessarily the will of the party. In other words, party supremacy in an era of party godfathers may well not be the path to democratic progress.

Finally, I will end with three well-known incidents in Nigeria's recent political life to illustrate that party supremacy is not always consistent with the advancement of democracy. The first is the saga that took place in Anambra

State in 2003 in which the leaders of one of the leading political parties in the state compelled a Governorship candidate to sign a prior letter of resignation in case he, on winning the election, failed to adhere to a number of agreed things. The candidate was even taken to a shrine to swear an oath to keep to the agreement. When as Governor he failed to keep to the pact, he was kidnapped and the letter of resignation tendered in the House of Assembly to support his replacement. This may be an unorthodox way of enforcing the will of the party, but it also illustrates how party supremacy could be used to undermine democracy.

The second illustration is the nomination of candidates for Governor by the People's Democratic Party in Rivers State in 2007. It has since become clear from the judgment of the Supreme Court that the party removed the winner of the primaries and replaced him with a favoured candidate. Against the admonitions and threats by the party, the legitimate winner of the primaries went to court and pursued the case to the Supreme Court. The Supreme Court subsequently determined the case only after the 2007 elections, deciding that the favoured candidate was not the legitimate candidate and therefore could not have rightly won the election. It then declared the legitimate winner of the primaries the winner of the Governorship election in Rivers State. Discounting the curiosity of this Supreme Court decision in declaring a Governor instead of ordering a re-election or better still the disqualification of the party from the election, this incident points to how party supremacy could be counter-democratic.

The final illustration has to do with the election of principal officers of the National Assembly in 2015. The ruling party had "anointed" specific individuals to become the principal officers. However, some members of the party felt that such a decision was not democratic. They therefore ignored party directives, allied with other parties and blocked the emergence of the party's favoured candidates as principal officers. This incident deeply divided opinions across Nigeria. Some observers vilified the recalcitrant legislators for gross indiscipline and for undermining party supremacy. However, many other observers praised the legislators and criticized the party for attempting to foist unpopular officers on the National Assembly.

CHAPTER 5

Corruption in Nigeria: Review, Causes, Effects and Solutions

Okwuagbala Uzochukwu Mike, BSc.

Introduction

Corruption is Nigeria's biggest challenge. It is clear to every citizen that the level of corruption in the country is high. It is found in every sector of society. This chapter presents corruption in the Federal Republic of Nigeria: its causes, effects and solutions. It covers areas where corruption manifests in the country, and how it has resulted to stunted growth in many sectors of the economy, backed up with facts and figures. The chapter is informative and offers suggestions as how to reduce the spread of corruption in the country.

What is corruption? Corruption is the dishonest or fraudulent conduct by those in power, typically involving bribery. It is the illegitimate use of power to benefit a private interest (Morris 1991). Corruption is the giving of a bribe to an official so that the truth will not be told. It involves the embezzlement of public funds for personal use and any acts which are considered to be criminal according to the law of a particular society.

Corruption is one of the economic crimes that are particularly subversive to the economic life of any society. Its commonest and meanest form is bribery, the taking of money or other forms of gratification as a condition or inducement for the performance of official act in favour of the person that offers the gratification (Hassan, Ebele & Raphael 2007).

According to Professor Ben Nwabueze, corruption can manifest in many ways, including unnecessary expensive and extravagant lifestyle, lavish ostentatious display of ill-gotten wealth, unaccounted-for bulging bank accounts, large personal donations at private functions not supported by visible means of income, ownership of private jet or fleet of expensive cars, palatial buildings, and so on (Nwabueze 2003).

Corruption is perhaps the most troubling 'disease' in Nigeria today, not because it is new, but because it has refused to yield to all manner of medications. Many say that it has become malignant and resistant to therapy, but I think that it is because the right therapy has not yet been administered. Others say that it might not respond to normal medication because of its malignancy (Nwaze 2011).

A Review of the State of Corruption in Nigeria

Transparency International, and other notable organizations that monitor corrupt practices around the world have ranked Nigeria, the most populous country in Africa, high in corruption. Such negative perceptions have sometimes had repercussions on Nigerians in diaspora, who have been perceived as also corrupt because of their country of origin.

Tabular Ranking of Corruption in Nigeria

Year	No of countries Surveyed	Transparency Score	Rank	Countries in the same category	Interpretation
2000	90	1.2	90	-	Nigeria was the world's most corrupt country in the year 2000.
2001	91	1.0	90	-	Nigeria was ranked the second-most corrupt nation in the year 2001.
2002	102	1.6	101	-	Nigeria was ranked the second-most corrupt nation in the year 2002.
2003	133	1.4	132	-	Nigeria was ranked the second-most corrupt nation in the year 2003.
2004	146	1.6	144	-	Nigeria was ranked the third-most corrupt nation in the year 2004.
2005	159	1.9	152	Cote d'Ivoire and Equatorial Guinea	By categorization, Nigeria ranked 8th most-corrupt nation in 2005.
2006	163	2.2	142	Angola, Congo Republic, Kenya, Kyrgyzstan, Pakistan, Sierra Leone, Tajikistan, and Turkmenistan	Nigeria ranked 21st most corrupt by categorization in 2006.
2007	180	2.2	147	Angola and Guinea-Bissau	Nigeria ranked 33rd most corrupt by group categorization in 2007.
2008	180	2.7	121	Nepal, Sao Tome and Principe, Togo and Viet Nam	Nigeria ranked 59th most corrupt by group categorization in 2008.
2009	180	2.5	130	Honduras, Lebanon, Libya, Maldives, Mauritania, Mozambique, Nicaragua, and Uganda	Nigeria ranked 50th most corrupt by group categorization in 2009.
2010	178	2.4	134	Azerbaijan, Bangladesh, Honduras, Philippines, Sierra Leone, Togo, Ukraine, Zimbabwe	Nigeria ranked 44th most corrupt by group categorization in 2010.
2011	183	2.4	143	Azerbaijan, Belarus, Comoros, Mauritania, Russia, Timor-Leste, Togo, and Uganda	Nigeria ranked 40th most corrupt by group categorization in 2011.
2012	176	27	139	Azerbaijan, Kenya, Nepal and Pakistan	Nigeria ranked 37th most corrupt by group categorization in 2012.
2013	177	25	144	Cameroon, Central African Republic, Iran, Papua New, Guinea and Ukraine	Nigeria ranked 33rd most corrupt by group categorization in 2013.
2014	175	27	136	Cameroon, Iran, Kyrgyzstan, Lebanon and Russia	Nigeria ranked 40th most corrupt by group categorization in 2014.
2015	168	27	136	Comoros and Tajikistan	Nigeria ranked 32nd most corrupt by group categorization in 2015

Table 5.1: Data provided in this table are correct and sourced from Transparency International website.

Using the table, from the year 2000 to 2011, the scoring index was from 0 to 10, where 10 represents free from corruption. The standard for grading how corrupt a country was changed from 2012 to 2015. Countries were scored by percentage, that is, by percentage basis ranging from 0 to 100. A score of 100 percent designates high transparency. An analysis of the anti-graft/anti-corruption laws in Nigeria shows that corruption will continue in spite of the laws, because the perpetrators do not fear any consequences (Oyinola 2011). Nigeria has had very poor Transparency International's corruption index ranking each year since 2000 to 2015. By contrast, in 2013, Denmark and New Zealand both scored highest at 91 percent each, meaning the countries were perceived to be clean and relatively transparent in outlook.

Corruption in Nigeria has brought untold hardships to the citizens of the country. Funds earmarked for specific projects have often been looted and diverted into the personal accounts of those charged with executing such projects. The $2.1billion arms deal is a case in point. This amount earmarked for the purchase of arms to counteract the activities of Boko Haram in North Eastern Nigeria, remains unaccounted for. The consequence of this is the loss of lives of several civilians and Nigerian soldiers, who have been inadequately armed in their fight against Boko Haram.

According to investigations by the Economic and Financial Crimes Commission, (EFCC), it has been discovered that 1.5 billion naira was paid from this fund into the account of the son of the former finance minister of the country. This news appeared in Sun Nigerian Newspaper on March 14, 2016. The evidence is depicted in the caption below:

Dasukigate: 1.5 Billion Traced to Son Of Former Finance Minister

— 14th March 2016

In another shocking revelation into the now-infamous investigation of the $2.1 billion arms deals funds (Dasukigate) it has been revealed that a whooping N1.5billion was paid to the account of the son of a former minister of finance.

The Economic and Financial Crimes Commission (EFCC) have decided to keep the names quiet so as not to put the investigation in danger.

EFCC claim that bureau de change operator who gave them the information, Salisu Umaru, said:

EFCC invited Mr. Salisu Umaru, the bureau de change operator who was involved in transmitting the funds into the account of the minister's son, and his statement after the meeting with EFCC was:

> *"I was invited by EFCC and when I reported, I was shown my company's account statement with Zenith Bank called Jabama Ada Global Nigeria Limited in which there was an inflow of N500million on 5/2/2015 and N1billion on 16/4/2015 into the account from the Office of the National Security Adviser. On the inflow of N500million into my company's account on 5/2/2015, I wish to state as follows: That on the same date (5/2/2015), I paid the equivalent of US$2,380,952 to the son of the minister, being the equivalent of the said N500million at the rate of N210 per dollar. I do not know what he used*

the money for. My own business is to buy and sell dollars. It is only the minister's son that can explain what the money was meant for. The minister's son signed and collected the said N500million" (Nwosu 2016).

Several other Nigerians ranging from high-ranking military officers to former ministers were arrested for various large amounts traced to their accounts from the 2.1 billion dollars. However, none of those involved in this scandal have been made to face the consequences of their actions. They are yet to serve their jail terms.

Faces of Corruption

There are different dimensions of corruption in Nigeria, and there is hardly any sector or facet of the society that is not affected.

Political Corruption

Corruption is rife in Nigerian politics, yet the politicians involved in corrupt practices appear to be above the law. They go free without punishment irrespective of the fact that there are laws that stipulate the penalties such offenders should face. Hassan et al in their book, "Nigeria's Reform Programme: Issues and Challenges" lamented thus on how corruption has bastardized the legal laws: "Corruption has broken loose of all legal barriers and restraints to become simply a buccaneering plunder brazenly perpetrated" (Hassan, Ebele & Olawepo 2007).

Other faces of corruption include embezzlement, bribery, rituals, rigging in elections and so on. Corruption is most visible in the political system. In both the Senate and the House of Representatives, corruption manifests at high levels through padding the national budget with hundreds of billions of naira, demanding incredible amounts from candidates undergoing confirmation hearings, pocketing hundreds of millions of naira designated for constituency projects, and from extorting hundreds of millions of naira through their oversight functions in several establishments.

Embezzlement of public funds in every sector is common. Many Nigerian (mis)leaders have helped boost the economies of other nations by depositing embezzled money in foreign banks. Facts and figures have shown that many of the men and women who rule Nigeria have embezzled funds and deposited them into foreign banks. After the death of the former Nigerian president, Sani Abacha, investigations led to the freezing of one of his foreign accounts containing over $100 million United States dollars (Hector 2004) that he stole. The Abacha administration in the 1990s notoriously looted upwards of $3 billion (Uzochukwu 2013). In 2005, the government of Switzerland returned to the government of Nigeria the sum of $722 million from one of his accounts in Switzerland. On July 29, 2016, the government of Switzerland signed a memorandum of understanding (MOU) with the Nigerian government to return another $321 million in another account of late Sani Abacha to Nigerian government. Unfortunately, many such funds have been abandoned to the foreign governments when the Nigerian leader or official dies, because they were maintained as nameless coded secret accounts.

Election rigging is a common phenomenon. During elections, the contestants hire thugs who go round the election polling stations to highjack the ballot boxes. When they steal these boxes, they then fill them with fake voters cards. In recent times, the new tactics that the contestants have adopted is buying voter's cards so that they can manipulate and use the cards for their own advantages. On many occasions politicians have bribed some top election officials to manipulate election results in their favour, including aspirants for president and governorship positions. When such cases appeared in court, the person who offered the judge the most bribe won the case.

Corruption in Universities and Colleges

Corruption parades itself in universities, polytechnics and

colleges in Nigeria. Most lecturers use the opportunity they have as lecturers to take advantage of students. Harassment of women by male lecturers, and the pressure to sleep with them is common. The most painful part of it is that some of them are married. Some of these married male lecturers offer female students good grades in exchange for sex.

Universities in Nigeria constantly complain about the funds allocated to them. Yet in many cases, the real problem is theft and mismanagement of funds. A lecturer in a university located in Anambra State who complained about the poor standard of the foundry in their department of Metallurgical and Materials Engineering had this to say: "What makes our foundry to be of low standard is corruption. An organization gave the department some money that would have been more than enough to upgrade and standardize the foundry, but I do not know what the management of the department did with the money." Corruption is one of the biggest challenges faced by the Nigerian education system.

Every university in Nigeria has a quota (maximum number of students) they can admit each year. How do some students find their way into the universities? Some are there not by merit, but through bribery called "sorting". Some rich men in the country bribe vice-chancellors and heads of departments to secure admission for their children. The consequence of this corrupt practice is that those who should be admitted on merit are often denied admission because their places have been taken up.

Heads of tertiary institutions in the Federal Republic of Nigeria have been found corrupt on many occasions. Some of them use the opportunities they have as the heads of the institutions for embezzlement of the institution's funds. Many of them do not follow due process in running the affairs of the institutions. A typical example of how these heads indulge in corruption is that involving the former Vice-Chancellor of Nnamdi Azikiwe University, Awka, (UNIZIK) Anambra state. In the year 2012, the former Vice-Chancellor of the university was investigated by EFCC for corrupt activities involving mismanagement of the university fund.

This ugly state of affairs appeared as headline news in some local newspapers and was documented by anti-corruption groups. Premium Times; *International Centre for Investigative Reporting, icirnigeria.org; 247Ureports, and others had the report detailed out in their publications.*

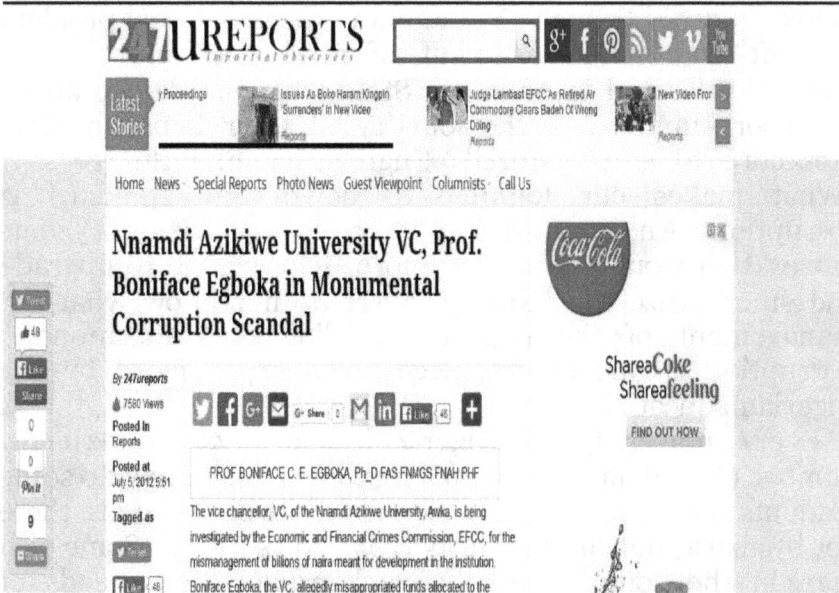

The above caption is the news report by 247Ureports on the corruption scandal. Quoting from the **International Centre for Investigative Reporting** on this corruption scandal, "The vice chancellor of the Nnamdi Azikiwe University, Awka, is being investigated by the Economic and Financial Crimes Commission (EFCC), for the mismanagement of billions of naira meant for development in the institution". Additional details from another publication stated, "Boniface Egboka, the VC, allegedly misappropriated funds allocated to the university through award of bogus and inflated contracts to himself through fronts and cronies, by selective bidding and fraudulent contract cost variations" (icirnigeria.org 2012). Such corrupt practices by Vice Chancellors are embarrassing for Nigerian universities because the citadel of learning in global best practices is a den of some of the worst corrupt practices.

Corruption in the Police Force

Corruption is prevalent amongst the police force in Nigeria. Bribery, intimidation, sexual harassment of young inmates in prisons, are some of the many forms of corruption in the police force. Given the bad experiences many Nigerians have had with policemen, the reputation of even the good ones amongst them have been tarnished.

The policemen who are sent on routine patrol duties cannot do so without collecting bribes from car owners and drivers. Their passion and purpose is to collect money from road users, not to make the roads secure. Bribes become compulsory even when your vehicle particulars are in order. Bus drivers must offer money before they continue with their journey. Bribery among Nigerian Police is routine. It is either you give money and go through with your vehicle or you refuse to do so and face the consequences by being unnecessarily delayed. In September 2015, a woman was shot dead by a policeman in Lagos state because her husband refused to give bribe to a team of eight policemen.

Corruption in the Nigerian police force has claimed lives in the country. According to the report, the woman and her husband were coming back from church that evening and when they refused to stop and offer bribe to the police, they were fired with gunshots, and the wife of the man was unlucky to be hit by the bullet. The tragic event claimed the life of the woman, and the husband was injured, and rushed to the hospital. This was reported in Daily Post news report of September 18, 2015. Idongesit, the woman died on the spot, while her husband, Godwin, was said to be gasping for breath at the Lagos State University Teaching Hospital, Ikeja, where he was taken for treatment. It was gathered that the couple was returning from a church programme on Wednesday in a tricycle belonging to the family when the incident happened" (Ameh 2015).

Corruption in Nigerian Football

Players are often not chosen by merit. It is all about who you know in top political offices or society. In the Nigerian Football Federation (NFF), corruption is the reason why Mr. A is elected as the coach of the team today and tomorrow the election is nullified and Mr. B chosen. Everybody wants to be at the head so that he will fill his pocket with the national cake. Reports and evidence have shown that there are corrupt practices in Nigerian football. A BBC news report had this to say: "A senior football official and a club administrator have been banned for 10 years following their involvement in corruption, the football authority has announced" (BBC Sport News 2013). Match-fixing and corruption are problems in Nigerian football and have led to sanctions against a number of clubs, referees and officials (Oluwashina 2013).

A referee (name withdrawn) who is currently a Catholic

priest serving in a parish in Anambra, once spoke about his experience on the level of corruption in football. According to the priest, he said that he narrowly escaped death when he officiated a match in the local league. He stated: "After the first half of the match, none of the two sides scored any goal. Before the beginning of the second half, some officials and young youths who were supporting the club at home side came and said to me: if you want to leave this pitch alive, make sure that you do anything possible to see that our club win this match." The young referee was scared of the threat and finally the home side won the match with a lone goal. The inability of Super Eagles of Nigeria to qualify for 2015 Africa Cup of Nations (AFCON) can be attributed to corruption.

Corruption in Churches

When churches are corrupt, what hope do Nigerians have? The truth is that not all the churches in the country are corrupt. Corruption is witnessed mainly in some "mushroom churches." Mushroom churches in this context are those churches, which do not have solid origin or foundation. They are not like Catholic, Anglican, or Orthodox churches. Mushroom churches are those churches which start when a person who calls himself a pastor goes and rents a room, decorates it, and convinces people to join him, that he has been given powers to perform signs and miracles from God. Some of the pastors go to the extent of using magical and devilish powers in running their church business in the name of God's power. They give the congregations what they want without them knowing the source of their so-called power. If there are women seeking the fruit of the womb, the babies may be given to them through devilish powers, and such babies would often be a source of much heartaches to their parents till death.

Pastors have on many occasions been caught in adultery and fornication. Through newspapers, television, and other channels, the immoral acts committed by Nigerian pastors have been publicized. In early November of 2014, there was a radio program from Blaze FM, Orifite, about a pastor that impregnated an 11-year-old girl. According to the report, the girl was impregnated by the pastor when her mother left her in the pastor's care for prayers, and went about her own business.

Internet Fraud

Fraudulent Internet activity is another face of corruption in Nigeria. Graduates and non-graduates who lack the knowledge and skills to help them secure gainful employment have taken to fraudulent activities over the Internet. These scammers have defrauded many Nigerian citizens, through posting false job offers on websites, and impersonating some religious leaders and extracting funds from vulnerable and unsuspecting citizens. According to the spiritual director of Adoration Ministry Enugu Nigeria (AMEN), Rev. Father Ejike Mbaka, some Nigerians impersonated him through websites and social media sites, specifically Facebook. He lamented that the bad guys used his picture to deceive people and collect money from them while claiming they were Fr. Mbaka. The notable reverend father made it clear that he was not on Facebook and neither did he own a website with his name. He went further to say that anyone caught in that act will dance to the music that he or she deserves, and the police have been alerted to find those criminals out.

Such acts are criminal and deserve serious punishment; hence both the Senate and members of House of Representatives are working hard to see that those caught face the punishments they deserve.

Corruption in the Customs Service

The customs service of Nigeria is the organization that is authorized to clear goods that are imported into the country. This group is not free from the menace of corruption. In most occasions, you must pay bribes to customs before your goods are cleared. Many containers that are retained by

164

customs belong to those not willing to pay the large amount of money being demanded as bribes.

Causes of Corruption

There are many factors that have propagated the growth of corruption in Nigeria. Different scholars have aired their views on the causes of corruption. Chuks Nwaze in his book, "Corruption in Nigeria Exposed" outlines the following as the causes of corruption in Nigeria (Nwaze 2011):

- Weak institutional enforcement framework
- Commanders without army
- Lack of ethical standard in government business
- Poor reward system and
- Extended family

In a larger view, the basic causes of corruption include, but are not limited to:

- Greed
- Poor youth empowerment
- Poverty
- Unemployment
- Inadequate payment and
- Weak law enforcement

Greed

Greed has caused a lot of crises in the world, including in Nigeria. It is because of greed and insatiability that political leaders embezzle from the funds they are supposed to use for national development. Politicians, businessmen and women as well as some educationists are covetous and never satisfied or contented. This attitude sometimes pushes them into the dirty game of corruption. If Nigerian politicians were less greedy, the rate of corruption will be reduced considerably.

Corruption among businessmen and women is mostly as a result of greed. They buy good quality products from the market and reduce the quality to sell to customers. The faking of the products they sell is because they want to make more money.

Greed cuts across other areas, including sexual affairs. This is in line with Nwaze's point about the extended family being one of the causes of corruption. A poor man who is sexually greedy can father up to fifteen children and thus forced into corrupt activities in order to find every possible means to take care of his large family.

Poor Youth Empowerment

Poor moral and economic youth empowerment contribute to corruption. Internet fraud, sexual harassment by male CEOs, and other inappropriate behavior are because Nigerians lack understanding on the importance of youth empowerment. When parents and governments empower youths both financially and morally, the level of corruption among them will diminish. Some Nigerian youths are morally depraved. As a result, they are ready to make money through every possible means. Forging of certificates, fraudulent activities among the youths and other social vices are because the youths are poorly empowered.

Poverty

Nigeria, a land supposedly flowing with milk and honey, as a result of its abundant endowment of crude oil and other natural resources, is paradoxically one of the world's poorest countries. A great proportion of its population live in abject poverty (Jike 2007).

According to international standards of poverty, a person is said to be poor when he lives below $1.25 (₦210, though it varies) per day. There are many poor people in Nigeria, and poverty pushes them into corruption. According to World Bank Group, in 2004, 63.1 percent of Nigerians were poor. The poverty level increased to 68 percent in 2010. Some people may engage in criminal activities because of poverty. It is one of the reasons why the poor youths in the country collect bribes to work as thugs for Nigerian politicians.

Unemployment

Unemployment is one of the major challenges in Nigeria. Every year, many graduates leave Nigerian universities without securing any job for months, and some years after. People are pushed into corrupt practices because of the high unemployment rate of about 60 percent.

The youths, and their parents are seriously lamenting the negative impact of unemployment in their lives. Some even crave death rather than suffering under the torment of unemployment in the country. Words cannot explain the level of punishment the citizens of Nigeria endure as a result of this menace.

In the country, some women have resorted to prostitution because of unemployment. They see this as the way out of their unemployment challenge.

Underpayment

Underpayment of workers in Nigeria is rampant because of the economic situation in the country. When an employee is underpayed, s(he) might resort to other means to make up for the shortfall, which might include engagement in corrupt practices.

Weak law enforcement

There are anti-corruption and law enforcement groups in Nigeria. However the problem is that some render themselves totally impotent by compromising their efficacy through collecting bribes from offenders they are supposed to prosecute. Chucks Nwaze in his book observed, "even with the preponderance of anti-corruption agencies (i.e

167

EFCC, ICPC, and CCB), not enough progress is being made in the war against corruption (Nwaze 2011).

Effects/Consequences of Corruption

Corruption has many negative effects. It causes disaster, poverty, and underdevelopment, amongst others, in any country. In the case of Nigeria, corruption has eaten deeply into the fabrics of the country, that it has almost paralysed the economy. Former President Olusegun Obasanjo on democracy day in 2003 observed, "corruption brings a nation and her people no good. Rather, it kills innovation and creativity, compromises public morality, contaminates individual and collective dignity, distorts national plan and erodes commitment to hard work and the dignity of labour" (President Olusegun Obasanjo in his Democracy Day Broadcast, 29th May, 2003). The negative consequences of corruption include:

- Poor investment
- Rise in poverty
- Poor national development
- National crises

Poor Investment

When reputable companies invest in a particular country such as Nigeria, the country experiences development. The unemployment rate in Nigeria would have been considerably reduced if investors were attracted to the country. Companies that would normally have invested in Nigeria are reluctant to do so because of too many uncertainties surrounding the country, including endemic corruption. But low investment breeds underdevelopment. Development is directly proportional to societal growth. When there is economic growth in a country, the citizens are better off.

Rise in Poverty

When heads of public services are busy laundering the money that is supposed to be used to create employment for the masses and reduce poverty, there will be rise in the poverty level in the country. Poverty is a direct result of massive corruption in Nigeria. A situation whereby the governor of a state uses public funds to promote his personal businesses will not yield good to the economic welfare of the citizens. Instead it exacerbates poverty for the people.

Poor National Development

Any country with high corruption is likely to experience developmental bankruptcy. A situation whereby some CEOs indulge in corrupt practices for personal gains, has the consequence of depleting the economic growth of the country. When Nigerian leaders keep on laundering the nation's money to foreign countries, there will be less economic development in Nigeria.

ERADICATING CORRUPTION IN NIGERIA.

Corrupt Nigerians underestimate the impact of their actions on other citizens. Corruption keeps the Nigerian nation underdeveloped, with serious and severe consequences of government-induced poverty on Nigerian citizens.

The WE THE PEOPLE Project.

From the various forms of corruption and pervasiveness of corruption in every sector and institution in Nigeria, it is clear that a new and different approach should be employed to combat corruption in Nigeria. The nation's law books are replete with many laws on bribery and corruption, with various punishment assigned to offenders. Nigeria has several law enforcement agencies, including specialized agencies to combat crime and corruption. None of these has dissuaded corrupt practices in Nigeria. President Buhari has invested significant effort, energy and resources in fighting corruption in Nigeria, but the evil continues unabated because the president cannot be everywhere in the nation at the same time as a watch dog of corruption to check continuing daily abuses in every sector everywhere in Nigeria. There is only one potential solution to bribery in Nigeria—personal accountability through a new breed of Nigerians who will personally commit to a new responsible way of life that will shun bribery and corruption in their daily lives as a life style.

The WE THE PEOPLE movement, under the non-governmental agency (NGO) named, "The People's Grassroots Association for a Corruption-Free Nigeria" is a nationwide movement of WE THE PEOPLE engineered by Nigerian intellectuals from both diaspora and all six geo-political zones of Nigeria to grow a new breed of Nigerian grassroots from every tribe and religion who will clean up Nigeria from bottom to top. This textbook, WE THE PEOPLE, has been produced as a teaching tool that will be used to educate the Nigerian masses to properly change their mindset and thereby create a nation of individually accountable people. Membership to this association is free for all Nigerians who understand the evils of bribery and corruption in Nigeria, accept to change their ways, and commit to the WE THE PEOPLE PLEDGE offered at the end of this book. The goals of the NGO, "The People's Grassroots Association for a Corruption-Free Nigeria include raising a critical mass of at least 50 million new Nigerians who together will clean up Nigeria from bottom to top. Our aim is to first clean the bottom, then the clean bottom will inevitably also clean the top. Only a clean united bottom can clean the top permanently. Nigerians have suffered for too long, and the Nigerian nation has been violated and bastardized by mindless corrupt leaders and legislatures who exemplified and glorified corrupt practices for the grassroots of Nigeria. Unfortunately, it is the grassroots of Nigeria that suffers disproportionately from the bad and horrible consequences of living in a very corrupt society. Since corruption has hurt the development of Nigeria and spread poverty and insecurity in Nigeria, WE THE PEOPLE must reject corruption with its evils, create a new breed of individually responsible and accountable grassroots, and clean up Nigeria from bottom to top, one committed person at a time, through the nationwide movement of the NGO, *'The People's Grassroots Association for a Corruption-Free Nigeria"*. Once you commit to the WE THE PEOPLE PLEDGE, help us to spread the word and get several people to read this book and also commit to the pledge and the movement. For additional information, please visit info@www.wethepeoplenigeria.org.

References

- Ameh C. G (2015). Policemen shoot at couple, kill wife for refusing to pay bribe. A publication of DailyPost, Nigeria
- Ben Nwabueze (2003). Constitutional Democracy in Africa. Vol. 3: 334. Spectrum Books, Nigeria
- Chuks Nwaze (2011). Corruption in Nigeria Exposed. Control & Surveillance Associate Limited, Lagos, Nigeria
- Danladi (2007). Nigeria Ranks 148 on the 2007 Corruption Perception Index. Naira Land Publication
- Dr. V.T Jike (2007). The Nigerian Sociological Review. Grace Communication International, Nigeria
- Hassan, Ebele & Olawepo (2007). Nigeria Reform Programme: Issues and Challenges. Vantage Publishers Ltd, Ibadan, Nigeria
- Hector, I. (2004). SKJ SAGA: Swiss Govt Freezes $ 100M Accounts. Vanguard, Nigeria
- **International Center for Investigative Reporting (2012).** Nnamdi Azikiwe University VC in Corruption Scandal. A publication of icirnigeria.org, Nigeria
- Maire Karl (2000). The House has fallen: Midnight in Nigeria. Publishers Weekly, New York, USA

- Morris, S.D. (1991). Corruption and Politics in Contemporary Mexico. University of Alabama Press, Tuscaloosa
- Uzochukwu, M. O. (2013). Challenges in Nigeria and Solutions on how to resolve them. Hubpages Inc.
- Oluwashina, O. (2013). Nigeria Official Banned for Bribe. BBC Sport News Lagos.
- Oyinola, O. A. (2011). Corruption Eradication in Nigeria: An Appraisal. Library Philosophy and Practice
- Philip Nwosu (2016), Dasukigate: 1.5 Billion Traced to Son Of Former Finance Minister. Sun News Publication, Nigeria
- President Olusegun Obasanjo on Democracy Day Broadcast on 29th May, 2003
- Section 52 of the Anti-Corruption Act
- Soni Daniel (2016), $2.1bN cash: Return home or be humiliated, EFCC warns fleeing corrupt ex-officials. A Publication of Vanguard, Nigeria

- The Storey Report. The Commission of Inquiry into the administration of Lagos Town Council
- Transparency International (2013). Corruption Perceptions Index 2013. Publication of Transparency International, Germany
- Transparency International (2014). Corruption Perceptions Index 2014, Publication of Transparency International, Germany
- Ureports (2012). Nnamdi Azikiwe University VC, Prof. Boniface Egboka in Monumental Corruption Scandal. A publication of 247Ureports.com, Nigeria
- Vanguard (2016). Fayose cautions Buhari over probe of military chiefs, says $2.1bn arms deal is a scam. A publication of Vanguard, Nigeria

World Bank Group. (2013), Poverty and Equity.

CHAPTER 6

Corruption in the National Assembly: Abuses in Budget Approvals, Confirmation Hearing, Oversight Duties, and Constituency Projects.

Lewis Obi

Barely a week after the National Assembly was inaugurated in June 1999, it was discovered that the Speaker of the House of Representastives, Alhaji Salisu Buhari, not only forged his education certificates but he had also falsified his age.

The nation had barely recovered from the shock of the Speaker being a forger before it was discovered that the President of the Senate, Evan(s) Enwerem, was an ex-convict. His successor, Dr. Chuba Okadigbo, a most articulate man, educated in some of the world's most famous universities, barely lasted a year when he, too, was removed for misappropriation of funds. Indeed, there were five presidents of the senate in seven years.

Ever since, the National Assembly has not recovered from being an organization of self-centered, power-obsessed men and women who do no more than grab whatever they could as quickly as they could. Because they do not believe in transparency as an important tenet of democracy their affairs are shrouded in secrecy, so much so that the Nigerian populace has no idea what they take home for emoluments. They do not believe that democracy has a future in Nigeria and so they make hay while the sun shines by grabbing whatever they can lay their hands upon. And since they have the power of the purse granted them by the Constitution they pay themselves the highest any legislature in the world could earn.

BUDGET PADDING

Thus, members of the National Assembly rarely fight for anything except for their individual welfare, and Nigeria was fortunate to get a glimpse into the way the budget padding system works through a fortuitous circumstance when the Speaker broke with a committee chairman. Because the Assembly is organized like a secret society, its affairs are always shrouded in secrecy. But on 20th July 2016, the Speaker of the House of Representatives, Dr. Yakubu Dogara, dismissed the Chairman of the powerful Appropriations Committee of the House, Mr. Abdulmumin Jibrin. The latter was alleged to have awarded to his Kiru/Bebeji Constituency in Kano State projects worth N4.1 billion.

The Speaker in announcing his sack admitted that Jibrin had approached him to say he could no longer cope with the pressure of the position, and wanted to resign. Rather than accept the resignation the Speaker proceeded to sack him; he said the House Leadership had decided to remove him. Jibrin was apparently displeased with the dramatized manner of his removal, especially when he had earlier offered to resign voluntarily.

Jibrin did not go quietly. Next day, he brought in a letter to explain why the House Leadership pushed him out. In doing so, he confirmed the worst fears Nigerians have had about budget padding by the National Assembly and the scope of the corruption in the institution. The four leaders of the House, Jibrin said, had unilaterally allocated to themselves N40 billion of the N100 billion allocated to the entire National Assembly for constituency projects. The leaders included Speaker Dogara himself, the Deputy Speaker, Yusuf Suleiman Lasun, the Chief Whip, Al-Hassan Ado Doguwa, and the Minority Leader, Leo Ogor.

He called on the Speaker to resign for creating the budget impasse which delayed the Appropriation Act 2016 and which many economists and observers hold responsible for the current economic recession. He held the Speaker responsible for the much discredited push by the National

Assembly to amend the Constitution in order to insert immunity clauses to protect the leaders of the National Assembly. Jibrin said his crime was his refusal to cover up the actions of the House leadership in their allocation of "wasteful projects worth N20 billion to their constituencies."

"My inability to admit into the budget almost N30 billion personal requests from Mr. Speaker and the other three principal officers also became an issue," he said.

"I gave the Speaker statistics of 2000 (two thousand) new projects introduced into the budget by less than 10 committee chairmen without the knowledge of their committee members. He did nothing about it because he was part of the mess yet he is talking about improving the budget system."

Dr. Junaid Mohammed once said that "ours is a parliament where members decree constituency projects for themselves, award constituency projects to their companies and make corruption more popular in Nigeria." And that is how the so-called constituency projects and the paddings schemes had worked.

State House correspondents cornered former President Olusegun Obasanjo who had come for a consultation with President Buhari and sought his views on the latest scandal. He told them that he has been vindicated. He has been a consistent critic. In 2012, he described the National Assembly as an institution filled with "rogues and armed robbers." In January 2016, as if he foresaw what was going to happen, Obasanjo wrote a letter to the President of the Senate, Dr. Bukola Saraki and House Speaker Dogara, accusing the federal lawmakers of corruption, greed and impunity. His grouse at that time was the extra cars which the National Assembly wanted to purchase for themselves, after they had each collected N8 million to buy a personal car. Now they wanted a car "for committee work." Obasanjo had suggested that a few pool cars in the National Assembly would meet every need of committees rather than spending nearly N8 billion for 469 cars at a time the nation was going through tough times and the economy was on the brink of a recession. As has been customary when anyone raised a finger against any action by the National Assembly, they all united in one voice to shout Obasanjo down, drown out the voice of others and went ahead and bought the luxury vehicles they wanted, most of them costing as much as N38 million apiece.

So, it was no surprise that 2000 projects could be inserted into the budget by "less than 10 committee chairmen without the knowledge of members of their committees," which is a further indication that even in the conspiracies to loot the treasury, the left hand often does not know what the right hand is doing.

The Speaker and Jibrin were said to have been good friends earlier in the life of the 8th Assembly. Jibrin said he thought the Speaker took great offence with him for meeting President Buhari without the Speaker's permission. This gives an inkling into the dictatorial structure of the House and how it is organized and run. But he said the meeting was a harmless meeting of committee chairmen involved in the budget process from both the House and the Senate, apparently called by the President to smoothen if not expedite the troubled 2016 budget process.

"Dogara took it extremely personal that we saw the President without his knowledge and went on to scuttle our efforts to help the president during the budget process because he wanted to be seen by the president as the only good man."

"He (Speaker Dogara) forgot that he sees heads of MDAs daily which he enjoys doing more than his job as Speaker for reasons best known to him anyway, without Mr. President's knowledge. That is how petty and narrow-minded Dogara can be. A coward, hypocrite and pretender of the highest order. Mr. President must be very careful with him. He wines with Mr. President and dines with Mr. President's enemies. I am glad I'm finally free from his emotional blackmail of constantly trying to make me see my appointment as appropriation chairman as a favour." With those words it became clear that for the first time in the 4th Republic, the gloves were off and that a fight between two members who know the inner workings of the National Assembly would be fascinating, and Nigeria may learn more of what actually goes on in this cult-like enclosure

The committee system has been a tool to loot the treasury and keep friends and allies in check. There are 96 different committees in a house of 360 members. Each has a N50 million expense account, the same number applies to the 109-member Senate. The committees are classed between the juicy and the less juicy; the juicy being those where members expect a great deal of monetary benefits of all kinds not excluding bribes from the ministries, departments and agencies (MDAs). It is through the instrumentalities of these MDA's that constituency projects and budget paddings turn into cash for the members. Indeed, Jibrin revealed some handwritten documents by House leaders which arbitrarily earmarked funds for "fictitious" projects hidden carefully in genuine projects by the executive branch. In one of the documents one of the leaders wrote in projects worth N594 million to be embedded in the ministries of Agriculture, Labour, and Trade and Investments, as well as in the National Boundary Commission. The only way to cash those paddings is by close co-operation with the officials in those various ministries, departments and agencies. It is therefore not a surprise that the Speaker spends a considerable length of time with government officials.

Abdulmumuni Jibrin was stating what most Nigerians already knew when he told Channels TV late in July 2016 that President Olusegun Obasanjo had been right and that,

"yes, we (National Assembly members) are corrupt...there is corruption in the House of Representatives, and not only is there corruption, there is institutional corruption... These are things that I can prove and it is what my struggle is about...the only thing is that we have been living in denial. I have been there for five years and I have seen a lot and I am happy that something has triggered it (the budget scandal) ... to address the issues at the National Assembly to force re-forms... This issue is going to lead to a revolution in the National Assembly."

"My problem was that I was not talking. I came to the National Assembly and I was made to believe that when one is chairman of finance, you have to live and die with certain information. Also, if you are chairman of Appropriation (Committee), you have to be custodian of information, meaning there are a lot of things you must not say."

It is truly remarkable how the National Assembly turned a democratic institution, the people's house, which ought to be open and transparent in all things and at all times, into an Ogboni Society cult-like secret coven.

Now the greed of the National Assembly is simply breathtaking. So far N480 billion of padding has been identified for the 469-member legislature, apparently, so members get a billion apiece. But by Jibrin's disclosures to the Sunday Punch, the Speaker, a man who often appeared to be innocent and faultless, would get N3 billion; the deputy speaker, N2.55 billion; House Leader and Chief Whip, N1.8 billion each; deputy leader and deputy chief whip, N1.5 billion each; minority leader and minority whip, N1.4 billion each; the deputy minority leader and deputy minority whip, N1.3 billion each, totaling N17.5 billion. These are separate from the N20 billion inserted in the so-called service-wide vote.

The N480 billion incorporates the 2,000 projects inserted by 10 standing committee chairmen. No one knows how much of these have already been cashed out, but National Assembly members have reportedly besieged Federal ministries and agencies trying to retrieve the inserted amounts. Two senators are reported to have made a fortune cashing out from the Cross River Basin Authority and the Sokoto Rima Basin Authority and the Small and Medium Enterprises Development Agencies of Nigeria. One pocketed N3.4 billion and the other N1.2 billion.

It needs to be said, and as Jibrin has continued to repeat, that the padding of the budget by the National Assembly is not a new phenomenon. The trouble this year appears to be the scale. In February 2013, the initial budget sent in by President Goodluck Jonathan was for N4.25 trillions but the lawmakers padded it with N63 billions bringing the final figure to N4.98 trillions.

But to Senate Leader Mohammed Ali-Ndume "the issue of budget padding is more of a media hype... it is more of personal thing between Dogara and Jibrin." An indication that much worse secrets lie beneath the iron-clad secrecy that has always surrounded the Senate.

Then the ruling All Progressives Congress (APC), which periodically acts as the alternate government, embarrassed by the scandal, summoned Jibrin on 2nd August 2016. In a tone reminiscent of the Communist Party Presidium, it warned Jibrin that "failure to and/or refusal to honour this invitation will amount to a decision you have made not to submit to the party." Jibrin was interrogated for four hours and told not to speak to the Press any more, which is often the first step to sweeping a scandal under the carpet.

The usual disinformation and mass manipulation of the scandal then began. The usual hired spinners arrived. One of them is called the National Youth Council of Nigeria, which stated that the nation's democracy was under trial following what it termed an alleged plot to destabilize the leadership of the House of Representatives by external forces which it did not name. The Council sent a petition to the Economic and Financial Crimes Commission (EFCC) accusing Jibrin of involvement in multi-million Naira contract. Other groups describing themselves as civil society organizations also ran to save the Speaker and one of such was named African Media Roundtable Initiative, and Coalition of Analysts and Media, and Civil Society Organizations. The other was called the Centre for Legislative Advocacy led by an Opeyemi Duke. These groups were defending the Speaker and the National Assembly because it was the responsibility of the National Assembly "to make appropriation" and that "there was nothing like padding in legislative terms." These organizations remind you of "Youths Earnestly" of the 1990s which tried hard to foist General Sani Abacha on Nigeria as an elected president.

The ruling party is trying to hush Jibrin. The National Assembly, in characteristic fraternity, has rallied round the Speaker. They are all in it together; Jibrin has spilled the beans – and, indeed, the milk. Only few voices are being heard calling the Speaker to resign. Jibrin feels he is been fenced off and unable to meet President Buhari to explain his stance. That is in line with the damage-control strategy of the ruling party. The government at first seemed to want to stay aloof and see where the chips would fall, but Jibrin's allegations continued to shock the nation and continued to discredit the National Assembly.

The President invited the Speaker and apparently reassured him. Emerging from the meeting the Speaker was so confident of his position he told the Press that budget "padding was not an offence." That started a second national outrage. But not enough to even spur a student's demonstration. As a matter of fact, the National Association of Nigerian Students pledged its support to the Speaker. It is a move which speaks volumes for the depth of the corruption in Nigeria, about the students themselves, and about the leadership of the National Assembly.

If Buhari ignores the scandal, although Nigerians are no more capable of being shocked by what their governments do, they would probably then make a determination that the Buhari fight against corruption has been eviscerated. The accusations against Dogara are many and credible. Jibrin has alleged that the Speaker "fraudulently diverted a federal government water project to your farm in Nasarawa" State. He also queried how the Speaker was funding the farm which has exploded from a six-hectare enterprise to more than 100 hectares complete with structures, and equipment worth billions of Naira.

Jibrin also disclosed that the Speaker collects N25 million every month. This must be additional to the regular emoluments which are thought to be about that figure. Many Nigerians know that the National Assembly is the highest paid legislature in the world, and earns eight times higher than its American counterpart. The irony of the legislature of the seventh poorest country in the world earning eight times higher than the world's richest countries has never been lost on anyone and underscores why the National Assembly is an anomaly.

Confirmation Hearings:

The truly sensational was the Mallam Nasir Ahmad El-Rufai case which shocked the country in September 2003 when the nominee wrote in a newspaper article that "When I was nominated for ministerial appointment a couple of legislators called me and said I made money as director-general of the Bureau for Public Enterprises, BPE, and so to make sure I got cleared I have to pay them N54 million".

The Senate referred the allegation to its Committee on Ethics, Privileges and Public Petitions headed by Olorunnimbe Mamora. After much delay and nail biting, the committee held a hearing at which El-Rufai was asked to name the people who asked him for bribes. He had no hesitation as he named Senator Ibrahim Mantu and Senator Jonathan Zwingina, Deputy Senate President and Deputy Senate Leader respectively. Those were among the powers that be in the National Assembly. It was as if El-Rufai had brought down the roof over his head.

The committee absolved their colleagues saying there was no hard evidence. David Ihenacho in a withering critique of the report of the committee said "the so-called Senate Committee on Ethics was in fact grossly unethical in the way it handled the El-Rufai allegation. The committee members criminally neglected all the ingredients of bribery that were abundantly available in the testimonies they had taken. For instance, Mantu acknowledged he had had meetings with Zwingina and El-Rufai in which the latter had solicited their support for confirmation. But the committee could not press him to confirm or deny whether there was a quid pro quo. Instead, the committee eased him into obfuscating the whole matter. The so-called members allowed Mantu to stand "logic and common sense" on their heads by claiming that since he did not collect the money he did not commit any offence.

At all events, El-Rufai was eventually confirmed and the business of demanding and receiving bribes apparently went on under the table. After what El-Rufai went through and the travesty of the committee's report, no nominee in his right mind would dare blow the whistle. Worse, a misguided section of the Press blamed El-Rufai for not providing "hard evidence," even when it was glaringly impossible to do so under the circumstances.

In April 2005 the Punch reported the case of the Education Minister, Prof. Fabian Osuji who paid N55 million to the Senate President, Adolphus Wabara and three senators in return for the approval and a boost to the Education ministry's budget. The tragic aspect of this case was that Prof. Osuji had on occasions proved to be a man of integrity. It was unclear how he could have been misled into thinking it was normal to pay bribes. He did not readily have the money. He borrowed N20 million from the National Universities Commission and made up the rest. Being innocent of such things, he went about distributing the money with a retinue of education ministry officials. Prof. Osuji was arrested and detained for four days by the EFCC and eventually dismissed by President Obasanjo and his case has not been decided. But the Senators went free except for Senate President Wabara who resigned the leadership of the Senate but stayed to serve out his term of office. He was, however, forced to refund the N20 million he took. The Senate did not even deign to enquire into this allegation against its members. But the government refused to prosecute the senators on the specious excuse that it would appear like an effort to undermine the legislative branch.

Oversight Corruption:

It was in May 2012 that Aruma Oteh, Director-General of the Nigerian Security and Exchange Commission had to face the House of Representatives Adhoc Committee on the Capital Market to answer questions. But all hell was let loose when she accused the committee chairman Herman Hembe and his deputy Ifeanyi Azubogu of demanding bribes from her twice. The first demand was for N39 million and the second for N5 million. Before then, she said, the committee chairman had collected some money and a business class air ticket to travel to the Dominican Republic for a seminar. The chairman eventually did not go for the seminar but he neither returned the ticket nor the money. The committee ended the dialogue there and then and began to question her qualifications and performance, brushing aside her weighty allegations. When the committee was done nitpicking on her, they passed a resolution recommending her dismissal by the President, because she dared to make public the demand for bribes by the members of the House. The House added a rider that should the President fail to sack her, the House would cease to recognize her as the director-general of the SEC. On return from recess the House reaffirmed its resolution and added an ultimatum of 14 days to the President. Not to be outdone, the Senate Committee also passed the same kind of resolution warning the President that if he did not dismiss her the Senate would no longer recognize or screen members of the commission's board. It was sheer brutal arm-twisting and a blatant abuse of power. But President Jonathan did not oblige them and Miss Oteh stayed till the end of her five-year tenure and was promptly snapped up by an international organization abroad.

The case of Farouk Lawan, the Chairman of the House Committee on the Monitoring of Petroleum Subsidy became another embarrassing case of bribery. The committee tried to establish the conduct of oil marketers who collected foreign exchange but failed to import petroleum products. Mr. Femi Otedola, former governor of Lagos State who was chairman of Zenon Oil and Gas Ltd was among those who bought foreign exchange from the Central Bank but had failed to import the products. Committee Chairman Lawan received $500,000 from Chief Otedola to remove his name from the list of offenders. Another member of the committee, Mr. Boniface Emenalo also collected another $120,000 from Otedola for a total of $620,000 bribe extorted from a company in the name of oversight function of the legislature.

At first Lawan denied receiving any money, unknown to him that the entire process of collecting the money by Lawan had been filmed by Otedola. Later after the video was released, Lawan admitted he received the money but it was as an exhibit to prove that Otedola was trying to corrupt members of the committee. Although Lawan was suspended from the House, the probe by the House has not yielded any report. The case against Lawan is still in the court.

Former President Olusegun Obasanjo has often offered it as his view that members of the National Assembly have lost every moral authority to conduct oversight functions on any government department or agency. And it is no surprise the scandalous financial abuse of $2.1 billion perpetrated in the office of the National Security Adviser, Col. Sambo Dasuki, which is now yielding sensational court cases. The two cash consignments seized by the Customs authorities in South Africa did not even generate any enquiry from the National Assembly.

In 2004, the late Senator Uche Chukwumerije, a man known for unimpeachable integrity, alleged that his colleague in the Senate, Chief Arthur Nzeribe, had gathered some members of the National Assembly in his official residence on 14th January 2004 offering each member N5 million to support the declaration of a state of emergency in Plateau State. The Senate made no effort to enquire into this allegation.

Dr. HarunaYerima deserves mention as a member of the House of Representatives who was a lone voice and who at a public gathering declared that some committees go about collecting bribes from ministries and parastatals to induce members into taking favourable decisions. He pointedly identified the Chairman of the House Committee on Communications for facilitating the distribution of MTN recharge cards to members. In his words: "Ministers and heads of parastatals are often asked to bring money so that their budgets can be passed. MTN bribes us every month. It brings recharge cards worth N7,500 for every member (The News 4th April 2005)."

Many members of the National Assembly do not imagine there could be anything resembling legislative integrity; or that their position is not to be used for their personal aggrandizement. They see their positions as the result of an investment as per former Senate President Adolphus Wabara: "Most of us came into the National Assembly with high expectations. It is an investment really to come into the National Assembly. When you go about campaigning and asking for votes, we don't get these votes for free. You spend some money. Most of us even sold houses. You come in through legitimate means but you can't recoup what you spend." (News 4 April 2005)

Representative Abdulmumin Jibrin, the erstwhile chairman of the House Appropriations Committee, is probably the instrument of Providence to save Nigerian democracy. His heart seems to be in the right place. But it is not a task he can accomplish alone. He needs the support of all patriotic Nigerians who should converge on Abuja in their hundreds of thousands, encircle the two chambers, and insist on the dissolution of the National Assembly and a total reformulation of the institution.

Our powerful national groups and change agents must stand up – the Nigerian Labour Congress, the Trade Union Congress, the Academic Staff Union of Universities, Petroleum and Gas Workers Unions National Council of Women Societies, Women in Nigeria, Nigerian Union of Journalists, National Union of Railway men, Civil Service Unions, Local Government Employee Unions. An interim Nigerian National Congress must be constituted from these patriotic organizations. Men and women of proven integrity from the six geo-political zones should strengthen the groups representatives and be legally proclaimed.

What has happened is obvious. The National Assembly having betrayed its mission after 17 years of shameless, unbridled corruption has lost its mandate and authority and therefore its legitimacy. The Nigerian people must reclaim their mandate and constitute a new body since the National Assembly has become destructive of the objectives of its founding, leaving the people no choice but to abolish it and institute a new legislature with a fresh mandate to provide them with safety, honesty, integrity in public administration, law, order and good government.

Conclusions

A referendum on the National Assembly has become imperative because Nigeria's rather fragile structure of democratic government might collapse from the pressure of the cost of government. The signs that the economy cannot sustain our current bureaucracies have appeared in state governments, two-thirds of which can no longer guarantee regular payment of salaries to civil servants and teachers.

What needs to be established is Nigeria's choice between a bicameral and a unicameral legislature. After 17 years and trillions of Naira spent on the Senate and the House, it doesn't quite appear there is anything the two chambers have done which a single chamber cannot do. We have had two chambers not because we needed them but because other countries have them. A second question which a referendum should also answer is whether it would not be more efficient to have the legislature as a part-time occupation and its remuneration fixed by an independent body free from the influences which have rendered the Revenue Mobilization and Fiscal Commission impotent.

A part-time schedule would appear to lessen the pressure of the do-or-die competition and attract men and women whose interest is to serve the people. Now the National Assembly is nothing but a business enterprise and the primary objective of members is to make money for themselves. And plenty do they make, being the highest paid legislature in the world. Now if the money-making factor is reduced considerably, it would free the legislators from being secretive about their earnings. They are secretive about their current earnings because the figures are embarrassing. The figures are embarrassing because they bear no resemblance to the realities of the Nigerian economy and international comparisons make them appear like something out of this world. For instance, the authoritative Economist magazine, has reported that the lowest paid Nigerian legislator earns 116 times of the income per capita, the proportion is 60 in Kenya, 30 in Ghana, and 18 in Indonesia. There is nothing to compare with that degree of disparity anywhere in the world.

It tells you at a glance that income inequality in Nigeria is probably the highest in the world.

Consider the following comparison of senators' annual pay worldwide, with the pay of senators in Nigeria:

* Sri Lanka – $5,100.00
* India – $11,200.00
* Malaysia – $25,300.00
* Thailand – $43,800.00
* Spain – $43,900.00
* Ghana – $46,500.00
* Saudi Arabia – $64,000.00
* Indonesia – $65,800.00
* Kenya – $74,500.00
* France – $85,900.00
* Sweden – $99 300.00
* South Africa – $104,000.00
* Britain – $105,400.00
* New Zealand – $112,500.00
* Israel – $114,800.00
* Germany – $119,500.00
* Ireland – $120,400.00
* Hong Kong – $130,700.00
* Japan – $149,700.00
* Canada – $154 000.00
* Singapore – $154,000.00
* Brazil – $157,600.00
* United States – $174,000.00
* Italy – $182,000.00
*Nigeria - $2,183,685.00

The details of the remuneration of an average Nigerian Senator is detailed below:

Monthly

* Basic Salary (B.S) – N2,484,245.50
* Hardship Allowance (50% of B.S) – N1,242,122.70
* Constituency Allowance (200% of B.S) – N4,968,509.00
* Newspapers Allowance (50% of B.S) – N1,242,122.70
* Wardrobe Allowance (25% of B.S) – N621,061.37
* Recess Allowance (10% of B.S) – N248,424.55
* Accommodation (200% of B.S) – N4,968,509.00
* Utilities (30% of B.S) – N828,081.83
* Domestic Staff (70% of B.S) – N1,863,184.12
* Entertainment (30% of B.S) – N828,081.83
* Personal Assistants (25% of B.S) – N621,061.12
* Vehicle Maintenance Allowance (75% of B.S) – N1,863,184.12
* Leave Allowance (10% of B.S) – N248,424.55
* Severance Gratuity (300% of B.S) – N7,452,736.50
* Car Allowance (400% of B.S) – N9,936,982.00
* **TOTAL MONTHLY SALARY = N29,479,749.00 ($181,974.00)**
* TOTAL YEARLY SALARY = N29,479,749.00 x 12 = N353,756,988.00 ($2,183,686.00)

The average salary of a Nigerian worker based on the national minimum wage is N18,000.00. So, the yearly salary is N18,000.00 x 12 = N216,000.00
Remember, yearly Salary of Nigerian Senator = N353,756,988.00
Proportion: N353,756,988.00/N216,000.00 = 1,638

It will take an average Nigerian worker 1,638 years to earn the yearly salary of a Nigerian Senator.

The president of the United States of America, the most powerful public servant of the largest economy in the world, earns $400,000 annually. In fact, the salary of the president of the United States was $200,000 until the most recent salary increase to $400,000 annually from $200,000 annually which took effect when George W. Bush became president. Additional provisions for the U.S president includes $50,000 for expense account, $100,000 for travel account, and $19,000 for entertainment, annually. This comes to a maximum total of $569,000 in salaries and benefits for the President of the United States of America. Compare this with annual salary of $2,183,685.00 for every Nigerian senator. Every Nigerian senator earns 383.7% the salary of the President of the United States of America. Senators in the United States of America earn $174,000 annually. A Nigerian senator earns 12.55 times, or 1,255% the salary of the United States senator.

In spite of this incredibly high salary for senators in a poor and developing economy where the average pay for grassroots is less than $360 annually, the national assembly is also a notorious cell-pool of corruption, scheming and amassing mind-blowing amounts to themselves through evil corrupt practices. Consider the following confessions from one member of the Nigerian national assembly, a former appropriations committee chairman who felt-out with his colleagues and decided to expose their ways, in his own words:

HOW WE SHARED NIGERIA'S MONEY BY HON. ABDULMUMIN JUBRIN

"I got N650 million as my running cost as the Chairman of Appropriation Committee.
■Speaker Yakubu Dogara got N1.5 billion,
■His Deputy Yusuf Lasun got N800 million.
■House Majority Leader Femi Gbajabiamila got N1.2 billion,
■Deputy Majorty Leader Buba Jibrin got N1.2 billion.
■House Whip Alhassan Ado Doguwa got N1.2 billion,
■Deputy House Whip got N700 million.
■House Minority Leader Leo Ogor got N1.2 billion,
■Deputy Minority Leader Onyema got N800 million.
■Minority Whip got N700 million,
■Deputy Minority Whip got N700 million.

I have documents to back up all these."

Then in a letter to his colleagues, following his written confession, he stated the following as a warning to them to come clean quickly by returning the massive amounts of money they stole together or face his legal action:

TO ALL HONOURABLE MEMBERS
HOUSE OF REPRESENTATIVES
NATIONAL ASSEMBLY
ABUJA

My dear Colleagues,

BURDEN OF PROOF OF EVIDENCE: RUNNING COST OF
HONOURABLE MEMBERS OF THE HOUSE OF REPRESENTATIVES

I wish to draw your attention to the fact that since you suspended me yesterday and the suggestion of the Ethics Committee report that my allegations were generalized and without proof, I have come under intense public scrutiny and pressure to prove that there exists systemic corruption in the House. I have taken it as a responsibility to prove to the public that the House is a den of systemic corruption. As colleagues, I have a bond with many of you and built a life long friendship.

I have some of you that I hold in high esteem. If you end up at the receiving end of the actions I will be taking up in the next few days, I want you to know there is nothing personal but commitment and fervent desire to ensure that corruption is wiped out of the House and reforms that will restore the battered image of the House and take back the House to the Nigerian people is implemented.

Consequent upon the above and before I proceed with the aggressive steps I intend to take, I hereby DEMAND that if you have illegally taken or stolen any money meant for the RUNNING COST OF YOUR OFFICES FOR YOUR ENTIRE STAY IN THE HOUSE, YOU SHOULD RETURN THE MONEY WITHIN ONE WEEK TO THE CLERK OF THE NATIONAL ASSEMBLY AND FOR THE PURPOSE OF CLARITY, I AM REFERRING TO ABOUT 10 MILLION NAIRA YOU COLLECT FROM TAX PAYERS' MONEY MONTHLY. THE CLERK WILL PROVIDE YOU WITH OFFICIAL ACCOUNT DETAILS, FAILURE OF WHICH I WILL TAKE NECESSARY ACTION TO ENSURE THAT YOU RETURN ANY MONEY STOLEN AND STAND WITNESS AGAINST YOU IN CASE OF PROSECUTION.

I have written to the Clerk of the National Assembly to stand by in anticipation. In the face of the revenue challenges and biting hardship the country is currently facing, there is no better time the country needs such money than now.

In the case of the Presiding and Principal Officers, in addition to my demand in this letter which applies to them too, I have written them yesterday and gave them 72 hours ULTIMATUM to make public the total amount they have received as running cost in their entire stay in the House, failure of which I will proceed with necessary legal action to compel them to make the total amount each of them have received public.
There are other issues of monumental corruption in the House that I will be raising in the following weeks which we must all deal with, but first lets get done with this one.

Thank you.
God bless.

Hon Abdulmumin Jibrin PhD MBA
APC-Kano
Kiru-Bebeji Federal Constituency
Kano

Unless the National Assembly is dissolved, nothing is going to change in Nigeria:

- It will not matter if the entire leadership of the House and Senate goes to prison for 10 years or more as they should over the current budget scandal. In China and elsewhere they probably would be executed. It will not matter, indeed, if half the members of both chambers went to prison. It is doubtful if a single member can be found who is innocent of this padding scandal. And it would be good if all of them could be jailed for a lengthy period. But I know this is the real world. It will not happen. Yet even if 99 per cent went to prison, the National Assembly would still come out a corrupt institution because there is corruption in its DNA.

- it will not matter what President Muhammadu Buhari does in the fight against corruption. The virus as long as it is in the National Assembly would remain in the body politic, growing and perpetuating itself. The National Assembly never pretended to join in the fight against corruption. This is why, with the exception of Senator Shehu Sani, not a single member declared his or her assets publicly, to follow President Buhari's and Vice-President Yemi Osibajo's worthy examples.

- it will not matter if Speaker Dogara, the Ali Baba in the House, resigns with the House leadership. It will not matter either if Senate President Bukola Saraki, the Ali Baba in the Senate, resigns with the Senate leadership. Anyone with the most rudimentary idea of the workings of a presidential system knows that the National Assembly has become the greatest danger to the survival of democracy in Nigeria.

- there would be no hope for democracy in Nigeria because democracy can only survive on truth and honesty. All our elections end up inconclusive and in litigation because there is no truth in them. Elections are marred by violence because someone wants to bend the truth with force.

The only ray of hope in the horizon is the WE THE PEOPLE nationwide project, led by the NGO, "The People's Grassroots Association for a Corruption-Free Nigeria". Through this book they will teach accountability and responsibility to a new breed of Nigerians who will clean up Nigeria from bottom to top. If you are unhappy with Nigeria, including the national assembly, join this association and work hard with them to create a new breed of Nigerians who will do the right thing for Nigeria and Nigerians.

CHAPTER 7

How Corruption Keeps Nigeria Underdeveloped: My Personal Experience

Prof. Peter U. Nwangwu, MSc Pharm.D PhD FACCP FASCP

Introduction

During the Nigerian-Biafra war, I had the opportunity to work as a paramedic at the Queen Elizabeth hospital, Umuahia. I was a young man of 18 years; my active duty at the hospital saved me from being conscripted as a soldier in the Biafra army. I worked in the hospital pharmacy where drugs and food were dispensed to the sick and malnourished. I was one of two young men deployed newly to join four ladies at the pharmacy to ensure that the food items were dispensed strictly according to physician prescription for the malnourished sick. Although I was a young man and a new staff, I was firm and very dedicated to my job. On my first day at work, I saw the supervisor pack a variety of food items and gave it to one of her friends who came to the pharmacy, without a physician's prescription as required. I stopped her friend from receiving the food items and demanded from my supervisor that I must see the physician prescription for the food items. The food items were returned. My supervisor trembled in shock and unbelief. Before the end of that working day she tendered her letter of resignation. That was the dawn of a new beginning of accountability at the Queen Elizabeth hospital pharmacy.

The news of what happened spread like a wild fire throughout the hospital and beyond. Before then many malnourished patients who actually needed the food items were deprived because the staff in the pharmacy gave the food items to their friends instead of the malnourished sick patients. I put a stop to that, at the tender age of 18. My commitment and passion for serving the malnourished sick and needy created a nice bond between me and the sick who were in dire need. This fine tender bond grew stronger daily as I served them with all my heart and I witnessed measurable change in their health and true gratitude in their hearts. This was the beginning of the genuine desire in my heart to invest myself and my resources to build a world-class hospital in Nigeria, where quality care will be accessible to all who need it.

Healthcare Problems in Nigeria

The problems of healthcare in Nigeria can be broken down to two broad crucial areas:

(a)   The problems of Quality of Healthcare, and
(b)   The problems of Accessibility to Healthcare

Problems with the quality of care would include the adequacy of healthcare facilities and systems, including healthcare policies at medical centers, adequacy of standard operating procedures at these centers, adequacy of the level and scope of care provided by physicians and nurses in light of current knowledge and accepted standards of medical practice in line with global best practices, evidence-based medical care, and current standards of medical practice as found in current world medical literature.

Problems with accessibility to care would include the adequacy of the numbers of healthcare facilities and the proper distribution of these facilities to allow easy and immediate access to a medical facility for every patient who needs one, the affordability, and therefore the accessibility of quality healthcare to all patients.

The warm and incredibly strong bonds I had developed with the sick and needy at Queen Elizabeth hospital, Umuahia, left an abiding challenge in my heart to establish a quality healthcare and accessible medical center in Nigeria, "The Peacemakers Medical Center". This vision grew with me, throughout my years of professional development. My calling was not to become a medical doctor, but to develop the medical infrastructure that will allow doctors practice good medicine in Nigeria, perpetually.

Brief Summary of my Academic and Professional Preparation for my Task

I had served as a Professor of Pharmacology and Toxicology at St. John's University, New York, before joining the drug industry. I worked on 42nd street in Midtown Manhattan in New York City at the world headquarters of American Home Products, a multi-billion-dollar conglomerate that included Wyeth Laboratories, and Ayerst Laboratories. Before my days at St. John's University I served as the Director of Clinical Research at Florida A&M University in Tallahassee, Florida. My educational preparation included two doctorate degrees – the professional Pharm.D or doctor of Pharmacy degree in clinical pharmacy and biopharmaceutics which is the terminal degree in professional pharmacy, and also the research Ph.D. or doctor of Philosophy degree in medical sciences, specializing in cardiovascular pharmacology. My master's degree was in medicinal chemistry and pharmacognosy, and also in pharmacodynamics and toxicology. I earned my bachelor's degree with honors in chemistry at the University of Nebraska, Lincoln. I was therefore properly trained and experienced in all areas of pharmacy, and had a sincere desire to make significant contribution to healthcare in Nigeria.

The Healthcare Project for Nigeria

It was while I served at St. John's University, New York in the early 80's that I became especially troubled about the state of healthcare services in Nigeria. I received many heart breaking reports of people who died needlessly from simple treatable conditions, and the enormous social burdens created by the premature death of heads of households. At first I felt quite helpless about the scope and magnitude of the problem. What can one man do to make a significant and measurable difference? But I eventually decided to pursue an idea that I felt would make significant contribution to alleviation of the problem. As you can appreciate, the key to making any significant and lasting impact on the problems of healthcare in Nigeria is having a dependable source of large sums of money – not just for the development of the proper healthcare infrastructure, but also for the perpetual maintenance of the infrastructure. I decided to set up a modern drug manufacturing company, which will have the capacity to earn significant sums of money, and the sensitivity to commit the profits from this enterprise to the development of the healthcare sector in Nigeria.

I still have in my files copies of letters I received from four state Governors in the United States expressing interest and outlining the benefits of locating my pharmaceutical manufacturing plant in their states. I visited their respective states, but eventually decided to locate the plant in Nigeria for only one reason: a local modern generic drug manufacturing plant in Nigeria would make available to our people a reliable source of affordable high quality essential drugs, which will markedly contribute to quality healthcare in Nigeria by alleviation of unnecessary drug scarcity. Therefore, in 1986, I resigned my appointment in New York and decided to commit large sums of money to the development of a modern drug manufacturing plant in Nigeria.

My Experience in Nigeria
Deciding the Location for a Drug Manufacturing Plant

When I arrived in Nigeria, my first task was deciding a location to site the plant. My initial considerations included choosing a site near a seaport to facilitate importation of raw materials, and ultimately exportation of some of the finished products to markets outside Nigeria. Other factors in consideration included availability of trained and responsible labor force, availability of power, clean water, telecommunication, and national transportation network for distribution of finished products. I was quite attracted to Lagos and Port Harcourt. I got my first shock when a reliable and informed friend quietly said to me: "I understand the factors you are using to select a site and they are sensible and legitimate. However, you must remember that you will import a lot of raw materials, and that import license is a very important issue. If you do not site your plant in the right state or location, you will never get the import license and hard currency you need to purchase raw materials for your operations." Several people confirmed his assertion. Eventually the project was sited in Jos, Northern Nigeria, not because the location we settled for has a seaport which we needed, but because it offered the promise of import license through significant connections to the government. We established our facilities. We had a nice and very modern drug manufacturing plant. I was properly introduced by a good friend in Jos, the late Chief Ezekiel Yusufu, to several key people in General Ibrahim Babanginda's government, especially several key ministers from Langtang, including General Domkat Bali, the Defence minister, General Jeremiah Useni, the Quarter master general of the Nigerian Army, and Colonel John Shagaya, the internal affairs minister.

Infrastructure for Drug Distribution

National distribution infrastructure for pharmaceuticals in Nigeria, such as reliable wholesalers, was very poor and inefficient, in the late 1980's. Therefore, selling to the federal government was attractive at the time. We put together a proposal for the ministry of defense. Fake drugs were rampant in Nigeria. We therefore proposed to manufacture private label products for the ministry of defense which will be supplied to the army, navy and air force. The first product was an analgesic branded Defadol. Benefits outlined for the ministry included:

(a) The product will be sold only to the defense ministry. So, if it was seen on the market the ministry would have legitimate grounds to arrest such sellers. This would cut down on pilferage and diversion which were rampant problems.

(b) Since the product was a private label brand made exclusively for the defense ministry, there will be no fears as to the quality of the product, which was significant in view of the fake drug crisis in Nigeria at the time.

Through a very elaborate process the proposal was approved by the director of medical services for the Nigerian Army, General Ajao, the quartermaster general, and the defence minister. Before signing the contract, the defence minister asked the ministry of health to analyze samples of our product and advise them if they should purchase the products. The analysis showed that the product quality was excellent and above reproach, and so the health ministry wrote a good letter of support for the product advising the minister of defence to proceed with final approval of the contract. The defence minister therefore approved the contract. It was a five-year contract to supply Defadol to the Nigerian Defence ministry for use by Army, Navy, and Air force hospitals nationwide.

Challenges of Implementation of the Contract for Drug Supply

After the minister approved and signed our contract he

passed it down to his permanent secretary for implementation. That was when our nightmares started. To cut a very long story short, our contract sat in a drawer in the office of the permanent secretary at that time, a man from Kano, for nearly two years because we refused to bribe anyone, specifically him the permanent secretary. We were advised to bribe the man by some people who knew him well; otherwise the project would not move forward. My position was that the project should stand on its merit, that the permanent secretary must do his job and implement a project that had already been approved by his boss, the minister. Little did I know that my firm position against bribery would cost me 18 months of utter frustration. The minister eventually knew what was going on. He supported my position. He was embarrassed by the events. Eventually the minister through approvals by the president negotiated removal of the permanent secretary. The man was moved to aviation and a new permanent secretary was appointed for defense. The defence minister sent for me after a new permanent secretary was appointed for defence. Upon arrival at his office, he sent for the new permanent secretary. In my presence, the minister told him about our project and how it had been delayed for too long unnecessarily. He directed him to implement the project

The permanent secretary asked me to wait for him in his office so he can finish other unrelated discussions with the minister. I thanked the minister and went down to the permanent secretary's office to wait for him. He came into his office shortly thereafter and asked one of his assistants to find our company's file. When they found the file and handed it to him, he asked one of his assistants to take me and the file to the director of Army, with clear instructions to process and implement the contract award, which was for five years.

When the matter was introduced to the director of Army in his office, he received me warmly, took the file from the messenger from the permanent secretary's office, and closed his office door after the messenger left his office. He welcomed me again. In a very direct manner, he said to me, "if you want this contract implemented, there are six people you must go and see. He named the permanent secretary first, and named himself as the sixth person, with four other people in-between. I asked him, what exactly do you have in mind, what do you mean by "see"? Without mincing words, he said, "This initial contract is for three million naira; therefore, you must give the permanent secretary N300,000 cash upfront". He went down the list of how much I must give each of the six people, including himself who he said will be willing to take only N60,000 because he will treat me like his friend. This was in the 1980's when naira had so much more value than now. When I expressed shock and outrage for the demand, he simply said that is the way it is, and then added, "after all in that your America where you have come from, there is no free lunch"! He emphasized that the permanent secretary will not sign-off on the contract implementation if I did not pay him at least N300,000 cash in advance, neither will any of the other four persons he named for me. I asked him, "will you be willing to play your own role and get the process started without receiving anything, since you want to treat me as a friend?" He said certainly, but warned me that without going to pay the permanent secretary N300,000, the project will not go anywhere.

We agreed that he will get the implementation process started. He assured me that by the following week our company file will be back to the permanent secretary's office waiting for his signature, which we will not get without paying him N300,000 cash up-front.

The following week I returned to the office of director of army at the defense headquarters to make sure he processed our file as required for the permanent secretary's signature. He confirmed that he did, but the permanent secretary had not signed the project. Armed with that useful information, I went straight to the permanent secretary's office. He remembered and welcomed me. I said to him, "sir, I have come to thank you for being a good man. Our project is moving forward since you came here as permanent secretary and I really want to thank you". He said "that's alright, you are welcome". Then I said, "sir, the director of army, told me that he has completed action on the file and that the file is currently in your office awaiting your signature". He asked, "are you sure?" I replied, "yes sir, very sure". He asked one of his assistants to search for and get the file for him. When they gave it to him, he signed it and asked the assistant to take me and the file to the director of army.

When we entered his office, the director of army took the file from the messenger from the permanent secretary's office, and closed the door behind him. When he left the director of army was really excited to see the permanent secretary's signature. In his excitement, he stated, "Prof, you are now in business. Your project is ready to fly!" Then, in a quieter and somber voice he asked, "tell me, how much money did you pay him?" I said, "nothing"! He replied, "Impossible, absolutely impossible"! He continued, "why are you treating me like a stranger? I was open with you and put everything on the table for you. Why are you hiding the amount you paid the man from me?" I responded, "I did not pay him a penny". He became more urgent and intense, "but it has never happened before, and cannot happen. Sign off on a three-million-naira project without collecting at least N300,000 from you? Impossible!"

I thanked him for his willingness to play his own role and present the paper-work for the project to the permanent secretary for his signature. I asked what the next steps were. He said committee will meet in a few weeks for formal approval of the implementation of the project. Two weeks after that I returned to the office of director of army. He confirmed that the committee met and approved the project implementation, but that the committee secretary has not typed and submitted the minutes of the committee's meeting. He gave me the name and office location of the committee's secretary. I got to this young lady and inquired about the status of the minutes of the committee's meeting? In a nonchalant and psychedelic manner, she responded, "I am very busy, and do not know when the minutes will be ready. I am flying into London for the weekend".

I was both amazed and angry at the level of indiscipline. A young lady, a glorified typist in an office who decides her own schedule for typing minutes of an important meeting by a committee, who has enough cash to fly into London for her weekends, and who cannot be held accountable by her superiors, including the director of army—whatever that designation really stands for. I reported her words to the director of army who simply resigned to the fact that the minutes will be ready whenever the girl produces it. I knew the girl was also waiting for me to bribe her before typing the minutes, but I ignored her totally and left. The project was finally implemented. We manufactured and delivered the products, and submitted our invoice.

Challenges with Payment for Drugs' Supply

Getting paid for the product we manufactured and supplied was another hell. Just signing the invoice and submitting it to the defence ministry was like pulling a wisdom tooth. Apparently we were supposed to bribe someone for that. A fine Yoruba gentleman, a Colonel in the army who was the Chief Pharmacist played his role well by checking the products and signing off as complete on the drugs we manufactured and supplied. The director of army medical services, a Major General, did not sign our bill for submission to the defense department. The General told me to see the Colonel. I was repeatedly advised by the Colonel to bribe the General, but I was not interested. On one occasion when I went back to complain to the Colonel, he said to me, "Sir, I treat you as my senior professional colleague in pharmacy. I have checked the drug inventory and signed my signature to confirm that everything is complete. Your invoice is waiting for the signature of my boss. All the grammar he is speaking to you is because he is waiting for something called 'the Nigerian factor'. Go and see him. If you do not have all the money, give him what you have now and tell him when you will bring the rest of the money. Simple."

This went on for weeks. I got a phone call from the Quarter master general of the Nigerian army, a Major General who I was friendly with. When I got to his office, he told me to go and see the Major General who was the Director of Army medical services. Reluctantly, I went to the General's house that evening to see him by paying him a social visit. I did not give him a penny. We chatted and talked about everything except my drug supply bill that was waiting for his approval signature for payment of the bill by the defence headquarters. In my mind and logic, I had obeyed Quarter master general by going to visit the director of medical services that evening, because I certainly saw him when I paid that social visit, as I was directed to go and see him. Several weeks passed, but the director of medical services continued to hold our bill, and did not sign it. We had entered December, and Christmas was fast approaching. My family was in the U.S and I missed my family and wanted to spend Christmas with them, unconditionally. I was hoping that the bill of the drugs we supplied will at least be signed and submitted for payment. That did not happen.

Finally, I wrote a comprehensive letter of protest to director of medical services, and copied his immediate boss, the quarter master general, and his boss's boss, the defense minister, hoping that the bosses will cause him to sign and submit the bill. The quarter master general immediately sent for me after he received and read the letter. When I got to his office, he asked me to sit down. Then he asked, "Doctor, what is wrong with you? I asked you to go and see the General, and you are writing this long letter and copying me. What do you think the letter will do for you? That man is a General and the director of medical services. He can frustrate you. Go and see the man, stop writing these long letters." I thanked him and left his office, and took the next available flight to return to my family in the U.S. After I left for the U.S, the bill was signed and submitted. It took at least two months for him to simply sign our invoice because we were unwilling to bribe anybody. In mid-January of the following year, I returned to Nigeria.

After the invoice was signed and submitted we were told there was no money to pay us for that quarter. Forty companies had already been short-listed for payment that quarter. Total sum to be paid amounted to over 40 million naira, but the total quarterly allocation released to the defence ministry by the government for payments that quarter was only 10 million naira. Our company was not even among the 40 companies short-listed for payment that quarter!

Let me briefly share with you how I got paid that quarter. I was introduced to the lady who handled the list of companies short-listed for payment. She apologized for my problems, and stated she only handles the list of short-listed companies after they are short-listed for payment, that she has no input on who is short-listed for payment, and does not participate in the meetings where those decisions are made. Therefore, she could not help me. But then she offered one thought. Since I have a working capital line of credit from my bank to produce and supply Defadol to the Nigerian defence, she suggested that I go to my bank and get a nasty foreclosure letter from the bank threatening to impound all my assets for non-payment. She wanted me to submit that letter to the permanent secretary at the Ministry of Defence, hoping that such letter will move the permanent secretary to pay us and protect our assets from foreclosure by the bank. I rushed off to my bank and asked for such letter, which they gladly issued to me.

I set up an appointment to meet with the permanent secretary in his office. I presented the ugly foreclosure threat letter from my bank and watched the permanent secretary read it. His response? "Well, that is too bad that the bank will liquidate your assets for non-payment. We see things like that and letters like this all the time, but we are not able to do anything about it." I was speechless. He continued, "Forty companies have been short-listed to be paid forty million naira. The Federal government gave us only ten million naira for this quarter. Out of that ten million, there are several companies I begged to hold off on checks issued to them last quarter because there was not enough money from last quarter to cover their checks. So I must first pay those people from this 10 million naira, before I even begin paying those that are short-listed for this quarter, and your company is not listed for payment this quarter." Incredible, I thought to myself.

An idea flew through my mind. The Nigerian president at that time, a military General, had just fallen out with his defence minister, a lieutenant General. The defence minister was one of the star ministers of the Nigerian president, and had served for long as reputable defence minister. In a general cabinet reshuffle, the President moved the defence minister from defence to Internal affairs as minister for internal affairs. The defence minister felt insulted, and simply walked away from the job and never returned. So the Nigerian president appointed himself as the acting defence minister. The idea that flew through my mind was to write a letter to the defence minister and tell him the problems I was having with his ministry.

The summary of the well-crafted letter was to tell the president that I was a professor of pharmacology in New York when I heard the Nigerian government appeal to well-trained Nigerians in diaspora to come home and help the government develop the country. I took the appeal of the government very seriously, resigned from my appointments in New York, came back to Nigeria with significant investment capital, and invested in a modern drug manufacturing company in Jos. I was thankful that the Nigerian defence department recognized and rewarded our effort by giving us a five-year contract to manufacture and supply a branded product to the defence. Based on that contract, I took a working capital line of credit from the bank, manufactured and supplied products to the defence department. The defence ministry has not paid me for products supplied to them, my bank is threatening to foreclose and sell off all our assets. I stated that the story of why the bank sold off all my assets after I resigned a safe and lucrative job in New York, and came back with all my capital to invest in modern drug manufacturing in Nigeria, will make a juicy front line page in every newspaper in Nigeria, and that will make the Nigerian president and his administration look very bad. The courier/dispatch rider at the defence headquarters was tipped to make sure that the letter was delivered to the president who was the acting defence minister.

Two weeks after this I returned to the defence headquarters, and went to the lady who handles short-listed companies for payments. She was ecstatic with joy. She told me a revised shortlist for payment came out nearly a week ago. She said when she looked it, she trembled with such excitement that the list fell off her hands. Even though my company was not listed in the first list of 40 companies to be paid from the 10 million naira allocated for that quarter, in the new shortlist that came out, my company name was listed as number one, and the directive was that my company will be paid every penny owed to it, and whatever balance left from the 10 million for the quarter should be paid the other 40 companies. Wow! It was a big relief. So I asked the lady, "what's next?" She said, "go and collect your money!" That's how we eventually got paid. After I got the check and converted the money to dollars by dividing it with the prevailing exchange rate, it was depressing to realize what I suffered and went through for such small amount of money in dollars. The bad feeling came from knowing how long it took to get the job done, the incredible costs to the company in accumulated interests on our working capital credit line, the opportunity costs, and the frustrations we endured. But I was consistent in refusing to bribe anyone as a precondition for them to do their job. After we were paid, I chose to go back and express gratitude by giving small envelopes to several people for the services they provided. That shocked many of them because according to them, I had no reason to come back to express such gratitude for services already rendered. Several expressed great respect and admiration for my principled manner of doing business.

Although the original contract was for five years, I was so discouraged and frustrated by my experiences that I decided to return permanently to the United States after collecting payment for the first supply of product. I did not return to Nigeria again until after 12 years.

The Lessons from my Experience

1. The most important lesson I learned from my experience is the problem of too much reliance on government contracts. In retrospect, I should never have gone to the government for anything. If I dealt strictly with the private sector on a cash-and-carry program, the outcome of my experience may have been different.

2. I returned to Nigeria 12 years after that experience. The terrain had changed so completely in terms of people who knew me and people I know. The second lesson from my experience came to me during that visit. I wished I did not leave; I wished I stayed. For two reasons:

    (a) Indians, Lebanese, Chinese and Italians were all over the place abusing the country and the resources of the country. They have no real vested interest in the country, but they are willing to stay in the country because of the enormous amounts of money they make in Nigeria. They will bribe everyone for everything, inflate their contract price to recover their bribery
    costs, and immediately repatriate their profits out of Nigeria regardless of the hard currency cost, and without any consideration whatsoever for the hard currency burden of their actions to the economy.

    (b) When you leave Nigeria, in some ways, Nigeria leaves you. It is like you have to start all over again from the beginning every time you leave that country for a prolonged period of time.

3.   Do I regret not bribing people to facilitate our project? No, absolutely not! Clearly if I elected to bribe as required, I would not have been frustrated the way I was. I had excellent contacts and a very good project that would have been extremely successful, and by today I would have made the financial adventures of the generals and politicians in that country seem like a child's play. But I stand here today to testify to you that no one needs that type of wealth, especially when acquired by theft, bribery and corrupt practices. I have my good conscience, and I can tell you that my good conscience is worth more than the entire Nigerian national treasury. You have a choice, not to be part of the decadence.

Here is my hypothesis on what I think is the problem with Nigeria and most Nigerians everywhere. We are a country of very insecure people. In our incredible and intense search for acceptance, significance, and emotional and psychological security, we go to any length to look better and be more powerful than the Akpans' next door. We want more money in our bank account than the Akpans' even if we have to take a bribe, steal, push cocaine or be a 419. Because of our psychological insecurity we have to show off our wealth so we can be seen to be wealthier and more powerful than the Akpans'. We must be called Engineer that, Architect so, or chief that, because we have a need to assert superiority over the common Mr. Akpan. This sad emotional insecurity problem has plagued our nation for too long, and has created a country of insane people. If we do not address that simple but profound national problem of emotional insecurity through proper dialogue and education, we will remain a country of artificial and vain people.

We need to understand that there is nothing wrong with being ordinary or simple. It is perfectly okay. As a matter of fact, it is wonderful to be ordinary. And let us begin with ourselves here in the Diaspora. I look forward to the day when a Nigerian will say, "It is okay for the other guy's idea to be better than mine. That's wonderful, he is a really gifted and profoundly intelligent guy – and I just love to learn from his profound wisdom and listen to him speak. He is more qualified to be our leader, and how I love to work with him, support and respect his ideas, and do whatever he wants me to do to help this organization grow!" That mindset and disposition is the only way to a new and prosperous Nigeria. A lot is at stake for everyone in the development of Nigeria into a safe, law-abiding, hospitable nation with basic amenities and functional services. The country is losing the services of many good Nigerians driven out of the country and scattered all over the world against the deepest desires of their heart. Increasing numbers of Nigerians die and are buried outside their fatherland against their will; some of them born outside Nigeria, die without the benefit of stepping their foot on Nigerian soil for even one day.

HOW BRIBERY KEEPS NIGERIA UNDER-DEVELOPED

My goal was to set up a modern generic pharmaceutical manufacturing factory in Nigeria, and to use the profits from that manufacturing plant to build and maintain a very modern and well-equipped world-class center of excellence for medical services. My vision was frustrated by demands for bribery everywhere in Nigeria, an evil I chose to refuse. By frustrating me out of Nigeria by demands for bribery, Nigeria was denied the opportunity of benefiting from my visions, and therefore remained underdeveloped in local pharmaceutical manufacturing, and world-class medical services. I know many other foreign investors who have been frustrated out of Nigeria by the level of corruption and demand for bribery. By not letting them stay and participate in the development of Nigeria through their investments, we lose their contribution, and Nigeria remains under-developed. Many investors and businessmen in different parts of the world are very afraid of coming to Nigeria because of the level of corruption. Malaysia, Singapore, Dubai are examples of places where investors took their money to and developed those countries because bribery and corruption there was not shouting and as widespread as in Nigeria. Bribery and Corruption is a national evil that is keeping Nigeria underdeveloped.

In closing my presentation in this chapter, I want to tell you about our beloved country Nigeria from the eyes of my children when I took them there from America many years ago. My youngest son at that time was 2 years old. He saw some chickens walking around in the compound and was so utterly captivated by this sight. He had never seen chickens walking around freely in a compound where people live. He asked his mother, my wife, if he could catch the chickens. His mom said, "By all means, go for it". This child spent half of the day diving after these chickens, which continued to jump and elude him, but he was having incredible fun trying to catch them. Towards the end of our visit to Nigeria, my family and I were all sitting around talking one day and I asked them a simple question. "Nigeria and America, which one do you like more?" My first son who was seven years old at the time was the first to answer. He had a funny smile on his face, and then he answered, "Nigeria". Out of curiosity, I asked, "Why do you like Nigeria more than America?" His answer was simple but profound. He said, "Because I can pee anywhere I want."

CHAPTER 8

The Roots and Foundations of Corruption in Nigeria: Corrective Tools for Mitigation

Obinna Ubani-Ebere, PhD RFG CABCS CACN CFS

Introduction

Corruption is an unconscionable advantage, profit or gain of injustice through the abuse of authority and power. However, corruption anywhere does not exist in a vacuum. There is always an underlying basis for corruption to exist, thrive and succeed in any society. Unfortunately, there is no nation on the planet earth that is immune against the threat and damage of corruption. The objectives of this chapter are to: (1) discuss the roots and foundations of corruption in the public and private sectors of Nigeria, (2) identify loopholes that breed corruption, (3) examine their consequences, and (4) propose corrective tools for mitigation of corruption in Nigeria.

The sudden death of empathy for decency, honesty, truthfulness, kindness, patriotism, equality, justice, and respect for the law created the opportunity that transformed Nigeria into a vineyard of moral delinquency, inhumanity, affliction, abduction, bomb attacks, kidnapping, infringement, injustice, indiscriminate and targeted killing. As a result, Nigeria has become a hub and fierce conduits of exploitation, crimes, extortion, bribery, frauds, nepotism, crookedness, rackets, shadiness, and skimming which are the serious symptoms of a sick society that squeezes the poorest of the poor and citizens that have no connections with the upper echelon of Nigeria.

Unfortunately, these moral corrosions, and the epidemic of corruption, trickle down from those that represent the aristocracy of Nigeria to the low class of Nigeria. The complexity and sophistication of the Nigerian brand of corruption is one of her great predicaments that make her a profoundly sick society.

Corruption is a product of greed that causes poverty and misery, disproportionately affecting the voiceless poor in the society, the repercussions of which have led to decades of damages of the social welfare and infrastructural system in Nigeria. It is wrong to treat corruption as a case of oversight or mistake in Nigeria. Corruption is an intentional action, willful act, and conscious neglect of established processes, laws and decency. It is a deliberate violation of laws, ethics, and codes of conduct for personal benefits or benefits for a few citizens at the expense of the majority. This poses a fundamental challenge, obstacle, and threat to the economic, political and social stability of Nigeria. The problem is that corruption breeds corruption as bribery begets bribery in a system where there is no transparent control, a culture of accountability, checks and balances, a system of watchdogs, watching the watchdogs, policing the police, or investigating the investigators to ensure best practices.

It has become commonplace to associate Nigeria with various forms of corruption, an association that has greatly damaged her global image and integrity.

Nigeria's Moral Diseases or Ethical Sickness

It is an undeniable global truth and reality that corruption is one of the main sources of economic, political, and social upheaval in any society. However, corruption in any country does not exist in a vacuum. Structural corruption in Nigeria is founded on a firm foundation composed of seven ethical sicknesses as shown in Figure 1.

Figure 1: The Foundations of Corruption

The first ethical sickness of Nigeria is an unending desire known as *'greed syndrome'*. Greed has no end, and remains the driver of corruption in many societies. Greed is the engine of corruption, and the ultimate common problem in today's modern society. The second ethical sickness is *selfish ambition*, which places self-interest ahead of the overall interest of the society at large. Selfish ambitions contaminate human motives. The third ethical sickness is *overindulgence*. Overindulgence breeds a materialistic culture of sacrificing morality to acquire material goods and financial wealth beyond their needs.

The fourth ethical sickness of Nigeria is euphemistically known as the *"get rich quick" mentality*. This mindset is the precursor to crimes driven by materialism. *Un-patriotism* is the fifth ethical sickness of Nigeria. This term is a characteristic of people who are not proud of their country and would be involved in schemes that threaten the existence of their country without any regret. The desire for *instant gratification* and grandiosity, which motivates corruption, is the sixth ethical disease of Nigeria. Finally, cultural and traditional value systems that *honor dishonest characters* that derive wealth from grand or petty corruption based on ill-gotten titles and recognition is the seventh ethical disease or moral sickness of Nigeria.

A community that tolerates dishonesty, or honors known thieves, looters, fraudsters, swindlers, embezzlers, forgers, drug dealers, child traffickers, corrupt politicians and public officials, without questioning the legitimacy of the sources of their wealth celebrates corruption in that community. These seven interrelated ethical diseases are highly embedded in the daily lives of people in Nigeria, and combine to form the structural foundation for corruption that makes Nigeria a hub for white collar scams, such as bribery, extortions, and 419, distribution of fake drugs, fraud, and forgery. These white collar crimes not only taint Nigeria's image and credibility but make her citizens suspect of fraud and wrong doings around the world, even when they are innocent.

Classification of Corruption in Nigeria

Corruption in Nigeria can be classified into ten correlated categories, which include:

1. ***Law Enforcement Corruption***
   Law enforcement corruption is an open transgression in Nigeria that begins from the international airport and the high and byways. Law enforcement misconduct perverts justice via crimes like bribery and extortion. Gross violations of Nigeria's statutes by law enforcement agencies directly contradict the oath to protect and defend, which makes this branch of government the "Dean of iniquity".

2. ***Political and Administrative Corruption***
   Political and administrative corruption is a scheme, whereby politicians and those who serve or work in the public office in Nigeria use their authority and power for private and personal advantages.

3. Organized Corruption

Organized corruption is one of the major threats to Nigerian economic, political, and social development. These crimes are well organized and sophisticated; and include kidnapping groups, piracy groups, terrorist groups, child factories, sex trafficking, and crude oil theft.

4. Financial Institution Corruption

Corruption of financial institutions is one of the scams and frauds that threaten Nigeria's financial system, diminishes faith in the banking industry, harms the economy, and promotes crime and youth unemployment. The financial institutions help politicians, government officials, and unscrupulous businesses that align themselves with bank officials to launder the nation's money to offshore banks.

Other forms of corruption in Nigeria include:

1. Business corruption, such as bribery for contracts.
2. Insurance corruption, which involves issuing fake and empty policies to car owners.
3. Insider corruption, which are crimes committed by those in the organization or department.
4. Minor corruption and petty crimes involving small quantities of money.
5. Grand corruption, which are large-scheme corruption involving huge amounts of fraud, perhaps at the high-ups of the government.
6. Chieftaincy title corruption, which is the type of corruption in Nigeria that has become a source of income for some monarchs who proliferate chieftaincy titles to individuals that give them money.
7. Electoral corruption, that involves election officials in Nigeria that collect bribes from candidates that pay the highest in order to skew

the outcome of the election.

8. Military corruption, involving the diversion of military resources by the military chiefs for private use.

9. 'Agbero' corruption, an unorganized corruption involving hooligans malingering or aggressively pestering and extorting money from people along the roads, motor parks and strategic locations in the name of government.

10. Payroll ghost corruption, which refers to ghost workers including deceased employees which appear on the government payrolls. The payroll corruption or crime hurts the federal, state and local government budgets.

11. Corruption of the medical industry, which occurs when patients come to public facilities and are illegally redirected or diverted to the private clinics, hospitals, or labs of the same doctors that were employed by the government. It is a serious professional scheme, which increases the ineffectiveness of the public medical facilities in Nigeria.

12. Religious corruption, a type of emerging corruption in Nigeria, which some leaders of these groups have used to cause family upheavals, brainwash and divide families by telling them that one of their siblings is the major cause of their misfortunes. These types of miracle extortion and frauds have caused serious devastations in some families.

Enabling Loopholes of Corruption in Nigeria

The Nigeria brand of corruption comes in different forms such as bribery, fraud/theft, extortion and blackmail, slush money, kickbacks, money laundering, forgery, kidnapping ransom, favoritism, nepotism, cronyism, piracy, facilitation payment, unwarranted rebates, excessive commissions, advanced fees, contract collusions.

216

These loopholes are used to award contracts, in which contractors collect full payment for alleged completed work, even without any evidence of one shovel on the site. Figure 2 presents the specific drivers of corruption in Nigeria.

Figure 2. Drivers of Corruption in Nigeria

Consequences of Corruption in Nigeria

Corruption is a culture of violence and dishonesty that is a serious threat to Nigeria's development. Its long-term impact on society transcends bribery and embezzlement. It promotes mediocrity and undermines the power of meritocracy in a society, thereby demoralizing and holding back those citizens who fight on merit, but are bypassed by the system that rewards criminals. Power and authority comes with severe intoxications, which impair good judgment and thoughts. The use of power for private gains, to punish enemies, ambush oppositions, and to pervert justice, are some of the dangerous weapons of corruption in Nigeria.

Corruption is a virulent infectious disease that has many severe economic, political, and social consequences. The outcome is injustice and corrosive perversion of justice that disables a society, hurts the poor and powerless citizens of Nigeria. The main actors in corruption schemes are politicians, legislatures, the presidency, governors, the judiciary, public institutions, the private sector, corporations, small businesses, individuals, law enforcement agencies, religious organizations, domestic and foreign banks as shown in figure 3. The challenge is that these actors hold strategic positions in the society and know exactly where and when to commit fraud or launder money. They are in the front lines of corruption that impose impediment to the society.

Figure 3: Actors in Corruption

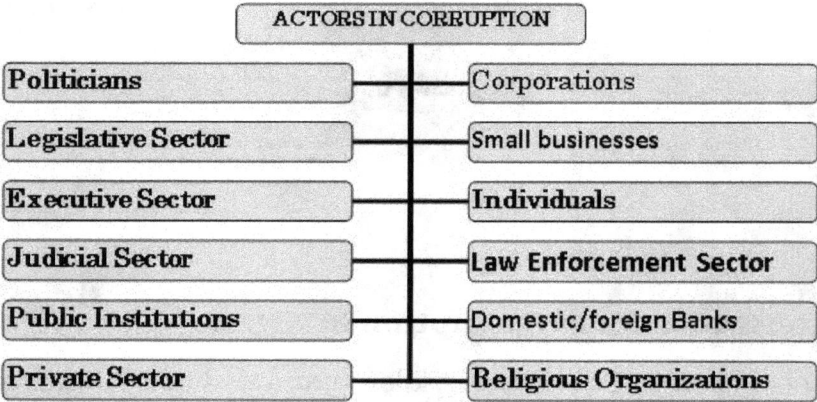

ACTORS IN CORRUPTION	
Politicians	Corporations
Legislative Sector	Small businesses
Executive Sector	Individuals
Judicial Sector	Law Enforcement Sector
Public Institutions	Domestic/foreign Banks
Private Sector	Religious Organizations

If corruption is the domain of governmental operations, it becomes the iniquity of the entire society when it goes unchallenged, because corruption easily survives, and succeeds in an unethical environment. Most leaders and citizens would certainly agree that the complex, dangerous nature of corruption in Nigeria underscores the importance of using strategic foresight and vision in articulating long-term plan in mitigating corruption and bribery in Nigeria.

The basic moral requirements that guide people to a good life are dead in Nigeria. These basic moral standard requirements include fairness, honesty, keeping contractual promises, self-confidence, trust, sincerity and respect. Without these standards, it would be easy for people to accept money and other values to pervert justices. Cheating is the mindset of corrupt minds and people, who refuse to play by the rule of law and follow established policies, laws and procedures.

Figure 4: Consequence of Corruption in Nigeria

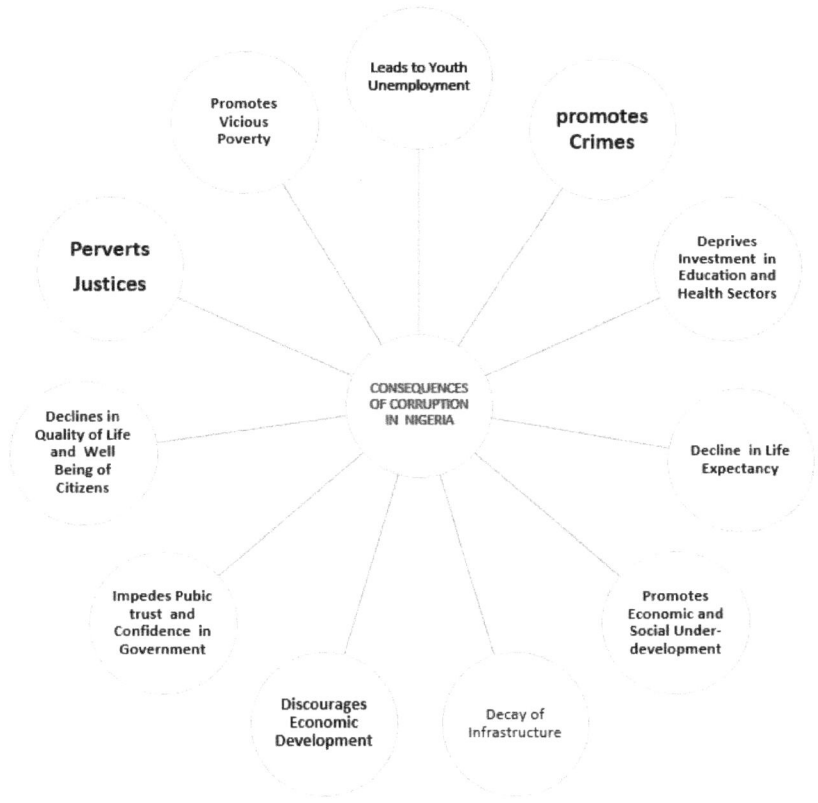

Leads to Youth Unemployment

Promotes Vicious Poverty

promotes Crimes

Perverts Justices

Deprives Investment in Education and Health Sectors

CONSEQUENCES OF CORRUPTION IN NIGERIA

Declines in Quality of Life and Well Being of Citizens

Decline in Life Expectancy

Impedes Pubic trust and Confidence in Government

Promotes Economic and Social Under-development

Discourages Economic Development

Decay of Infrastructure

Corruption is the trademark of an unscrupulous society. Though few people in Nigeria today will refuse kickbacks and bribery, those citizens who subscribe to the spirit of moral responsibility and accountability that reject corruption or refuse bribery or kickbacks are good citizens of the society. Unfortunately, no institution in Nigeria is free of corruption, nepotism, and bribery, be it the government institutions, parastatals, law enforcement agencies, departments, corporations, financial institutions, bankers, private businesses, educational institutions, teachers, professors, lecturers, executive, legislators, members of judiciary or religious institutions, hospitals, and private clinics.

Mitigation of corruption in Nigeria must require the culture of transparency that properly aligns with the culture of accountability. While the task of mitigating corruption in Nigeria is complex and complicated, the task of transforming a society politically, socially and economically is not simple, and both must be aligned for a positive outcome. The long-term solutions for curing the economic, political and moral or social diseases that produce corruption in Nigeria require foresight, and must be based on a new culture, vision and proactive, reactive and realistic strategies. If the strategic goal of a country is to achieve social justice and equity through the reduction of corruption and other activities of moral turpitude in the 21st century, then building a culture of accountability will be the critical prerequisite to achieving the quality and scale of response required to accomplish it.

The vision and culture of transforming Nigeria has many significant justifications or reasons that go beyond the economic, political and social empowerment of the Nigerian citizens. The struggle to transform a society is the total responsibility of "we the people" hence it is the people's common fight to reclaim their country back from corrupt politicians. The sociology of Nigerian politics sadly was changed by PDP to a winner takes all system, which ignores, and abandons every other citizen outside the cronyism. APC is doing the same. In the meantime, the country and WE THE PEOPLE suffer. Power belongs to the people; it is the inalienable rights of every citizen of Nigeria to actively participate in the affairs and management of government of the people for the people and by the people. Courageous citizens are those who are willing to take the risk to preserve the dignity of their country and reclaim and reconnect with their government. Building a culture of accountability, social justice and strong nonselective prosecution of wrong doings based on tribalism, religiosity, partisan politics or sectionalism in the minds of "we the people of Nigeria" is the prerequisite for reducing the frequent incidences of corruption, bribery and other forms moral turpitudes in Nigeria. Furthermore, Nigeria cannot accomplish the complex and complicated objective of achieving a change that reduces corruption and other activities of moral turpitude, unless there is change and new commitment in the attitudes, behaviors, values and actions of a new breed of "we the people" of Nigeria who are willing to respect the laws, follow the establish process, code of conducts and ethics of the society that allow every citizen equity and social justice.

Accountability and transparency has never been the cornerstone of the Nigerian society since her independence in 1960. That is why corruption has become the opium and worst infectious disease in Nigeria. Building transparency and accountability in the public and private sectors is a strategic anti-corruption weapon. Without a culture of accountability, internal controls and oversights, leaders and gatekeepers of the society will continue to run amuck in their behaviors and actions in discharging their day-to-day functions and responsibilities for "we the people of Nigeria".

Five Principles of Developing a Culture of Accountability and Transparency

Reduction of corruption and crimes will not take place in any society without the culture of accountability and transparency. There are five key principles or elements in developing a culture of accountability and transparency, which can reduce corruption, bribery and other insidious crimes in Nigeria.

Political Accountability

The first principle in developing a culture of accountability and transparency is *political accountability*, which is a requirement that enables public officials or elected officials to be wise stewards, be accountable, and to emphasize good stewardships in the gate- keeping and managing of government resources. The following are some of the common elements of culture of public accountability and transparency that will lead to change:

1. Common sense democracy or participatory governance in which the supreme powers are invested in the people, and power is directly or indirectly controlled by the people.
2. Transparent leadership that ensures people's confidence and trust in the government as well as leadership.
3. Freedom of speech, communication and press that allows citizens to make constructive criticisms of their leaders and government without retributions.
4. Incorporating the doctrine of checks and balances in the government in order to eliminate the tyranny of corruption, bribery and criminality.
5. A system that encourages or promotes tolerance and shared leadership, as well as the inclusion of the welfare of every citizen should become a way of governance.
6. Mandatory disclosure and verifiable net worth, wealth or financial status of public officials before going to the office and after office must be an essential requirement for all holding public office.
7. The establishment of enforceable code of ethics or system that will deter the abuse of power in office from top-to-bottom.
8. Absolute rejection of monocracy (instead of democracy) should be part of the new social

and political culture.

9. The establishment of citizens' bill of rights should be a core requirement for peace and stability.
10. Strong law enforcement and policing of all crimes and abuse of due process should be a high priority of the government.
11. Instituting independent judiciary or legal system capable of potent prosecution of all crimes of corruption in the public and private sectors will reestablish the people's confidence in the government.

Economic Accountability

The second principle in building a culture of accountability and transparency is *economic accountability*, which holds those who manage the economy, including financial institutions, ministry of finance, stock markets and the central bank accountable, and protects the institutions against fraud and embezzlement, including moving the Nigerian economy from single product economy to a diversified economy with strong manufacturing and export, including reducing Nigeria's dependence on importation of finished products. In addition, the economic accountability in Nigeria should include anti-poverty policies that help the poor for upward mobility.

Social accountability

The third principle of developing a culture of accountability and transparency, which aims at reducing corruption, fraud and criminal abuses of the system in Nigeria is *social accountability*. This is the building of accountability that relies on civic engagement, participation of ordinary citizens, and civil society organizations as well as stakeholders who act as watchdogs to the system.

In addition, social accountability creates avenue for social upward vertical and horizontal mobility, demolishes the culture of vicious poverty through economic, political and social empowerment; creates the Nigerian brand of social security, increase access to appropriate education and affordable healthcare as well as access to affordable non fake medicine in Nigeria. Social accountability also requires corporations and businesses to show a sense of corporate social responsibility that employs moral conscience and ethics in their operations; develops policies that encourage gender equity and equality as well as policies that encourage mind and mental decolonization of Nigeria's citizens against foreign made goods while promoting human rights.

Religious accountability

The fourth principle of building a culture of transparency and accountability is *religious accountability*, which holds religious leaders and their members accountable by influencing and instigating peace, hope and high moral grounds that impede frauds, bribery and other forms of corruption in Nigeria. Additionally, religious accountability does not promote religious discrimination or tribalism, does not incite riot and inter-religious conflicts or altercations and does not support religious xenophobia in Nigeria.

Corruption in Nigeria transcends ethnic and religious boundaries, political divisions, education and class. However, in the absence of integrity in the operations of government, and public services as well as private businesses, there are still a few men and women of exemplary conduct in the society, who stand their ground on the angle of truth, lead with distinction in honesty, undisputable integrity, serve the society with clean hands, free from corruption, bribery and tinted morality worthy of emulation in Nigeria.

Judicial accountability

The fifth principle of building a culture of transparency and accountability for mitigating corruption, bribery and fraud is *judicial accountability*, which is defined (www.lawteacher.co.uk) as "the costs that a judge expects to incur in case his/her behavior and/or his/her decisions deviate too much from a generally recognized standard, or the letter of the law" .

The lack of judicial-will to swiftly try and convict former governors, legislators, and public officials who colluded with the financial institutions, corporations, and some business operators to loot, defraud, steal and launder Nigerian money abroad is a national disgrace and evil in any anti-corruption, anti-fraud, anti-bribery, anti-money laundering or anti-graft activities in Nigeria. As long as corruption, bribery, fraud, extortion and kickbacks run in the arteries and blood streams of judges and court officials, justice from Nigeria judiciary will remain an article on the auction block for the highest bidder.

In his keynote address titled "Promoting Magistrate Court Ethics, Integrity and Improving Citizens' Access to Justice" to Socio-Economic Rights and Accountability Project (SERAP) in collaboration with the Royal Netherlands Embassy on February 9, 2012, the Chief Justice of Nigeria, Justice Dahiru Musdapher stated:

> "Corruption in the Justice sector is a keystone to corruption throughout society. Without an honest criminal justice system, the wealthy, especially the corrupt, can escape the consequences of their crimes. Such impunity reduces the perceived cost of corruption. The risk that corrupt activity will result in imprisonment and accompanying public humiliation is minimal. The gains from corruption are therefore trouble if corruption, kickbacks, bribery and other forms of graft trickle into the Supreme Court, which is the apex court and court of last resort not discounted, and there is thus little reason beyond personal integrity not to engage in corrupt acts"

While the tyranny of judiciary injustice is dangerous and unacceptable, any executive and legislative controls on the

Judicial system should not exist, as it perverts justice, impedes accountability, responsibility, transparency, fairness, equity, efficiency, effectiveness and integrity in judicial functions and responsibilities. Therefore, judicial independence and accountability must be respected and enforced to preserve the integrity of the judicial system, without any political interference in order to prevent the entrenchment of corrosive corruption, fraud, and influences of bribery in the judicial system, which, pervert justices, and blind judges in rendering truthful decisions or writing fair opinions based on the evidence of the law on cases before their courts, especially in cases related to elections in Nigeria. Figure 5 summarizes the seven principles of developing a culture of accountability and transparency for mitigating corruption and bribery in Nigeria.

A country emerges as a paper tiger legal system if laws are not enforced, abandoned or ignored due to corruption or influences of bribery and kickbacks. For the Nigerian Judicial System to be truly independent within the confines of separation of power between, legislature, executive and judiciary, as enshrined in the 1999 constitution, and be accountable to "we the people of Nigeria," or operate meaningfully on the great framework of values of accountability, transparency, responsibility, integrity, equity, fair judicial system, it should be free from the executive and legislative controls.

Figure 5: Seven Principles of Accountability and Transparency

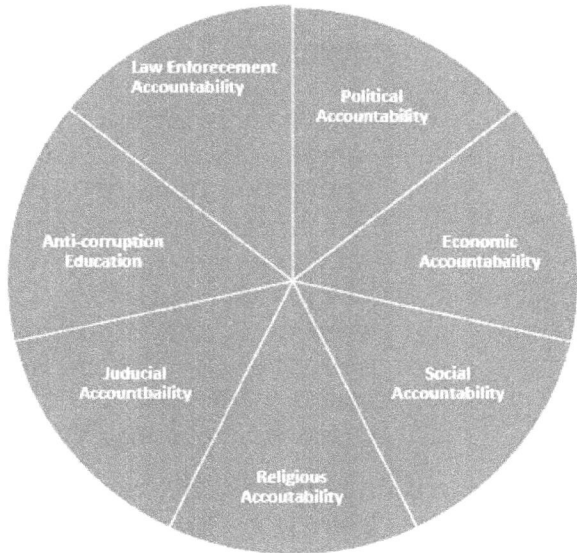

According to Association of Certified Fraud Examiners:

"Individuals working in Law Enforcement are central in the investigation step of the fraud examination process. "Law enforcement individuals perform a variety of tasks, such as collecting evidence and testifying in court. Individuals in law enforcement may work for the State or Federal government as a special agent, while others may work for local police departments. At times, they may even work undercover. The nature of work often depends on place of employment, location, size of organization, in addition to a variety of other factors. Special Agents may specialize in a particular area, or work in a variety of different fields".

Institutionally, Nigeria has what it takes to mitigate corruption, frauds, bribery, crimes and all forms of graft. The Nigerian Anti-Corruption Agencies(ACAs) include 1) the Nigerian Police Force (NPF), 2) Independent Corrupt

Practices Commission(ICPC), 3) Economic and Financial Crimes Commission (EFCC), 4) Code of Conduct Bureau (CCB), 5) The National Drug Law Enforcement Agency (NDLEA and 6) The Nigeria Customs as well as Nigeria Financial Intelligence Unit (NFIU), which monitor compliance with Anti-money laundering/combating the financing of the terrorism. Each of these agencies has great mission. For example, from the ICPC Official Website:

> "Corruption in Nigeria undermines democratic institutions, retards economic development and contributes to government instability. Corruption attacks the foundation of democratic institutions by distorting electoral processes, perverting the rule of law, and creating bureaucratic quagmires whose only reason for existence is the soliciting of bribes."

While corruption cannot be completely eradicated in any society, the risk of corruption, negatively affects the economic, political and social environment. However, it can be reduced or controlled with judicial-will and tenacious law enforcement. Mitigating corruption in Nigeria is a monumental task and challenge, and even tougher if judiciary and law enforcement entrusted to lead the fight are equally infected by the sick society amongst its ranks and file. Figure 6 shows the six major anti-corruption agencies (ACAs) in Nigeria.

Figure 6: Anti-Corruption Agencies (ACAs)

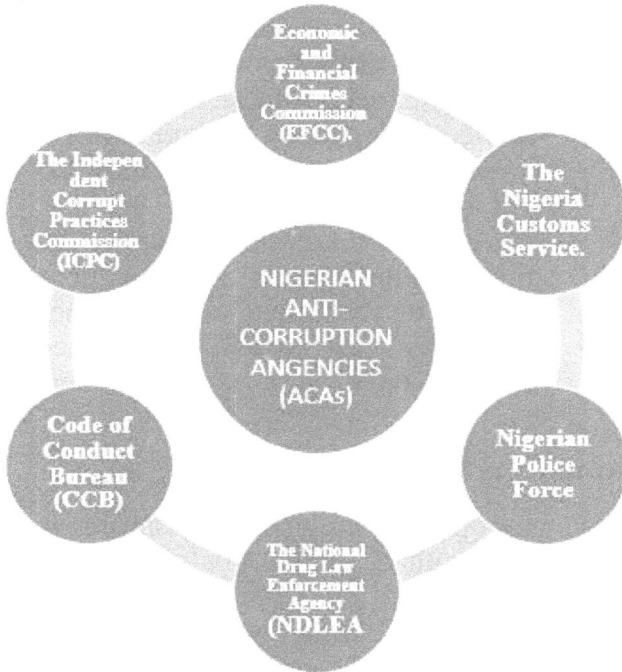

These agencies have interrelated goals of ridding Nigeria of economic and financial crimes including money laundering and terrorism. While these agencies work hard to achieve their mission and goals, their continuing effectiveness will depend on the following elements:

1. ACAs must determine to work together and in tandem, and must be efficient in resources management, deterrence and prevention of corruption and crimes.
2. The intra-agencies sharing information strengthens the capacity and capability to deter and prevent crimes.
3. Tenacity and transparency, showing swift justice and discipline amongst law enforcement ranks,

who otherwise bring shame on the agencies through corruption. They must improve the image and integrity of these agencies, because a police force that cannot police itself or its own staff, and hold them accountable for their own misconduct is ineffective, dubious and untrustworthy; they impose doubt on the integrity of the law enforcement.
4. ACAs must increase their credibility by going after the pending cases of corrupt politicians (big fishes), or the upper crusts of the government for corruption cases which remain inconclusive for the past 16 years.

Conclusions

Nigeria's corruption problems are complex and complicated, which will require both qualitative and quantitative approaches of mitigation. First, no action to reduce the risk of corruption in Nigeria will work unless the federal government takes the lead. Second, the fight against corruption will be long term and should be planned. One long-term goal of anti-corruption is the need to establish an anti-corruption course, which will be mandatory for every Nigerian and foreigners who want to do business in Nigeria.

Since corruption in Nigeria is essentially the use of authority and public office for personal advantage and private gains, there is a need to establish the Nigerian National Institute for Anti-Corruption (NNIAC) to provide anti-corruption education, training and awareness on the deadly impacts of corruption on Nigeria's Development. Such institutes will also be instrumental in introducing anti-corruption curriculum or programs from primary school to universities as well as making it compulsory for every applicant seeking a job both in private and public institution or organization to take one class in anti-corruption. Third, good governance is lethal to corruption. Fourth, frequent rigorous risk assessment, due diligence and internal control are other tools to reduce corruption.

Fifth, introducing bank secrecy act, which mandates financial institutions to report any susceptible transactions to anti-graft agencies will close some loopholes that enable money laundering in Nigeria. Sixth, making transparency and openness a culture of management and operation of the government is an indispensable weapon against corruption.

Finally, laws without enforcement are paper tigers. To be proactive, we must be defensive, or offensive against corruption and bribery as a necessary condition to reduce incidences of corruption; however, laws and rules cannot be enforced by wood or tree. You need human beings with a good heart who are willing to carry out their responsibilities ethically. Without such commitment, the outcomes of any corruption risk mitigations will be Dejavu in Nigeria.

It is sometimes good to be cowardly and that is not necessarily a bad thing. Anybody that rejects bribery is a good coward. The application of the rule in governance is the function of the federal, state and local government of Nigeria. The absence of accountability, transparency and openness in government builds the highway for corruption. Corruption is fightable in Nigeria but it will require determination from the upper level of government. However, Nigeria has no government at this time, because of massive corruption in government. What can WE THE PEOPLE do in the absence of government?

The problem is that present day WE THE PEOPLE in Nigeria are corrupt, and divided by tribal, religious, and political party affiliations. So the country bleeds because present day WE THE PEOPLE are totally impotent from their corruption and tribal, religious, and political party affiliations. Nigeria is weeping badly for a new breed of WE THE PEOPLE. Nigeria is pleading for a new breed of WE THE PEOPLE, individuals who will renounce corruption, religious, tribal, and political party affiliations, one person at a time, and commit to loving and saving Nigeria. No one person can save Nigeria alone. None of the existing political parties can save Nigeria. Only a new breed of committed WE THE PEOPLE can save Nigeria. We can clean Nigeria from bottom-to-top. One clean person at a time, WE THE

PEOPLE will build to a formidable force of 50 million clean Nigerians who are united in their determination to save Nigeria. They will save Nigeria by exercising their vote to clean the top from a clean bottom. A new breed of clean WE THE PEOPLE shall in a nationwide movement vote out of office all corrupt leaders, beginning from the presidency to the local government chairmen, including all corrupt governors and national assembly law makers. A clean executive and legislature will appoint and confirm a clean judiciary. We can do it. We must do it. Will you be part of the new breed of WE THE PEOPLE who will save Nigeria?

CHAPTER 9

The Benefits of Building a New Nigeria that will Bring Back Most Nigerians in the Diaspora

Prof. Elewechi Okike, PhD MPhil MSc BSc FHEA FRSA MNIM

Prof. Aminu S. Mikailu, PhD MSc BSc

We are all probably familiar with the saying 'there's no place like home'. This is true. After a long day's work, most of us look forward to the prospect of returning to our homes. In fact, it is said that 'the English man's home is his castle'. There is no feeling as awful as finding the prospect of returning home after work, daunting. Yet this is the reality of many men and women, who have serious challenges in their homes and other nexus of relationships.

Sadly, this analogy epitomises the situation that many distinguished Nigerians scattered across the globe find themselves. They find the prospect of returning to their homeland daunting because of the political, economic and social malaise in the country. The society is ridden with corruption at the highest levels and criminal activity is rife. The political climate is very unstable and tribal and religious conflicts are always looming on the horizon. The infrastructure is very poor or in some cases non-existent. The safety of life and/or property is never guaranteed. This is despite the fact that the country is endowed with so much in terms of natural and human resources. Besides, it is the largest producer of oil in Africa, and the 6th largest globally.

Whilst this chapter explores the benefits of building a new Nigeria that will bring back most Nigerians in diaspora (NIDs), it is not possible within the constraints of the chapter to present what this 'new Nigeria' would look like and all the potential benefits that would accrue to Nigeria when most NIDs return to the country. Nevertheless, it presents some of the most cogent reasons why an extra-ordinary number of Nigerians are in diaspora and how their return to the country will bring about noticeable positive change and economic and social development in the country.

Are Nigerians in diaspora out of the country by choice or by default? There are not many NIDs, who do not love their country. It is usually the case that during festive seasons it is sometimes difficult to find seats on planes en-route Nigeria. Although the political, economic and social environment of Nigeria prevent many Nigerians in diaspora from making the final return back to the country, many still like to visit home. Even whilst in diaspora, many Nigerians have close family, friends as well as investments and other developmental projects in Nigeria. In 2012, Nigerians in the Diaspora contributed more to Nigeria's economy than 34 of the 36 states, having remitted the sum of $12 billion. Only Lagos and Rivers states had higher GDP's[12].

Nigeria has so much to offer in terms of natural and human resources. It is endowed with every type of resource that most countries only dream about. Even the weather is favourable for all types of agricultural and socio-economic development. Yet, in spite of these natural endowments, many Nigerians find the prospect of returning to their homeland daunting. Majority would like to return to their country to contribute to its economic and social development, if the environment was conducive and enabling.

Reasons Why Many Nigerians Remain in Diaspora

Most NIDs who left the country to study did so not with the intention of staying away indefinitely, but rather to acquire the necessary knowledge and skills, including the expertise in their various disciplines to enable them return and contribute to the development of their country. Some of

[12]http://www.nigeriandiaspora.com/index.php

these people were beneficiaries of scholarships from either the Federal Government of Nigeria, when the economy was buoyant, or beneficiaries of other scholarship schemes, including those of the Commonwealth. These scholarships were awarded to scholars and academics, who had distinguished themselves in their academic disciplines, to enable them to study abroad and return to Nigeria and contribute to its growth and development.

In the days when the country's environment was stable, conducive and enabling, some of these scholars after successfully completing their studies did not stay back, not even to attend the graduation ceremonies of the institutions they attended. They were keen and enthusiastic to return home to the task of nation building. But not so now! With an environment that is mostly unstable, bedevilled with all sorts of vices, including the insecurity of life and property, many have been forced to stay back against their will.

Some were forced to leave the country in search of green pastures under the various military dictatorships, as living in the country became unbearable for them. Since attaining independence in 1960, Nigeria has grappled with the problems and crisis deeply rooted in religious, tribalism and other ethnic tensions. These tensions led to successive military coups, including tribal and religious unrests. In addition, the country has had a long history of gross mismanagement of the economy, with endemic corruption at all levels of government (Okike, 2004)[13]. Hence, in spite of the country's potentials for wealth, the country was ranked 152nd in the Human Capital Development Index in 2014, and thus one of the poorest countries in the world. In 1997, the ranking was 141st. This is despite the fact that the country is Africa's largest producer of oil, and boasts of the richest man and the richest woman in Africa.

Besides, political instability in the country, and endemic corruption, there is also the problem of the lack of integrity

---

[13] Okike, E.N.M. (2004) "Management of crisis: the response of the auditing profession in Nigeria to the challenge to its legitimacy", *Accounting, Auditing & Accountability Journal*, Vol.17 No.5, pp.705-730.

in leadership, leading to the lack of transparency, poor accountability and governance in the management of the nation's economic resources. The consequence of this state of affairs is the inability of the government to provide essential services to aid the economic and social development of the country. The wealth of the nation has for long been in the hands of a few elites, leaving majority of Nigerians in abject poverty. Lack of adequate infrastructure, poor and/or inadequate supply of energy, housing and transportation challenges, a declining educational system, poor medical facilities, little or no opportunities for growth and personal development across all levels of society, the lack of discipline amongst most Nigerians, little or no regard for the rule of law and order, an unreliable judicial system, resulting in weak or non-existent law enforcement and the insecurity of life and property are some of the conditions making it difficult for many Nigerians in diaspora to return to their homeland to contribute to the task of rebuilding the nation.

Achievements of Nigerians in Diaspora

This state of affairs is the reason for the massive 'brain drain' from Nigeria[14], and most of these brains have gone ahead and distinguished themselves in all fields of human endeavour across the globe. Many of them have become the best medical doctors, lawyers, accountants, pharmacists, professors, engineers and so on in different countries around the world, including the United States of America, the United Kingdom, Germany, Canada, France, to mention just a few.

The list of such Nigerians is endless. One can mention a few of them such as Professor Peter Nwangwu, the Editor of this book, *WE THE PEOPLE*. Born of Igbo parents from Anambra State of Nigeria, Peter Nwangwu was born in

---

[14] However, 'brain drain' is not unique to Nigeria. It has been identified as a problem facing both developing and industrialised countries. See Tettey, Wisdom J. (2003) "Africa's options: return, retention or diaspora", http://www.scidev.net/global/policy-brief/africa-s-options-return-retention-or-diaspora-.html

Umuahia, Abia State, Nigeria. He attended Anglican Grammar School, Umuahia, and Methodist College, Uzuakoli, where he became the pioneer recipient of the Best Student of the Year award in 1970. He moved to the United States in 1972 and had his college education at the University of Nebraska at Lincoln, where he was elected into the university's honor roll beginning from his first year, and also into the national scholastic honor society, Phi Eta Sigma, the exclusive academic honorary for selected men in American universities. Peter made history when he became the first student at the university to earn his bachelor's degree in chemistry after only two years of university education after high school. He made more history when he became the first student in the over 100-year history of that university to earn the Pharm.D. and Ph.D. degrees simultaneously. He was one of twelve Nigerians selected and documented in a reference book 'The Nigerian-Americans', authored by Professor Ogbaa and published by Greenwood Press, as those who have made the greatest positive impact and contributions to the American Society. Nwangwu invented two new techniques in pharmacology that are still used worldwide, developed seven new antiarrhythmic drugs that are protected by U.S patents, and was the first scientist to document and publish murine ventricular tachycardia, which has become a relevant model of human cardiomyopathies for studies in cardiovascular disease worldwide. His research inventions are used or quoted by professors at distinguished universities including Harvard, the number one university in the world, Cornell university, and university of Pennsylvania.

Peter is one of those Nigerians in diaspora, who are very passionate about making a difference in Nigeria, and seeing the country change for the better. Championing and commissioning the publication of this book, WE THE PEOPLE, bears testimony to this fact. During the tenure of Professor Chinedu Nebo as Vice Chancellor of the University of Nigeria, Peter served as Professor of Pharmacology, Toxicology and Clinical Pharmacy; Chief Development Officer, University of Nigeria; and President and Chief Executive Officer, University of Nigeria Research and

Economic Development (UNRED) Foundation. He was a Presidential Candidate for one of the political parties in Nigeria during the 2011 elections that saw Goodluck Jonathan elected as President.

Also in the United States, a female Nigerian, Deputy Inspector Ms Olufunmilo Obe is the Commander of the 28th Precinct in the New York Police Department. She is the first black from sub-Saharan Africa to have occupied such a position in the history of New York Police Department. Given what we know about the State of New York, to have a Nigerian occupy such an office presents Nigeria with an incredible opportunity to have her input in helping to revamp the Police sector in Nigeria.

In the UK, many Nigerians are exerting a lot of influence and helping to shape policy in the country. A glaring example is Chuka Ummuna, an active member of the Labour Party, who joined the UK parliament in 2010. He was the Shadow Business Secretary from 2011 to 2015, but resigned after the Labour Party lost the election in 2015 and Jeremy Corbyn took over from Ed Miliband as Labour Leader. Chuka is a qualified and experienced solicitor, with a keen interest in economic policy and reform. He was a member of the Treasury Select Committee, and has been known to challenge companies and institutions with dodgy accounting and tax avoidance policies. He also features regularly in the local newspapers. He had put himself forward as the Labour Leader after the resignation of Ed Miliband, although he withdrew his candidature three days later. Nevertheless, he has the potential to become the first black Prime Minister in the UK.

In addition to Chuka, there are others such as Chi Onwurah, also a Nigerian member of the UK parliament. She is the first black MP in Newcastle, and was elected into the UK parliament in 2010. Chi Onwurah is a qualified Electrical Engineer, with experience in telecommunications sector, prior to joining the UK parliament. She also occupied Shadow Cabinet positions, including as junior shadow minister for Business, Innovation and skills. Similarly, the Mayor of Brent in 2012-2013 was Mr Michael Adeyeye, a

Nigerian. Also in the UK, the author of this chapter, Professor Elewechi Okike established Book Aid for Africa (BAFA), as a UK registered Charity (Non-profit organisation) about ten years ago, to promote excellence in education in Africa. The Charity has shipped over 200,000 books to all levels of educational institutions across Africa. Nigerian institutions have been the greatest beneficiaries of the Charity's donations. One can go on and on identifying the impact that Nigerians in diaspora are making all over the world.

In the USA, Nigerians are the most educated ethnic group, at 60 percent, beating the national average of most Americans, which is 30 percent. In most of the Ivy League schools in the US, Nigerians are leading the rest in educational attainments. In the UK, the Imafidon family has been named the smartest in the whole country[15]. At 9 years old, the Imafidon twins, Peter and Paula Imafidon made history as the youngest children in British history to attend high school. They were the youngest to ever pass the University of Cambridge's advanced mathematics examination after they took part in the Excellence in Education program. The eldest child of the Imafidons graduated from high school at age 10. And at 11 years old, Christina Imafidon was the youngest student in history to attend a British University. These children are much older now and are actively involved in mentoring and coaching other children. Anne-Marie, the oldest child is involved in S.T.E.M. (Science, Technology, Engineering and Mathematics) program to help fulfill the need for science female leaders. She is currently occupying a top position at an international Investment Bank in the UK[16].

Nigerians in Diaspora and Nation-Building

Whilst not every Nigerian in diaspora can return home, the

[15] http://africanspotlight.com/2013/03/13/meet-the-nigerian-family-reported-as-the-smartest-in-britain/

[16] http://www.konnectafrica.net/paula-and-peter-imafidon/

onus lies with the Nigerian government to find the best possible way to tap into the resourcefulness of these Nigerians so that they can make meaningful contributions to the development of the nation. There are currently a number of strategy toolkits that set out practical advice for governments, foundations, corporations and individuals who wish to engage and harness the power of their diaspora[17]. The Nigerian government can take advantage of these toolkits to identify how best to engage meaningfully with NIDs and harness their wealth of experience and expertise.

NIDs have a lot to contribute to nation building and would love to return to their homeland to help lift the country out of the conundrum in which it has found itself over the years. As a matter of fact, Okoli (2015)[18] notes that time is of the essence in getting Nigerian professionals in diaspora back to aid the country's development because, according to him 'Nigerian professionals in Diaspora who would play an active role in the rebuilding process only have a few years of usefulness left in them'. He urges the Nigerian government 'to fish out those Nigerian professionals who are not chronically corrupt and engage them to be the outside change that would not look at faces when implementing viable reforms' (p.140). Okoli reiterates that 'if the Nigerian government cannot find ways to harness the potentials of Nigerians At Large and Nigerian professionals in Diaspora, then the country will not benefit from ... people born between 1946 to 1964, who were instrumental in building the global village'.

Adelaja (2015)[19] also lends his support to the need for the newly elected government in Nigeria to accelerate the process of creating a conducive environment that would encourage NIDs to return to contribute to the development of the nation. He warns that 'if African governments don't move fast to begin to encourage our Diaspora to return, it

---

[17] http://diasporamatters.com/publications-resources-2/
[18] Okoli, Christopher (2015) *Nigerian Promising Era*.
[19] Adelaja, Sunday (2015) 'How to take Nigeria from the third world to the first world through Diaspora'
https://www.facebook.com/pastor.sunday.adelaja/posts/10152911999473845

could be too late to gain their expertise'. He provides evidence of prominent Nigerians who died in diaspora and never had the opportunity to bless the country with their wealth of experience. One of them was a renowned neurosurgeon in the US, who had the intention of returning to the country, at age 50, but never made it.

Many NIDs are forced to remain outside of the country although they would gladly have returned home, and have produced second and third generations of children, some of whom have never visited the country because of the fear of the many aforementioned evils bedevilling the country. According to Adelaja (2015), these 'second, third and fourth generation immigrants get quickly absorbed in their new environment and culture. They tend to lose touch with their countries of origin'. Hence he suggests that 'our best bet is to entice the first generation immigrants, who still have cultural and emotional attachments with their homeland, to return and participate in the political, economic and social processes going on at home'.

How do we entice these people to return to their homeland? Tettey (2003) suggests providing incentives 'which go beyond verbal appeals to patriotism, and encompass recruitment drives as well as concrete measures to provide attractive conditions for those who return'. But he warns that such incentives might be counter-productive and lead to further 'brain drain' because it could undermine those who remain in the country. 'They may feel that their loyalty goes unrewarded while returnees are offered incentive packages'.

It is currently estimated[20] that there are about 5 million to 15 million Nigerians in diaspora. Adelaja (2015) puts the estimate at 15 to 17 million. The largest populations of Nigerians can be found in the UK, USA and South Africa. This emigration from Nigeria has been at a cost to Nigeria of

---

[20] http://www.nigeriandiaspora.com/index.php. This website notes that because of limited research, there is a lack of proper understanding of the size, location, demographics, etc. of Nigerians in Diaspora.

the best, brightest and most able[21]. Yet the effect of brain drain in Nigeria on the country's socio-economic development will be impossible to quantify.

However, the return of civil rule and the introduction of some semblance of democracy after the first democratic elections in 1999 gave hope to many NIDs.

Following the socio-economic reforms of the Obasanjo government (the first civilian government after many years of military dictatorships) between 1999 and 2003 and the renewed calls for NIDs to return home and contribute to nation building, some returned to Nigeria. Besides, the economic downturn in many countries provided the opportunity for some NIDs to return to Nigeria to explore opportunities to join the various efforts of the government in revamping the nation's economy.

It is heart-warming to know that the present administration (led by President Muhammadu Buhari) is keen to bring about positive change in the Nigerian economy that will require the contributions of NIDs. The new President met with Nigerians in diaspora when he visited the USA and said he wanted NIDs to work with the Nigerian government and help rebuild the country. The 7th National Assembly passed the Diaspora Commission Bill into law. It is now evident that NIDs that most governments previously ignored (and in some cases denigrated) are increasingly seen as agents of national development. They possess immense human, material, intellectual and professional resources. Many of them are extremely skilled and have added immeasurable value to their countries of residence. Also, they have attained the highest level of professionalism in developed nations, which should help facilitate economic and social development in Nigeria. Their role in the economic and social development of Nigeria cannot be undermined, nor can it be over-emphasized. The onus rests with the government to put structures in place that would facilitate a closer relationship between NIDs and the country.

---

[21] http://www.nigeriandiaspora.com/index.php.

The Economist [22] reports that India is a trailblazer in tapping into the wealth of its citizens in diaspora. It has an entire ministry for its emigrants. This ministry is responsible for the success of India's IT industry built by Indians 'lured home from Silicon Valley and Europe'.

What kind of environment would entice Nigerians in diaspora to return home?

It would be impossible to identify every possible action that needs to be taken to entice NIDs to want to return to Nigeria. Nevertheless some key issues are identified here:

Security: the Nigerian government must understand the importance of making the country safe and secure. There have been too many incidents of kidnapping (and even murder) of highly resourceful persons in Nigeria, including expatriates, in exchange for huge sums of money.

Integrity in Leadership: The government must be seen to promote integrity across board and must lead by example. How can anyone work with people that cannot be trusted? Most NIDs reside and work in countries where there is a strong element of trust in everyday interactions. Unfortunately, this is an area where NIDs can face one of their greatest challenges if not addressed.

Good Governance: poor accountability and governance have been major issues affecting the country. NIDs are based in countries where leaders are held accountable and can be removed from office by the electorate if found wanting. The government must be ready to enforce good governance and hold public officers accountable for their actions.

---

[22] http://www.economist.com/news/britain/21611102-some-5m-britons-live-abroad-country-could-do-far-more-exploit-its-high-flying-expats-and

Openness and Transparency: Nigerian public officers are generally not known to be open and transparent. It will be difficult for NIDs to return to Nigeria to work in an environment that lacks openness and transparency.

Reliable Judicial System: NIDs have been exposed to democratic and functional systems of government all over the world, where no one is above the law. This is fundamental if NIDs are to return to support development initiatives in Nigeria. There should be the opportunity for recourse to the law, when necessary. But where the judicial system is not reliable, it gives room for injustice to thrive, and most NIDs would not want to work in such an environment.

Law, Order and Discipline: Most Nigerians are generally known to lack order and discipline. They flamboyantly break the law and damn the consequences because they know they can bribe their way out. People drive recklessly even on the wrong side of the road, without fear of any reprisals. Under the military rule of the current President (Muhammadu Buhari) and his deputy, Late General Idiagbon in the early 1980s, they identified indiscipline as the greatest problem facing Nigerians, hence they launched a War Against Indiscipline (WAI) campaign, which saw the type of law enforcement, order and discipline that has never been replicated in Nigeria ever since. Many Nigerians recall that era as one of the most orderly they have ever experienced. Most NIDs are used to working in environments where there is law and order and people are disciplined, cultured and respectful. Returning to a country that lack order and discipline is not a likely prospect for most NIDs.

Adequate Enforcement Mechanisms: Nigeria is not lacking in laws. In fact there are many of them. It is whether or not they are enforced that matters. In a country where corruption is rife, and officials can be bribed, law enforcement is slack. Working in an environment where the

244

law enforcement mechanism is weak, can lead to frustration and NIDs would not succumb to such an environment.

Educational Infrastructure: If NIDs are to make meaningful contributions to the country, there is the need for adequate infrastructures to be in place especially in the education sectors. Many have decried the poor state of the education sector in the country. Many institutions lack basic infrastructure like decent classrooms and equipment, including learning resources. More needs to be done to ensure that institutions of learning are adequately resourced to enable NIDs wanting to join the sector on their return to do so and make meaningful contributions.

Business Infrastructure: small and medium-sized enterprises (SMEs) are the backbone of any economy. Therefore, adequate support mechanisms must be in place as well as opportunities for growth and development. Do SMEs in Nigeria have access to the most up to date technology to enable them compete effectively in today's global business community? NIDs have the potential to contribute effectively to this sector. What opportunities and incentives are available for any of them desiring to establish a business in Nigeria, and entering into local partnerships with established local businesses? Such collaborations have the potential to create job opportunities and contribute to the development of the economy.

Physical Infrastructure: The issue of inadequate infrastructure such as buildings, power supply, good roads and water, amongst others is one that has plagued Nigeria over the years. Many buildings are dilapidated; power supply is very erratic and sometimes may not be available for days; the roads are so poor that they are death traps. Many Nigerians have lost their lives as a result of the poor state of some Nigerian roads. Inadequate supply poses a health risk at the public hospitals that are poorly resourced. NIDs would be more productive and motivated to work in an environment where there is adequate infrastructure in place.

Research and Development Opportunities: Most NIDs reside in countries where enormous value is placed on research, hence research opportunities are available to continuously bring about improvements in the system, and people work with the latest and most up to date technologies. The Nigerian government must be seen to be committed to providing research and development opportunities, as no Nigerian in diaspora would like to return to the country and get 'stuck in the rot', and not able to keep abreast of developments in his/her field.

When these fundamental issues are addressed in Nigeria, one can look forward to a 'new Nigeria' that has the potential to attract majority of Nigerians back to their homeland. As mentioned earlier, there can never be a better substitute for one's home – 'there's no place like home'. It will be difficult and perhaps impossible to quantify the benefits that will accrue to Nigeria if most NIDs returned to the country.

Nigerians in diaspora can contribute in many areas to the country's development, including, but not limited to:

- Agriculture
- Construction
- Creative Industries
- Education and Training
- Health
- Information Communication Technology (ICT)
- Manufacturing
- Professional Services
- Security

They would gladly contribute meaningfully in any of these areas, including those not listed, where they perceive they can add value, and bring their skills to bear, to support initiatives of the government in any of these areas.

Nigerians in diaspora 'constitute a huge source of

knowledge, skills and experience which can be tapped into' (Abraham, 2015)[23]. These are experienced and well-educated men and women scattered across the globe that have distinguished themselves in their subject disciplines, and worked at top organisations and institutions across the world. Many of them are the 'crème de la crème' in their professions and fields of endeavour. Returning to Nigeria with their wealth of experience and expertise has the potential to transform Nigeria from a third world country to a first world country (Adelaja, 2015).

We are potentially looking at the situation where Nigeria will experience exponential growth in each of these sectors, and create job opportunities for many Nigerians, as these NIDs bring in their wealth of experience and their expertise into each of these sectors. The agricultural sector would once again be a major player amongst Nigeria's exports and contribute to the local economy, more than it did before the discovery of oil. The construction industry that is currently booming will do even much better. The creative industries will take on more sophistication and expand further across the globe. As for the education sector, Nigeria's institutions of learning would once again be well-resourced citadels of learning, with inputs from many distinguished academics in diaspora, and produce world-class scholars, as it always did in the past. With the support and contribution of NIDs, the ailing health sector in Nigeria will be revamped and better resourced. The situation where Nigerians travel to places like India and South Africa for medical treatment will cease to exist because Nigeria's top class medical experts in diaspora are back home. Similarly, the ICT, manufacturing, professional services and the security sectors in the country will thrive as NIDs contribute their skills and expertise to these sectors.

It has therefore been suggested (Abraham, 2015) that a 'Diaspora engagement strategy' be developed, as a platform for systematically engaging NIDs to ensure their maximum

---

and effective contribution to the Nigerian economy. It appears that their enormous human and financial resources potentials are yet under-utilised.

Besides human resources, the country is Africa's largest producer of oil, and is endowed with mineral resources of all sorts. When both the human and natural resources are properly managed, Nigeria will be a formidable force to be reckoned with.

Whilst in an ideal world, it would be beneficial for all NIDs with the wealth of experience and expertise required to aid the development of the nation to return to Nigeria to support the country's developmental programmes, it is not likely that every Nigerian in diaspora would like to return home. Nevertheless, there is the potential opportunity for them to contribute to policies and be involved in supporting development initiatives in other ways. For example, many NIDs eager to contribute to nation building have formed organisations in the countries in which they reside, including organisations such as Nigerians in Diaspora Organisation Americas (NIDOA). Some of these organisations are fully engaged in providing solutions that will assist Nigeria in many ways.

Adelaja (2015) suggests that the government should set up 'a Ministry of Diaspora and Integration', which would help build a bridge between Nigerians at home and NIDs. Such an initiative will help to stimulate investments into Nigeria. He states that countries like India, the Philippines and Mexico have such a policy in relation to their diaspora.

The reality is that Nigerians in diaspora are keen to support the government's efforts to develop the country. However, the environment has to be conducive and enabling for them to be able to do so. For example, simply trying to open a local deposit account can be quite challenging. Hopefully, with digitization within the banking sector, this should ease the bottleneck experienced in trying to open such accounts in Nigeria. This notwithstanding, it is reported (Adelaja, 2015) that NIDs around the world remitted $21 billion into the country's economy in 2013. Yet he opines that 'as big as $21 billion sounds, there is no doubt that these

Nigerians in diaspora are capable of producing greater wealth if they bring back their expertise and skills to Nigeria'.

Nigerians in diaspora would like to know that the government is committed to creating a corrupt-free environment, where everyone can be held accountable and no one is seen to be above the law; a Nigeria where leaders govern with integrity, openness and transparency; a Nigeria where there is order and discipline and the rule of law is maintained; a Nigeria in which the country's resources are used to benefit everyone and not just a few. In other words, a 'new Nigeria' that they can proudly return to. When this happens, we shall find that NIDs will start emigrating back to their country and we can all begin to look forward to contributing our quota in making Nigeria the 'Giant of Africa', not just based on the size of its population, but a true giant that will be a major player in the global economic and political scene.

WE THE PEOPLE is nationwide movement of concerned Nigerians, engineered by Nigerian intellectuals and professionals, to create a new responsible Nigeria by growing a new breed of honest and corrupt-free Nigerian grassroots, one person at a time. The movement believes that the most effective way to clean up Nigeria is a bottom-to-top approach, because only a clean bottom can clean the top. Through this movement, we will mobilize the critical mass of a new breed of WE THE PEOPLE of all tribes and religions who will use their enormous voting power to remove all corrupt leaders and legislatures from office, and replace them with honest men and women of integrity. This movement offers incredible opportunities to Nigerians in Diaspora to join hands and save their homeland, Nigeria, through the WE THE PEOPLE movement. Power belongs to the people. Since Nigeria has suffered direly in the hands of bad leaders and politicians, thereby forcing many decent Nigerians out of their own country into the Diaspora against their will, it is time for WE THE PEOPLE to take back their land by voting out in mass all the old and corrupt politicians and leaders who have held Nigeria hostage.

For additional information on how to join the WE THE

PEOPLE movement and participate in building a New Nigeria, a Nigeria that is corrupt-free, law-abiding with level-playing field for all; a Nigeria led by clean cerebral intellectuals, with dynamic economy, great security, functional and adequate infrastructure; a Nigeria that will become the pride of black men and women worldwide, read the Postface at the end of the last chapter in this book. But please don't jump to read the Postface, keep reading every chapter in this book until you get to the Postface. Nigerians in Diaspora cannot miss this divine opportunity to join WE THE PEOPLE to clean up Nigeria for their benefit, the benefit of their children and grand-children, and the emancipation of Nigeria and Nigerians everywhere.

CHAPTER 10

Towards a Holistic Development Trajectory for Nigeria

Prof. Damian U. Opata, MA(English) MA(Philosophy)

Introduction.

I thank Professor Peter Nwangwu for inviting me to contribute to this very ambitious book project. He asked that I write on: "How Enduring Change was Achieved in Other Countries Such as Singapore, Malaysia, Dubai, China, etc." What I understand my task to be is that I should discuss ways in which Nigeria could learn from the Asian model(s) of development. But I believe that what is critical is how Nigeria can propel forward to greatness, and that there are several ways through which this can be achieved. I also think that the way to this greatness is beyond the Asian models.

Speaking on the Asian model, let me say that I have certain reservations about it. This is particularly so because the Asian model has been famously called a miracle, implying that its development success was unexpected, that the route to it may have violated all tested development models, and indeed, that it is as a result of God's intervention. Timothy Taylor is one of several scholars who have raised questions about possible lessons other nations could learn from the Asian example. In a lecture titled "Lessons from the East Asian (Rumpled) Tigers, he says:

> "The focus of this lecture is on East Asia's (tiger) economies: Hong Kong, the Republic of Korea, Singapore, Taiwan, Indonesia, Malaysia and Thailand. These jurisdictions differ in many ways, but what they have in common is that as a group, they have experienced the most rapid sustained growth of any economies at any given time. Thus,

> they have become the focus of intense study, looking for lessons that might be applied elsewhere".

The argument over the policy lessons to be derived from the tigers typically divide up between those who believe that the main cause is fundamental factors like savings and investment, human, capital, technology transfer, and relatively free markets, and those who believe that it has more to do with government industrial policy. A prestigious study from the World Bank found that while the fundamental economic factors are of primary importance, there were serious situations in which government intervention makes a difference.

The East Asian economies suffered a financial and economic meltdown in 1997, complete with plunging stockmarkets and economies in recession. This downturn has raised a number of questions about the East Asian model of economic development; apparently, it is not quite as robust as many economists would have believed in the early 1990s. But there is some reason to believe that if these economists seize upon this downturn as a political justification for making some long-needed reforms, they will be able to return to "tiger" status within a few years (1).

On a final introductory note, Wonik Kim has effectively argued that, "The predominant explanation [for the success of the Asian model] has been provided by the developmental state theory" (2). If this is so, it then cannot be that this model is at the same time describable as a miracle, except of course the miracle inheres from the way it was applied to the concerned Asian countries. Whatever be the case, it cannot be described as a miracle in the sense of violating all theories of development. Incidentally, Kim goes on to state that

> "Although the previous studies in this research paradigm are successful in identifying the positive features of the East Asian state apparatus that contributed to phenomenal economic growth, they have neglected the question of the origins of the developmental state. Taking this issue

252

seriously, I have conducted a macro-historical comparison between Northeast Asia and Southeast Asia. Based on the theoretical framework of comparative colonialism recently developed in the field of political economy, I argue that the developmental state fundamentally requires relative income equality as the initial socio-economic condition ... While most Southeast Asian countries inherited 'extractive colonial institutions' [like Nigeria] that perpetuated income inequality, Korea and Taiwan were able to break away from the colonial legacy, which allowed the emergence of the developmental state" (2).

Moreover, as has been noted by Taylor in the excerpt cited above, the economies of these 'tigers' crashed and plunged their states into a recession. He is optimistic that the downturn in those economies could be used as a 'political justification for making long-needed reforms", but then, he does not recommend it as a model for other countries or nations in search of models for development.

Based on these considerations, I have convinced myself that I have to go beyond the developmental state theory of East Asia model to explore ways through which Nigeria can grow in the right direction. Of course, my added reason is that I am not a fan of most development models being forced upon or suggested for adoption by Africa in general and Nigeria in particular. This is why I have decided to modify the topic to read: "Towards a Holistic Development Trajectory for Nigeria". This would enable me to make suggestions that I consider useful for achieving growth, wellbeing, security, and unity in Nigeria.

Diagnosis of the Nigeria situation

In a paper titled, "A Plan for 'Re-Organization' of Nigeria", Ayodeji Olukoju presents the best and most comprehensive summary of the diagnosis of the crisis bedevilling Nigeria's development efforts. According to him, and I quote him extensively:

"The palpable political, social and economic crises manifest themselves in various forms: the collapse of physical and social infrastructure, the high incidence of vandalization of public property, the sporadic bouts of ethno-religious blood-letting, the increasingly fatal and menacing combat over resource control, the suffocating reality of corruption in public life, social insecurity expressed in the high incidence of armed robbery, assassination, ritual murder, kidnapping and even the abduction of the incumbent governor of a state, gross indiscipline that pervades national life, including an extreme form of youth restiveness, the collapse of formal and informal education at all levels, high rate of unemployment, the brutality and corruption of security personnel, a desecration of values, especially those long cherished, the brazen worship of Mammon, intensified religiosity without a marked improvement in the spiritual and social quality of the individual and the society, the steady disintegration of the family, an insatiable thirst for foreign commodities and cultures, including the current vogue of female (semi)nudity and single parenthood, the glorification of fraud – rigged elections, manipulated electoral process, the uncontrolled spate of examination malpractices, distress in the banking / finance sector occasioned by the looting of the till, advance fee fraud, counterfeiting of drugs and currency, arson as a way of covering up fraud and criminal activity or of settling political scores, the debasement of the judicial process, cronyism and primitive accumulation. Double standards, wrong-headed policies, the

254

privatisation of the state and its apparatus have been elevated to an art and canonized" (4).

This piece, written in 2003, that is thirteen years ago, still largely describes the Nigerian condition. Undoubtedly, different intervening governments have addressed these issues in one form or the other, but they keep persisting unsolved. The incidence of fake drugs has been reduced, but not eliminated; a lot has gone into refurbishing the education sector, but it appears the goal is far from being reached; the electoral process has been addressed, and in spite of electronic card readers, the problems linger, at least with an increasing incidence of inconclusive elections; the introduction of computer based testing system appears to be reducing the incidence of examination malpractice, but Nigeria is not yet out of it; the current administration of President Mohammed Buhari is frontally fighting corruption, but it is largely greeted with cynicism in terms of perceived lop-sidedness of the approach and uncertainty about whether recovered loot would be judiciously used; a lot of reform has taken place in the banking sector in spite of the current woeful state of the naira, and an assaulted stock market, and indeed, various aspects of the physical and social infrastructure have been steadily addressed, but a lot more still needs to be done.

There is hardly any doubt that the problems identified by Olukoju are critical to development efforts of any nation, but his paper does not address the genesis of the problems he has so succinctly enunciated. I will address two of the critical origins of Nigeria's development problem in this chapter. The first has to do with Nigeria's insertion into western modernity through colonialism, that is to say, its coloniality of being. The second which largely derives from the first has to do with the development paradigm Nigeria has adopted as well its links with globalisation. I will now develop these points.

On the Development Discourse

Jan Nederveen Pieterse, drawing largely from W. Sachs'

writings, states:

> "The idea of development stands like a ruin in
> the intellectual landscape. Delusion and
> disappointment, failures and crime have been the
> steady companion of development and they tell a
> common story: it did not work. Moreover, the
> historical conditions which catapulted the idea
> into prominence have vanished: development has
> become outdated" (Sachs, 1992:1) (360).

On their own, Andrea Cornwall and Debora Eade, in a preface to their edited book, *Deconstructing Development Discourse: Buzzwords and Fuzzwords*, state as follows:

> "The extraordinary thing about Development is
> that it is simultaneously descriptive and
> normative, concrete and yet aspirational, intuitive
> and clunkily pedestrian, capable of expressing the
> most deeply held convictions or of being simply
> 'full of sound and fury, signifying nothing'. This
> very elasticity makes it almost the ideal post-
> modern medium, even as it embodies a
> modernising agenda " (ix).

All this makes the term 'development' very suspect and at the same time very attractive, even seductive. Hence, it will be extremely difficult to do away with it as the discursive regime with which nations will engage and track their progress. The term has become a privileged campaign instrument used by government to woo the people and by the private sector and NGOs to secure funding. The greatest problem attendant on discourses on development is that the term is of colonial origin, and scholars have not done enough to domesticate it. The search for appropriate models to deliver it has been characterised by a dependency syndrome, and on a tacit acceptance of the divide between the developed and the developing based on criteria enunciated by the developed. It is either that there is a call for the adoption of a dominant development model, or there is a call for adopting / adapting a mix of development models from the so-called developed countries. The development discursive regime has therefore succeeded in enthroning such notions as 'underdeveloped', 'developing', and 'developed', all of which have been used to describe different countries, nations, and regions in the world. Unfortunately, these other terms have received universal approval. I do not subscribe to that universal classification of some nations as 'developed', 'under-developed' or 'developing', mainly because no nation ceases to develop. And if this is true, it means that discourse on development is a comparative thing invented by the powerful to tag the weak. Development discourse the way it is currently framed is a discourse driven by power and the powerful.

The development discourse I want to adopt here is the one that inheres from an Igbo worldview about human positioning and human wellbeing in the world. While doing this, I realise that the Igbo is situate in a globalising world, an inter-connected world. There are five key terms that I want to appropriate from Igbo worldview. These are: *udo* (peace), *ifunanya* (love), *oganiru* (progress / matching with the future), *I di n'otu* (being united), and *eme onye ka emere ibe ya* (treating a person as his or her kind has been treated). For me, these are values and principles needed in Nigeria. These are the beliefs and truths individuals and groups wish to see in their lives. These are not restricted to economics or politics; they are all-embracing. They give lie to the fact that all a person wants is economic development or democracy as a form of political development. They also affirm the partiality of all development models and that human life and welfare are best seen in relational terms.

The most embracing of all the terms listed above is *oganiru* (progress / matching with the future). It is a difficult term to translate adequately to English. *Oganiru* among the Igbo is largely measured by (1) increase in the number of people in a family / village/ town / or community, (2) long life, (3) and things or the wherewithal with which to sustain life. It is important to note that these three things are a constant in the traditional morning prayers and kola invocation of most Igbo people. The things with which to sustain life are usually captured as *aku na – uba* (wealth and prosperity). However, health and physical fitness are prayed for to enable an individual to actualise them. In the same vein, *ako na – uche, umeala, ak'* (reason and thought, humility, and strong will) are also asked for to enable an individual to become rich and prosperous. The desire is accompanied by the means of achieving it.

Increase in the population of a family is an essential ingredient of *oganiru*. This is why the Igbo have a saying: *onye nani anaghi egbuyi egbuyi*; an individual does not form a long cue / line. That is also why they say: *igwe bu ike*, plurality is strength, or a big population constitutes strength. In contemporary western development discourse, the having of many children is frowned upon despite the fact that three of the greatest world economies in the world, America, China and India have a share of the world's largest population. What is needed is the expansion and technological improvement of the productive base, not birth control in the manner of prescribing not more than four children per mother. This could be achieved if the will is there. An Igbo folk tale already ridiculed the idea of population control. This is captured in the story in which there was famine in the land of animals. In order to have enough food, the animals decided that every one of them should kill its mother so that they would have enough to feed on. Only the wise dog decided not to obey this directive, and only the dog fared well during the period of the famine, until the Tortoise discovered its secret. The lesson is that instead of the animals finding a way to increase food supply to feed their teeming population, they decided on birth control, one of the ways recommended to alleviate poverty in contemporary development discourse, as if the traditional Igbo did not practice its own system of birth control. Come to think of it: doing away with the mothers is the surest way to effective population control; not asking a mother, a woman, or a family not to have more than four children even when the capacity to feed even double that number is available.

Indeed, it is the case that a big population is better placed to provide the wherewithal for the preservation and sustenance of life. A big population easily presents a diverse plurality of ways of thinking and doing things, ways of competitive gaming, and ways of defending itself. Economic booms take place in large population centres, and even when there is environmental pollution or degradation, they receive greater attention by governments. If it comes to pooling resources together, their collective strength is enormous. In international relations, big populations are respected and feared, even among themselves. They make mince of small populations. There is strength in being big. Ask China; Ask America; Ask India. And let America or Great Britain leave Israel alone, and see what their Arab nations will do with her. Then look at the elevated position of the three dominant ethnic groups in Nigeria. The Igbo knew when they framed the statement: *Igwe bu ike*; strength lies in the many. So, what is needed is the strategy and technique of improving the productive base of the economy.

It is important to dwell briefly on the statement, *eme onye ka emere ibe ya*; that is, treating a person as his or her kind is treated. This is a very important framing of the notion of equality. It recognises that people may be born equal, but that they belong to different classes and occupations, and therefore deserve appropriate treatment according to who they are and what they do. For instance, a titled man should be accorded the respect accorded to titled men; a baby must be accorded the respect he or she deserves. This is the idea that frames the Igbo proverb; *nwata kwo aka, o soro eze rie*; when a child washes his hands, he dines with kings. This of course arises from the notion that all human beings are born equal, but some achieve fame more than others. In dealing with such people, recognition must be given to what they have achieved.

The idea of *I di n'otu*, unity, was easily achievable in traditional closed societies. The populations were largely homogenous, and citizens had intimate knowledge of one another, or at least of the segments that made up a community. The communal ethic was strong, and people were bonded through social solidarity networks. This naturally lessened the incidence of criminality. The strife and conflicts that obtained were not enough to call for separate and independent communities. Among the Igbo, such calls now emanate from the government – driven creation of chiefdoms that are called autonomous communities, as if the community from which they are being carved were not autonomous. Many communities have embraced this because they do not want to be left behind, especially as chiefs are paid stipends by governments.

All the issues so far could and did operate well in traditional closed societies where individuals had access to land, water bodies, and other natural resources upon which they drew from for their survival. In such societies, there was no role for the state, because there were no states. Individual struggle for self and family was the norm. *Oganiru* for a community was not measured in abstract terms, but on the progress made by individuals, which could be extrapolated to apply to the community. In other words, that a society was moving forward was determined on the number of individuals in that society who were making visible progress. A society making progress would be characterised as one that had more births than deaths and more material things that could sustain life. Indeed, a society that looked back on its past and compared it with the present and convinced itself that the present was better than the past in virtually all its ramifications would consider itself as making good progress.

All that changed with colonisation, the harbinger of modernization in Nigeria, and the originator of state and state-propelled development. The creation of administrative headquarters, the development of cities and urban areas, and the concentration of social amenities in such centres led to massive migration to them. The trend has continued to grow, and globalisation and regional interconnectedness are more and more increasing such 'massification' in these centres. Nigeria is heavily entangled in the modernization net. This is why it cannot easily escape from development models which have led to the development of areas she wants to borrow from. All the models could roughly fall into two broad categories: state-driven development and non-state-driven development. It is within this line of thinking that I intend to proffer my modest suggestions through which Nigeria's development ambition could be substantially met.

Some Possible Approaches to a Solution

Science is an essentially anarchistic enterprise: theoretical anarchism is more humanitarian and more likely to encourage progress than its law-and –order alternatives (Paul Feyerabend 17).

Where once a few strong columns could hold up the weight of the world, now a dynamic mix of materials, shapes, and structures are needed ... For me, smart power meant choosing the right combination of tools – diplomatic, economic, military, political, legal, and cultural – for each situation (Hillary Rodham Clinton 33).

Anaro ofu ebe ekiri mmuo (One does not stand in one place to watch a masquerade / an embodied being) - An Igbo Proverb.

These quotations speak to ways of achieving peace, love, unity, and progressively embracing the future. Nigeria is a multi-ethnic, multi-religious country. Its colonial and amalgamated nature makes it a complex case in terms of appropriate development models that could take it out of the woods. An eclectic use of the 'smart power' model as advocated by Hillary Rodham Clinton would seem to me to be the key to success in Nigeria. Different approaches should be applied to different sectors of the economy.

To start with, Nigeria should develop both state and private development think tanks whose major function would be to study the best functioning sectors in different countries and nations with a view to adapting them to different sectors of the Nigerian situation. Such think tanks should be looking at societies with best human longevity, societies that have most peace, societies that have the best operating health systems for the citizens, societies that have best employment records, and indeed, societies with identified advantages in different sectors of development. This is so because no known nation or country will have the best operating systems in all sectors of the society. This would translate to the Igbo adage that no person can be both taller and shorter than another person at the same time. The policy of seeking the best systems wherever they are found also suggests that no one model of development is perfect, and that no one development model can do the magic or miracle of development.

Let us take, for example, one of the most important aspects of development, peace. Without enduring peace, no country can really claim to have developed. The Global peace Index, 2016, ranked Nigeria as the fourth country in the world with the highest number of "internal conflict deaths". In Africa, Botswana and Mauritius are rated as highly peaceful countries. In the world, Iceland, Denmark, and Austria are rated as the three most peaceful countries in the world. What Nigeria needs to do is to study these countries, many of them multi-ethnic and multi-religious, and find out what factors have contributed to the achievement of peace. Thereafter, Nigeria should find ways of adjusting these findings in terms of the ways they are implemented in these countries, and explore ways of adapting them to the Nigeria situation. In doing that, it will not be sufficient, for instance, to say that the features that make for peace in countries are those listed in Global Peace Index, 2016. These include: well-functioning government, sound business environment, low levels of corruption, acceptance of the rights of others, high levels of human capital, good relations with neighbours, free flow of information, and equitable distribution of resources. What is more critical is to find out what specific constituents of these features are, and how each of them is implemented to achieve peace in the countries where they are found. Thereafter, Nigeria should study ways of successfully adapting them to fit the Nigeria context. This approach to peace building should complement Nigeria's studied position on the needed internal conditions for peace building.

Agriculture is one of the areas recommended for adoption by

developing countries. In a paper titled, "Strategies for Agricultural Development", Vernon W. Ruttan and Yujiro Hayami identified four general models of agricultural development: the conservation model, the urban industrial impact model, the diffusion model, and the high-payoff input model. There may be some others. Now in the same paper, they argue that:

> "There is clear evidence that technology can be developed to facilitate the substitution of relatively abundant (hence cheap) factors for relatively scarce (hence expensive) factors in the economy. The constraints imposed on agricultural development by an inelastic supply of land have, in economies such as Japan and Taiwan, been offset by the development of high-yielding crop varieties designed for substitution of fertilizer for land. The constraints imposed by an inelastic supply of labor, in countries such as the United States, Canada, and Australia, have been offset by advances leading to the substitution of animal and mechanical power for labor. ... It seems reasonable, following Hick, to call techniques designed to facilitate the substitution of other inputs for labor, "labor-saving," and those designed to facilitate the substitution of other inputs for land, "land-saving." (132 – 133).

Definitely, these models have their advantages and disadvantages, and I am not here concerned with whether there are newer models or not, but with the fact if the two models are not combinable in one place, then the one that best fits a people and their context should be adopted. The same goes for the four models identified by Ruttan and Hayami. This is consistent with the approach I am recommending in this paper: that any model, no matter where found, that fits any sector of the economy should be adapted to the Nigerian situation. Indeed, in some sectors like Agriculture where the soil and weather conditions are widely different like in Nigeria, a multiplicity of models that fit particular regions or local government areas should be adapted.

Ifunanya is mentioned as the next thing the Igbo pray and wish for in their families and communities. It is usually translated as 'Love", but I doubt whether the full meaning is captured therein. It suggests a lot of things: mutual respect, willingness to help the other, the unconditional acceptance of the existence of the other as he or she is, the ability and disposition to feel at ease in the presence of another, tolerance, love of one another, etc. These features are also desirable ones in the Nigerian Federation. I believe very strongly that what a people want in their prayers is very important for them, and that whatever this thing is should be incorporated as a feature of measuring their development success. It is needful to engage linguistic anthropologists to see what different ethnic groups in Nigeria pray for in their family and communal prayers, articulate them, and find ways of ensuring that these things are realised at family and communal levels. I have searched to see whether there are such equivalents in development discourse, and the nearest I see are 'friendly' and 'tolerance; sometimes, 'happiness index' is mentioned, but none of these captures the Igbo notion of *ifunanya*.

The lesson one could learn from this is that development is many a time determined by the world view of a people, and that it is therefore, very highly culture-dependent, at least when not seen in global terms. This is one further reason that makes dependence on a one-to one adoption of foreign models of development a dicey thing. Each country must have its character, and that in a positive way for each to be happy in its own dispensation. But it is well known that colonisation and modernization as well as global imperialism will continue to affect and impact on the character of a people. What is worrisome is when under pressure from these forces, people change what is indexically positive about themselves. When such happens, the people affirm their under-development themselves. The lessons embodied in the Igbo notion of *ifunanya* are not yet signalled as one of the

264

indices of measuring development in the development discourse; yet it is a privileged desideratum among the Igbo, and indeed, very needful in a multi-ethnic and multi-religious Nigeria.

Ka eme onye ka emere ibe ya, treating each person according to character, gender, and rank is one which goes beyond legality and legal provisions for individual rights. It also goes beyond the notion of equality of persons. This goes well for a homogenous society. A classic example can be found in the fictional narrative, *Things Fall Apart* by Chinua Achebe. In the novel, a disadvantaged Okonkwo goes to Obierika to borrow some seed yams. Obierika gives Okonkwo double the number of seed yams he requests because he knows that Okonkwo is very hardworking. Obierika does not fail to mention to Okonkwo that he would not have given the seed yams to him were he found to be lazy. In a modern state society, this would simply translate to aid, but in the novel it is a recognition of treating the hardworker as other hardworkers could be treated. All the same, there are many human rights models, especially the natural rights approach and the political approach. Again, borrowing from biblical metaphor, "all models fall short of the glory of God".

Conclusion

The upshot of what I have been trying to say is that Nigeria does not need only one model of development, especially as most development models are skewed towards economics. I argue that Nigeria should be free to borrow any fitting model from anywhere in the world, and that when such is the case, there should be a selective adaptation of such in different sectors of the Nigerian polity. Whether such approach is anarchistic in the sense proposed for science by Feyerabend, or whether it is 'smart power' as called by Hillary Rodham Clinton and recommended for America does not matter to me. What is important is not the label, the cloth, but the substance, in this case, achieving Nigeria's development ambition. As the Igbo proverb has it: *onye ejile oba, manya ru m*; meaning, whoever has the cup, let the palm wine reach me. Whatever method that is adopted for development, and so long as such is adapted in a non-harmful way (the entire essence of adaptation), let development come.

The WE THE PEOPLE movement in Nigeria is a new movement of Nigerian grassroots engineered by Nigerian intellectuals and professionals at home and in the diaspora which cuts across ethnic and religious boundaries. It seeks to grow a new breed of WE THE PEOPLE in Nigeria through education that will change the mindset of Nigerians, one person at a time. It seeks to clean up Nigeria from bottom-to-top, and eventually raise a critical mass of a new breed of WE THE PEOPLE who will speak and act with one voice, regardless of their ethnic and religious persuasions. Their first crucial task is to use the power of their united votes nationwide to vote out corrupt politicians and legislatures, and vote in decent clean men and women of integrity in a massive nationwide movement of WE THE PEOPLE to take back their nation Nigeria from corrupt bad eggs at all levels of government nationwide. Once this important first step is achieved, the task of developing Nigeria into a truly safe, prosperous and corrupt-free nation will be achieved beyond measure and imagination.

References

Clinton, Hillary Rodham. *Hard Choices*. New York: Simon & Schuster, 2014.

Cornwall, Andrea and Deborah Eade. Ed. *Deconstructing Development Discourse: Buzzwords and Fuzzwords. Warwickshire"* Practical Action Publishing and Oxfam, 2010.

Feyerabend, Paul. Against Method: *Outline of an Anarchic Theory of Knowledge*. London: Verso, 1978; Third Impression, 1980.

Kim, Wonik. "Rethinking Colonialism and the Origins of the Development State in East Asia". *Journal of Contemporary*

Asia, Vol. 39, No. 3 (2009), 383 – 399. Web. July 17, 2016.

Olukoju, Ayodeji. "A Plan for the 'Re-Organization' of Nigeria." Text of the First faculty of Arts and Education Distinguished Guest lecture, Adekunle Ajasin University, Akungba- Akoko, Ondo State, Nigeria, 27 November 2003. Akugba-Akoko: First Academy Press.

Pieterse, Jan Nerdeveen. "My Paradigm or Yours? Alternative Development, Post-Development, Reflexive Development."*Development and Change*. Vol. 20 (1998), 343 – 373. Web. July 17, 2016.

Ruttan Vernon W. and Yujiro Hayami. "Strategies for Agricultural Development". Revised version of a "*paper prepared for the Food Research Institute's Conference on Strategies for Agricultural Development in the 1970s*." Web. August 8, 2016.

Taylor, Timothy. The Great Courses, Teaching that engages the mind: **Contemporary Economic Issues**, Part IV. Chantily, VA: The Teaching Company, 1998. Web. July 17, 2016.

CHAPTER 11

Lessons from History - The French Revolution and the Total Transformation of France

Inam AKRASI

There are lessons from the History of other Nations and peoples that We the People, of Nigeria, in embarking on this great mobilization and movement, can learn and draw from on how the experiences of other peoples and nations in mass revolt against unjust established order led to the total transformation of their countries. History has shown that We the People Movement is a powerful instrument of change. The most spectacular historical example of this People Movement that permanently changed a country for the good of the general population, the mass of the people of the country, is the French Revolution of 1789 that ushered in the total transformation of France from a post-feudalistic society of high-level social inequalities and privileges for a few, to a modern Country that we know today as one of the World's powers. But France was not always a developed, democratic country of "Liberté, Eqalité et Fraternité" (Liberty, Equality and Brotherhood), offering liberty and equal opportunities to the citizens, reduced gap between the rich and the poor, respect of the rule of law and order, efficient public administrative systems, accountability and transparency in administrative acts of public officers and authorities, with a well-respected institutional system of control of constitutionality of laws as well as of legality of administrative decisions and actions, a Country almost totally free of corruption of public Officials, as is the case today.

It was the mass mobilization of *le peuple*, with the loud cries of *"pouvoir au people"* (power to the people!), fired by the well-assimilated ideas and ideals of the Enlightenment philosophers and thinkers expressed in their writings and in the *"salons"*, veritable arena of ideas on good government and governance, social equality, individual freedom and liberties, control and limitation of powers of the governors vis-à-vis the governed, etc., such as Montesquieu (*L'Esprit des Lois*), Jean-Jacques Rousseau (*Contrat social*), Voltaire (*Traité sur la Tolérance*), Diderot (*L'Encyclopédie*), etc., that stormed the Bastille Fortress, a symbol of the Monarchy's arbitral powers, on 14 July 1789 to seize weapons and gun powders to violently pull down the "Ancien Régime", the Old Regime, and all its oppressive and unjust manifestations, that brought up a new set of committed people into government and governance, and created the conditions for this political, economic and social new France that exists till today.

This singular historical example of the oppressed population shouting "We the People ... " and expressing their strong will in action that changed the destiny of a whole Nation of France, is a big encouragement to the people of Nigeria who have the legitimate natural right to ask themselves some pertinent questions: What do We the People have right to in Nigeria of today where the poor can hardly afford three square meals a day and the rich can afford imported Champagne; where health-care facilities are not available to meet the needs of the poor whereas the rich can fly out for Overseas treatment; where poorly equipped public schools are the only option for the children of the poor families whereas the rich readily send their children to well-equipped private, fee-paying schools and from there to Private Universities or move to higher institutions abroad; where the masses can only count on crowded 'molue' buses on pot-holed, bad roads to go to their destinations while the rich settle at the back of their air-conditioned, chauffeur-driven SUV; such car models as recently demanded by Members of National Assembly at the expense of We the people? How far and in what manner does this country, Nigeria, belong also to us, We the People? What is our stake in the destiny of the country? Should we forge the destiny of this Nation for us, or without us and against us?

The population of pre-Revolution France, especially the *Tiers-Etat* (the Third Estate) and the emerging *bourgeoisie*, faced with the absolutism of the Kings that ruled over them: Louis X1V (reigned 1643 -1715), Louis XV (reigned 1715 – 1774), Louis XV1 (reigned 1774 – 1792), suffering from high level of taxation, which the nobility was exempted from paying, (just like the Nigerian rich today who hardly pay taxes), watching the affluence and the ostentatious life styles of both the Royal Court and the Second Estate (the Clergy and the Nobility), confronted with the poor cereal (grain) harvest especially of 1775 that sparked off the high cost of bread, the staple food of the people especially of the poor, (like the current high cost of garri in Nigeria), asked themselves questions that led them to challenge *l'ordre établi* (the established order) and that ignited riots on the Streets of Paris and social unrests in the whole country, starting from Paris, which culminated in the storming of the Bastille Fortress, an event that is considered by specialists as the high point of the beginning of the French Revolution.

The French population of pre-Revolution France was no doubt justified to consider their country a society of privileges for the few at the expense of "We the People". Because the public treasury was empty as the Royal Court, which spent from the public purse to sustain their lavish life style without counting, and the nobility were exempted from the tax burden that was necessary to shore up the empty State treasury that both the French assistance to the Americans in their uprising against the British colonialists for their Independence and the Seven Years' War (1756 - 1763), the European conflict over building of Overseas Empires that France was deeply involved in and lost, exacerbated.

In Nigeria today, the fall in oil prices on the international markets plus the poor public financial management and embezzlement of public funds of past administrations at both the Federal and State levels have also put the Nation in a very difficult financial situation. In fact, as in pre-Revolution France, the Nigerian public treasury of most

270

States, except Lagos, is empty. In spite of the economic crisis that caused much suffering to *le peuple* and the bankruptcy of the Monarchy, that is, the State, that limited the King's ability to provide even *le pain* (bread) that the poor peasant population expected of him, the ruling elites, still enjoying their privileges, like the Nigerian State Governors today, failed to read properly the handwriting on the wall regarding the inevitable reaction of the suffering population in the face of their misery, social and economic difficulties.

The same Revolutionary situation: social inequalities, financial difficulties of the State to meet its obligations to the population, high public debt profile, heavy tax burden on only a section of the population in absence of a just tax reform system, lavish life style of the Monarchy and the ruling class in the face of the suffering of the ordinary population, etc, that pushed *le peuple* of France to revolt in 1789 against the established political order and *Ancien Régime's* political and social structures, prevails in Nigeria today. For in today's Nigeria, there are the few rich and extremely rich who are really "enjoying life", while the mass of the population, that is, We the People, are really suffering. With so many State Governments owing their workers their monthly salaries, in some cases many months in arrears, where is the hope of survival for We the People?

On July 7, 2016, Socio-Economic Rights and Acountability Project (SERAP), a civil society organization in Nigeria, petitioned the International Criminal Court, ICC, accusing 11 state governments in Nigeria of owing workers in their states salaries for work done for the state by the workers, committing crimes against humanity, and making life impossible for the workers and their families. The eleven governors dragged to court before the ICC are: Rauf Agbesola of Osun state, Olusegun Mimiko of Ondo state, Ayodele Fayose of Ekiti state, Abdufatah Ahmed of Kwara state, Abiola Ajimobi of Oyo state, Nyesom Wike of Rivers state, Seriaka Dickson of Bayelsa state, Samuel Ortom of Bunue state, Mohammed Abubakar of Bauchi state, Yahaya Bello of Kogi state, and Simon Lalong of Plateau state. While these governors refuse to pay the workers in their states for alleged lack of money, most of them are busy using the money to accumulate personal property for themselves, like Fayose of Ekiti state who while not paying workers in his state, personally acquired with public funds new real estate of over 2.3 billion naira within his first six weeks in office as governor, according to EFCC. How can our anger not be expressed? How can the common man's desire for change be curtailed?

A National daily recently carried the following headlines: *"Water turned an enemy to the inhabitants of Saburi 1, a slum settlement in Abuja Municipal Area Council as 37 people died after drinking contaminated water."* The article went on to state what reflects the condition of life of the majority of We the People in Nigeria: *"... none of the victims was brought to the clinic as most of the villagers always complained of being too poor to pay medical bills ..."* (The Sun Newspaper of 27th April, 2016).

Yes, We the People are too poor even to go to the Hospital for treatment. We lack basic amenities in our communities. We find it difficult to offer ourselves three-square, well-balanced meals a day. Our housing conditions do not afford us the luxury of owing private generators to generate our own electricity in the face of the rampant failure of the public utility system. Hence, most of the time we are in darkness without corresponding reduction in our electricity bills.

Our cup of frustration, like that of the French population in 1789, is full. The French took up arms against the Monarchy and the established Old Régime in a very violent and bloody Revolution. Although the Revolution resulted in the total transformation of France, putting in place new political, governmental and social order that remain till today, such as a Republican form of Government replacing the Monarchy, new Constitution for the country, Declaration of Rights of the Citizens guaranteed by the Constitution, abolition of the stratified "Estates", ("Ordres" and "Corps") with their unjust privileges, amongst others.

The bloody nature of that revolution included the Reign of Terror, summary execution, even of the King Louis XV1 and the Queen, Marie-Antoinette, deportation and deaths of thousands of people. The French revolution resulted in powerful change and transformation as a result of the united will of the people mobilized in a popular Movement, under strong leadership like Robespierre, Danton, Camille Desmoulins.

Former president Olusegun Obasanjo has warned Nigerian leaders to mend their ways and become better leaders, to avoid a strong massive revolution in Nigeria that will be totally out of control. He feared for his own life and cautioned that there will be no safety net for any former or current leader associated with the decadence in Nigeria if eventually such a massive revolution erupts.

The WE THE PEOPLE movement in Nigeria as envisaged by the leadership of the movement is not an armed uprising as in the French revolution. It is our hope that by changing Nigeria for good through our no-arms conflict movement, we will forestall the possibility of armed revolution at any time in the future.

Through education and dialogue, we want to raise a new breed of honest and corruption-free Nigerians who will convince their fellow Nigerians, one person at a time, to commit to doing the right thing in their personal lives to bring about a new and clean Nigeria. As we mobilize this force of clean Nigerians, the new WE THE PEOPLE, our movement will clean Nigeria from bottom to top. It is a clean bottom that will produce a clean top. Our goal is to raise a critical mass of 50 million clean Nigerians in this movement, which will transform Nigeria irrevocably. From this 50 million new Nigerians of every tribe and religion, from every ward of every local government in Nigeria, we will have men and women of integrity who will run for elected office, and be voted for by the new breed of WE THE PEOPLE in a powerful movement to use the power of the ballot to put only men and women of integrity into positions of leadership everywhere in Nigeria, for a clean and law-abiding Nigeria. A lot of hard work is required, but it can be done, it will be done. It is the only way to change Nigeria—from bottom to top. Only a clean bottom can produce a clean top, and hold it totally accountable to WE THE PEOPLE. Let's have a clean bottom so we can have a clean top in Nigeria, for the good and benefit of we the people, the grassroots of the federal republic of Nigeria. Power belongs to the people. If you are interested in a new Nigeria, if you want to be part of the new breed of WE THE PEOPLE, send us your name, email and phone number using: info@wethepeoplenigeria.org. We will register you as a member of this non-governmental organization (NGO) and send you additional detail on this important non-conflict movement to save our country Nigeria.

CHAPTER 12

The New Breed of WE THE PEOPLE: The Character and Commitments required to Build a New Democratic and Progressive Nigeria.

Professor Grace Chibiko Offorma, BA.Ed M.Ed Ph.D

Professor Uduogie Michael Ivowi, PhD FNTI

Introduction

Nigeria is a sovereign nation that is blessed by God with rich soil, good climate and weather, and endowed with many mineral resources. The country is so rich in solid minerals, such as coal, tin, zinc, bitumen, silicon, columbites, tantalite, lead and many others that if explored and harnessed will contribute to technological development of the country (Offorma, 2013). It is estimated that the population is about 170 million people of various ethnic groups, religions, cultures, languages and traditions. In fact, there are about 250 languages in Nigeria; but we still communicate effectively and understand ourselves very well; thanks to EDUCATION.

Nigeria is blessed because she does not experience any of the very harsh natural disasters that occur in other countries of the world, such as tornadoes, as in the United States of America (USA) (Carolina and Isaac); earthquakes, as in India and Pakistan; infernos, as in Australia; tsunamis, as in Japan. Nigeria is blessed with flat land with rich soil, assorted fruits and vegetables that are seasonal. The fruits take their turns to mature in such a way that they are abundant and many are wasted due to lack of storage system or technology to package them in a more sustainable state. The country has sometimes experienced floods, such as that which occurred in 2012, including landslides in some parts of the country. These are not as devastating as the natural disasters experienced by other countries of the world. God has really blessed Nigeria and endowed her with the wherewithal for good and sustainable livelihood.

Nigeria is also blessed with human capital. There are many institutions of learning ranging from nursery to university. These institutions train and produce the work force at different levels, needed in the country and elsewhere. She has produced tremendous human capital that can promote her development in every sphere of life. Nigerians are found in other countries, making waves, though there are others who disgrace the country by their unwholesome behaviours.

Again, Nigeria has a Constitution, which is binding on all including WE THE PEOPLE and the leaders at different levels of government because the Constitution asserts in its first chapter that:

> We the people of the *Federal Republic* of Nigeria having firmly and solemnly resolved, to live in unity and harmony as one indivisible and indissoluble sovereign nation under God, dedicated to the promotion of inter-African solidarity, world peace, international co-operation and understanding
> And to provide for a Constitution for the purpose of promoting the good government and welfare of all persons in our country, on the principles of freedom, equality and justice, and for the purpose of consolidating the unity of our people, do hereby make, enact and give to ourselves the following Constitution: - (FGN, 1999).

It is the responsibility of the leaders to respect the Constitution. All their programmes must be geared towards the wellbeing of We the People. After all, the people voted them into power.

But one thing is clear; the society is dynamic and not static and there is need for people to change according to the positive demands and aspirations that emerge from the society. The 1999 Constitution is still operative *but people have been clamouring for the implementation of the accepted changes recommended by the National Conference of 2014 for Constitutional Review. If we are our brothers' keepers, why should we not listen to the demands of the people? Nigerian government is a democratic one and so must listen to the people to understand their needs and aspirations. The government is not autocratic. Ignoring the people can result to insecurity, war and other vices, some of* which are already being experienced in Nigeria today.

This chapter is focused on WE THE PEOPLE: The character and commitments required of this new breed of WE THE PEOPLE to build a democratic and progressive Nigeria. The contents include the concept of We the People, character and commitments required of the new breed of WE THE PEOPLE to bring the required change in attitude, behavior and dispositions in WE THE PEOPLE, conclusion and recommendations.

Concept and Character of We the People

We the People refer to Nigerians, bona fide men and women that own the land called Nigeria. The Federal Republic of Nigeria is estimated to have a population of about 170 million citizens, who are born and planted in the land of Nigeria. God has endowed this black race with intelligence, creative and entrepreneurial spirit, adaptation, capabilities and hospitable tendencies. We the People are their brothers' keepers and can accommodate others. For example, Nigeria has been playing many big brotherly roles in Africa. That is one of the reasons Nigeria is called 'the Giant of Africa'. We the People of Nigeria are loved and blessed by God.

Though they speak different languages, yet they perfectly understand themselves. They have a dream: to make Nigeria a great nation, where care, love, equity, oneness, fairness, justice and peace reign. They are patriotic and very ready to render selfless services to Nigeria. We the People may be divergent in their culture, language, ethnicity and religion, but their sense of unity, and aspiration binds them together into members of a sovereign nation.

Despite these positive attributes of We the people, they are indolent, dying in silence! We the People are aware of the impunities that are unleashed by our representatives the people voted into power, their indiscipline, neglect of duties, intimidation of the people that supported them during their campaign, dishonesty, greed and avarice, but We the people are afraid to tell them to their faces, that they have disappointed and failed us. Most of them are not more intelligent than some of We the people. According to Chidoka (2015, p. 6), "despite its vast resources and advantages, Nigeria is yet to perform at its highest potential."

We the People have developed 'shock absorbers' and condoned bad governance. The people undergo a lot of hardships, hunger, poverty, unemployment, and ignorance due to lack of good education, which is their fundamental right, though neglected by the leaders. They pay lip service to the geese that lay the golden eggs. Through education, economic, political, and social developments are driven. They live in very poor environmental conditions, with very poor health care and services, very bad roads, lack of good quality drinking water, erratic electricity supply, poor and inadequate accommodation. The civil and some public servants are owed salaries for months, yet they work for the government. The pensioners are not paid and they suffer and die. Yet these are the people that rendered valuable services that contributed to the development of the country, when they were young.

These issues are as a result of bad leadership. According to Achebe (1983),

> the trouble with Nigeria is simply and squarely a failure of leadership. There is nothing basically wrong with the Nigerian character.

There is nothing wrong with the Nigerian land or climate or water or air or anything else. The Nigerian problem is the unwillingness or inability of its leaders to rise to their responsibilities, to the challenge of personal example which are the hallmarks of true leadership p.1.

We the People are committed and dedicated to their responsibilities, they are God fearing, hardworking, honest, humane, humble, respectful and visionary. They are open to constructive criticisms, have listening ears and possess discernible spirit. They are quick to taking actions to avert looming dangers that will hurt other Nigerians. They seek dialogues in serious social, political, environmental and economic issues that may hamper development or introduce disharmony in the society.

They have a common goal: to see Nigeria develop as a great nation, harbouring good people who are their brothers' keepers. We the People carry everybody along in the scheme of things: social, economic, political endeavours. Their policy is: 'leave no one behind'.

Commitments Required to Build a New Democratic and Progressive Nigeria

We commence this section, defining what we mean by commitment. Commitment can be defined as a pursuit of one's pledge, irrespective of the hurdles one would have to jump. It involves having a vision and working very hard to attain the vision. According to on-line Webster Dictionary/Thesaurus, commitment is adherence to one's pledge or duty; or something one must embark upon because of prior agreement. A simple illustration of commitment is one who attends meetings of one's professional association and makes useful contributions to promote the association. The dictionary gives the following as the synonyms of commitment: allegiances, fidelity, constancy, faithfulness, dedication, fastness, devotion, fondness, love and so on. These behaviors depict faith in what one wants to achieve or attain.

It is an act of pledging, engaging oneself, a pledge or promise, obligation. Commitment is a character trait, which sustains one to be steadfast and sincere to a purpose. It calls for emotional or intellectual engagement of one to a course of action. It is what propels one in life's journey, as one remains dogged in the presence of the ups and downs of life, in a bid to attain one's goals or one's dreams. When we commit to certain purpose or course of action, we are committing to personal values, beliefs, principles and behaviors that reflect them.

Sincere relationships call for commitment. The relationships can be with ourselves, with other members of the family, with friends or between a leader and the led. Some people betray their relationship by not being committed. Such people are called fair weather friends. They become close to their friends in plenty but disappear when the going is tough. They opt out, or abandon the relationship. For leaders, commitment should be their watchword. They cannot afford to sell out or derail from the promises they made to the led when they were seeking their votes.

Commitment demands a lot of sacrifices, such as sleepless nights, denial of some pleasures, selflessness, and even taking some risks, just for the wellbeing of others. According to Najt (2011) a difference between interest and commitment exists. When one is interested in doing something, one does it at his or her convenience. When one is committed to something, one does not give any excuses, but focuses on the results or deliverables. One implication of commitment is that it is result-oriented, irrespective of the challenges on the way. Najt believes that when we understand our purpose, we must garner our strength and courage to face the odds, because the reward for commitment is that one gets what one has given. So what are the commitments of We the People?

Commitments of We the People

From the above discussions, we can sift some of the commitments expected of We the People, the new breed of Nigerians. The commitments include: good governance, quality and inclusive education, human capital development, fiscal federalism, commitment to people, organizations, institutions, enterprises, enhancement of food production and food security, abhorrence of corruption, tribalism, social injustice, indiscipline, and to shunning mediocrity.

Good Governance

We would look at the Nigerian Pledge to draw some commitments from it. The pledge reads thus:

I pledge to Nigeria, my country
To be faithful, loyal and honest
To serve Nigeria with all my strength
To defend her unity and uphold her honour and glory
So help me God.

This is a beautiful piece that contains what it takes to be a committed Nigerian. At assumption of public offices, people are requested to recite this Pledge; and they do. But they quickly forget this oath taken by them. Faithfulness, loyalty and honesty are all ingredients of commitment. A patriotic Nigerian should exhibit these values in his/her life, and dealings with other people. Most of our leaders are not faithful and loyal to their campaign promises when they win and get elected to their offices. This is not the character of We the People. The commitment of We the People is to uphold and live in line with these noble words of the Nigerian Pledge. The leaders should uphold the oath taken at assumption of office. They should be servant leaders, not greedy, selfish and insensitive leaders that steal money from the country's treasury; the money meant to provide for the needs of the people; and they do not care about the welfare of the citizens.

To serve Nigeria with all my strength, implies no reservation or pretense in rendering service to the nation or to the citizens. The leaders are supposed to be servant leaders, expending their energies in serving the led, sacrificing their time, energy, intellectual power, leisure, and at times sleep, to render service for the wellbeing of the citizens. This demands honesty of purpose, dedication and commitment to their responsibilities. An example that comes to my mind is what was reported by Ekpunobi (2012) about the flooding of 2012 in Nigeria. About fourteen (14) out of thirty-six (36) states, experienced great flooding, whereby property, farmlands, residences and even schools were drowned by flood. Anambra State was one of them. This information reached the then Governor, Mr Peter Obi by about 3.00am on the fateful day. He left his residence with his team, and went to the community, entered the flood that was above his knee with his men to render service to his people.

Figure.1: His Excellency, Mr Peter Obi and his Team in flood Waters

Good governance is another commitment of the new breed of Nigerians. This means the responsibilities of the government or governing bodies in meeting the needs of the people. It deals with viable economies and political bodies. According to the United Nations (UN) (2009), good governance has eight characteristics, namely: consensus oriented, participatory, following the Rule of Law, effective and efficient, accountability, transparent, responsive, equitable and inclusive. These can also be regarded as the ingredients of democracy. The Deputy Senate President of the Federal

Republic of Nigeria, Distinguished Senator Ike Ekeremadu (2014), sees the core ideals of democracy as transparency and accountability. He continues by saying that 'whenever leaders fail to provide effective leadership, they damage their relationship with the public and alienate themselves from those that matter most in democracy - the citizens' p.6. The new breed of Nigerians would be committed to good governance; working hard to ensure that elections are free, fair and transparent. The grass root would abhor ballot box snatching, thuggery, intimidation, abuse of human rights and shooting of the opponent.

The commitment of We the People will be to demonstrate democracy, through good governance. Only transparent people will be voted into power, not 'money bags' that buy people's consciences. Nobody will sell his/her conscience because of personal aggrandizement or the gains to be derived from corrupt politicians. Every Nigerian will be carried along through responsive, equitable, inclusive and consensus oriented governance. These promote development because an efficient and effective leader would be accountable to the led and would respect the Rule of Law. These will make for peace and security, because the resources are equitably distributed, no section of the country will be marginalized. There will be meritocracy and healthy competition among We the People. These will engender love, trust, honesty and dedication to duties.

Quality and Inclusive Education

It is said that ignorance is a disease and more expensive than literacy. The leaders forget that it is more difficult to lead ignorant people, because they are never on the same page with them. They may not understand government policies meant for their wellbeing. This misunderstanding may bring about confusion, disharmony, disobedience, disrespect, anger, insurgency, and other vices and social ills as witnessed in some communities. Nigeria is a very rich country. What makes us poor are our negative attitude, insincerity, avarice, greed, dishonesty. The commitment of

We the People will be to eradicate all these through provision of equitable and inclusive education, by providing the crucial infrastructure, facilities, learner-friendly environment, trained and motivated teachers to implement the policies. The school curricula will address the needs of We the People, thus producing functional and patriotic Nigerians. We are blessed and it is our belief that Nigeria is richly endowed to provide what it takes to educate the people.

The new breed of We the People will be committed to quality and inclusive education that will facilitate lifelong learning. The current Illiteracy in Nigeria will be tackled as that is the major challenge of We the People. There is need to educate all the citizens, so as to make them aware of their rights. It is written in the Bible that 'my people perish because of ignorance'. This type of education is a veritable tool for enhancement of all aspects of development. It also facilitates the grooming of the citizens to become knowledgeable, imbibe the right values, skills and attitudes for a sustainable livelihood. Education according to the Federal Government of Nigeria (FGN, 2004), 'is an instrument 'par excellence' for effective national development' P.4. Quality and inclusive education will be the focus of We the People so as to prepare Nigerians who are patriotic, and are committed to the progress and peaceful living of the people. The government will formulate educational policies and other policies for We the People to guide them and make them faithful to the policies by ensuring that all the tenets of the policies are implemented to the letter.

There must be positive political will to support education, by making all the necessary provisions to attain the goals of education. We the People must be treated to good quality and inclusive education. No one should be left behind, even the special education needs children will be trained according to their endowments. There is ability in their disabilities. Such children should not be neglected. The government pretends that they are providing for them, but they are starved of the necessary equipment, facilities, workshops, studios and qualified human resources to train them. These are needed to promote their education. Nigeria failed to attain the Millennium Development Goal 2 (MDGs) because of insincerity, negligence, dishonesty and lack of commitment. In short, it is the lack of political will on the part of government and other education authorities that make us unable to implement policies to attain our stated objectives.

Today, the United Nations has launched other development goals to consolidate the gains from the MDGs. Sustainable Development Goals (SDGs) which is the new dispensation that will run for the next fifteen (15) years. Nigeria is among the nations that signed the initiatives and accepted to start the implementation by January 2016. No poverty is the first goal. The Ministry of Labor is calling on all unemployed youth to come and register with them to receive five thousand Naira as a monthly allowance. We do not see sufficient seriousness of the government in this plan of giving unemployed youths some welfare package to cushion the effect of lack of employment.

Human Capital Development

Quality and inclusive education would promote production of human capital. Human capital development is derived from quality education because education is the hub of all other developments. Onah (2011) posits that human capital development "is not just any change in the human condition that would qualify as development, but one that results in an improvement of the quality of human life" p.22. Intitutions of learning produce a nation's work force. Most leaders of institutions are not interested in the quality of their products. Their focus is on how much money they can make. They are not committed to production of people who will work in different sectors of the economy. Their major reason is that the government does not bring enough subventions. The staff and students can embark on some projects that can generate some funds for effective implementation of the programmes. By so doing, the students acquire essential skills that would give them a competitve edge when they graduate. The commitment of We the People will be to effectively equip the schools; and of course the institutional leaders will be from We the People, committed to the cause of the nation and ready to make sacrifices to produce both middle and high level manpower that will pilot the business of the nation and exploit the God-given resources in their environments.

Fiscal Federalism

It is interesting to note that every state of the federation has some mineral resources, which they can harness and use the proceeds to improve the lives of the people. Unfortunately, these minerals belong to the Federal Government under the policy of Fiscal Federalism. Thus the state governors and even the Local Government Chairmen are often powerless in harnessing these natural endowments, which can contribute greatly in generating revenue for the states to meet their obligations to their people.

Table 1 reveals the mineral endowments of each state, which should be harnessed and used to enhance the life of the people.

Table 1: States and Mineral Endowments

State	Minerals
Abia	limestone, marble, laterite, phosphate, petroleum, etc
Akwa Ibom	clay, silica, natural gas, glass sand, petroleum, etc
Anambra	stone, petroleum, lignite, natural gas, etc
Bauchi	tantalite, iron ore, columbite, lead, coal etc
Bayelsa	Salt, silica sand, natural gas, petroleum
Benue	sulphate, crude salt, calcium, sulphate, zinc ore, etc
Borno	sapphire, topaz, uranium, gold, aquamarine, etc
Cross River	salt, limestone, gold, sharp sand, mica, etc);
Delta	Kaoline, laterite, gravel, natural gas, petroleum

Ebonyi	lead, zinc ore, granite, kaoline, petroleum, etc
Edo	copper, gold, granite, gypsum, petroleum, etc
Ekiti	clay, bauxite, columbite, kaoline, granite, etc
Enugu	iron ore, crude oil, coal, petroleum, clay, etc
FCT- Abuja	limestone, granite, marble, mica, salt, etc
Gombe	graphite, kaoline, uranium coal, gypsum, etc
Imo	crude oil, salt, marble, natural gas, kaoline, etc
Jigawa	granite, silica, iron ore, potash, limestone, etc
Kano	clay, laterite, silica sand, tin ore, kaolite, etc
Katsina	Gold, gypsum, kaoline, diamond, uranium, etc
Kebbi	iron ore, salt, clay, phosphate, gold
Kwara	clay, quartz, marble, gold, tantalite. Etc
Lagos	bitumen, gravel, sharp sand, laterite, petroleum, etc
Nasarawa	emerald, garnet, sapphire, topaz, coal, etc
Niger	iron ore, gold, graphite, asbestos, marble, etc
Ogun	mica, silica sand, limestone, quartz, koaline, etc
Ondo	Marble, gold, clay, lignite, diorite, etc
Osun	clay, granite, talc, quartz, limestone, etc
Oyo	clay, granite, iron ore, kaoline, marble, dolomite, etc
Plateau	quartz, marble, mica, kaoline, columbite, etc
Rivers	Petroleum, natural gas, silica sand, glass sand clay, etc
Sokoto	clay, salt, limestone, phosphate, gypsum, etc
Taraba	sapphire, columbite, gypsum, limestone, lead/zinc ore, etc
Yobe	salt, limestone, iron ore, granite, shale, uranium, etc
Zamfara	gold, granite, chromites, clay, spring water, etc

Source: Raw Materials Research Development Council, (RMRDC) in Ikekweremadu, 2014 p.28.

We the People will empower the states to harness the various minerals in their different environment. That will go a long way to provide the needed employment opportunities to the citizens. Then, insurgency, restiveness, armed robbery, kidnapping, hired assassination, damage of oil pipe lines, thuggery and other social ills will be curtailed, as the perpetrators will be gainfully employed and busy and will not have time to engage in such heinous activities. Also, the practice of local government council officials waiting till the end of the month to collect their subventions and share them amongst themselves will be curtailed and the money used for its intended purposes.

Commitment to People, Organization, Institutions and Enterprises

This commitment refers to recognition of the worth of people, organizations, institutions and enterprises. There have been cases where leaders set-up their critics or even eliminate them. The victims may be media men, community leaders, and heads of institutions or enterprises. This is unwholesome and should not be the case in a civilized country. Democracy thrives in peaceful existence of all and contributions of all to the development of the society. Two examples are the cases of Dele Giwa (a media person) and Bola Ige (legal luminary), both of whom were allegedly assassinated because they voiced out some of the ills of the respective governments. Appointments to public offices should be done with the aim of adding value to the administration of the country. It should not be done on the basis of relationships, but based on competence. The present regime has relegated the youth to the background and that is why they are agitating. Many party loyalists, old friends and relations are appointed as ministers, directors, and so on, even when they are very old or incompetent to hold such offices. Many of them are not even computer literate; and so how can they function effectively? Competence is a factor in good governance. A team of competent public officials can put their heads together to change the economy of a nation. Olaniyan (2007, p.28) strongly agrees that "a key factor for ensuring that transparency and accountability support good governance, development, and democracy is the nature of the relationship between the two key actors in development - the people and the government".

There is no doubt that Nigerian youths have contributed

tremendously to the development of the country. The youths tried to defend Nigeria in the pre-and post-independence era. They fought for our independence and for our sovereignty. Youth movements such as Nigerian Youth Movements, West African Students' Union were piloted by youths who championed the struggle for Nigeria's independence from the British colonial rule. The Rt. Hon. Dr. Anamdi Azikiwe, Chief Obafemi Awolowo, Ahmadu Bello, Anthony Enahoro made their respective contributions to Nigeria's political and economic domains at a time they were all youths. They fought the British colonial masters when they were in their twenties and thirties. Olujuwon and Noah (2010, p.8) added that "in sports and other social endeavours, the youths were making great impact, selling Nigeria to the outside world as a country with great talents and promise".

Today, the youths get enmeshed in social ills; they reflect what is happening in the society. Nigeria is sinking into crises of underdevelopment; this affects the youth. The Nigerian youth can be used to measure the state of socio-political status of the country. Their energies and activism are channeled towards counter-productive directions. They are involved in crimes, violence, fraud, drug abuse (which is very rampart, even in the villages), cultism, examination malpractice (a cankerworm that has eaten deep into many students), embezzlement, opportunism, acts of gangsters, armed robbery, kidnapping, materialism, pipeline vandalism, and so on. Unemployment is raging and many youths turned into loafers. The adults are not helping matters. Their life style is deceitful and misleading. They forget what the Bible says about misleading the innocent ones. It is better that a big stone is tied to the neck of the person and he/she thrown into the ocean than to mislead the innocent. So what legacies are the adults leaving for the younger generation? The youths are of a nation are its most productive asset, yet in Nigeria they constitute the bulk of the unemployed. Therefore, the economic meltdown and down turn have had a tremendous effect on them, pushing them into criminal activities, as their means of survival.

We the People will have listening ears and be able to sift the truth from the fallacy, accept criticisms and implement any worthwhile change for better. There is an adage that says, *Vox populi, vox dei* (the people's voice is God's voice). Everybody must be carried along to show real democracy at work. We the People will appoint people to public positions based on competence, not on relationships or loyalty. We live in a digital world and if Nigeria is to participate in the global scheme of things and remain relevant, public officers must be computer literate, as that will facilitate effective administration and communication. The youths must be involved in the programme of activities for the development of Nigeria.

Enhancement of Food Production and Food Security

The first and second goals of the Post-2015 Development Agenda are to "end poverty in all its forms everywhere; end hunger, achieve food security and improve nutrition and promote sustainable agriculture" The third goal is linked to the first two. It is "ensure healthy lives and promote well-being for all at all ages" (Kamau and Donoghue, 2015). It is well known that healthy eating promotes the health of the people. If enough food is produced in Nigeria, the problem of hunger and ill health will be solved. These can be achieved through effective agriculture. There are so many street beggars in Nigeria and this is because of hunger and poverty. But will the 'peanuts' given to the beggars by the wealthy in the name of charity improve the situation of the poor? We believe that it is better to teach one how to fish than giving fish to one. At the beginning of this chapter we stated that Nigeria is blessed with good soil, weather and water; Nigerian soil is very rich for sustainable agriculture that will result in enormous food production that will help to eradicate poverty and hunger.

Agriculture has remained an important aspect of any economy. Unfortunately, Nigeria is operating a mono-economy, based on the oil and gas. In the 60s and 70s,

Nigeria was booming with agricultural produce and was exporting palm oil, palm kennel, rubber, cotton, cocoa, ground nuts and others. There were cottage industries that were using the raw materials to produce quality 'made in Nigerian' goods. Today, most of them have folded up due to inadequate electricity supply. Malaysia is one of the world producers of palm oil; they collected the seeds from Nigeria. Unfortunately as soon as Nigeria discovered oil, farms were abandoned for the villagers, who barely farmed for their personal sustenance, and unable to generate sufficient food for the country's growing population. Viable agricultural programmes and activities in any nation are capable of sustaining the food supply and reserves needed for the welfare of the citizens (Justice, Development and Peace Caritas (JDPC), Catholic Diocese of Nsukka, 2014).

Nigerians despise agriculture, and would rather consume imported food, most of which contain preservatives or are so polished that their food values are destroyed or reduced. Such foods do not support good health. Our fore fathers lived healthier and longer than us despite the improvements in technology, medicine and hygiene. This is attributed to our life style, the kind of things we eat and drink. In Nigeria, for example rice is produced in Abakaliki (Ebonyi State); Omogho and Aguleri (Anambra State); Adani (Enugu State); Makurdi and Oturkpo (Benue State) to mention but a few. Nigeria has the capacity to produce sufficient rice to feed her people, and still have enough to export. Unfortunately, people prefer foreign rice, which is polished and the only food value is carbohydrate. God has blessed us with nutritious fruits, vegetables, seeds and grains. The commodity profile of Nigeria is diverse; such crops as cassava, cowpea, cashew, 'acha' soyabean, maize, sorghum, plantain, and banana are produced in different parts of the country. We the people will be committed to promotion of agriculture. After all, there are so many graduates of Agriculture and allied disciplines who are ready to embark on agriculture if motivated. Challenges experienced in agriculture, such as poor access to credit facility, technical inputs, machines and farm implements, poor infrastructure, water supply, bad and inconsistent agricultural policies, uncontrollable grazing of animals and destruction of farm crops and so on, will be dealt with by We the People. Our local resources will be explored and converted to valuable conditions. We the People will highly support agribusiness, which is money spinning and so will improve the country's economy. The kind of Songhai farms in Republic of Benin will be multiplied in Nigeria to produce food, meat, vegetables and fruits. With the biotechnology being developed, fast-yielding plants will be cultivated, to adapt to climate change effects. Food security will be attained; agricultural industries will be put in place and many young Nigerians will be gainfully employed. When people feed well, they are happy and healthy. Many of the social ills will disappear and there will be peace.

Abhorrence of Corruption, Tribalism, Social Injustice, Indiscipline, and Mediocrity

We have discussed these social ills in the different sections of this chapter. They form a clog in the wheel of development and progress of our nation, Nigeria, and in deed in any country that does not fight against them. Corruption is seen in every sector of the economy. It is a cankerworm that has eaten deep into the fabric of the society. Nduka (2016) quoting the Vice President of the Federal Republic of Nigeria in an article published in the Guardian of March 7, 2016, wrote "Nigeria is a system where the norm is corrupt behaviour across all arms of formal system of governance and the private sector is a strong collaborator" p.10. Nduka has blamed Heads of State, governors and top civil servants, ministers and the legislators, politicians, the judiciary, top bankers, and business men, the military establishment, the academia and teaching profession as well as parents and guardians, who have helped to debase the standard of education by being accomplices to various examination malpractices and corrupt practices in various walks of life in Nigeria.

We the People actually have a big responsibility to

contend with. But we are not daunted. We are committed to rebuild Nigeria and groom a new breed of Nigerians that are patriotic and committed to the cause of our dear country, who are ready to make some sacrifices for the development and progress of our nation. We the People will shun tribalism, indiscipline, mediocrity and social injustices. We the people will be their brothers' keepers and will embark on job creation to create employment opportunities. If people are helped to put food on their tables, most of the social ills will stop. We are one of the countries of "youth advantage". Nigeria accounts for 47% of West Africa's population and the youth and the working-age are in the majority, as posited by Manyinka, Woetzel, Dobbs, Remes, Labaye, and Jordan (2015). Our youths must be well trained and groomed to contribute to the development of this country.

Conclusion

The cure of the ills of Nigeria lies with us, We the People. We are the foundation blocks. Development of any building commences from the foundation. So We the people will take the bull by the horn and drive our dream for Nigeria to fruition. In conclusion, let us revisit our national anthem, which has all the information we need to rebuild a peaceful and progressive Nigeria. We the People should try to commit the words of the anthem to memory and pray it every day, thus:

Arise O Compatriots
Nigeria's call obey
To serve our father land
With love and strength and faith
The labour of our heroes past
Shall never be in vain
To serve with heart and might
One nation bound in freedom
Peace and unity.

O God of creation

Direct our Nobel cause
Guide our leaders right
Help our youth the truth to know
In love and honesty to grow
And living just and true
Great lofty heights attain
To build a nation
Where peace and justice reign.

If our prayers are answered, Nigeria will be great again. It will be a home for all: no discrimination, no tribalism, no unemployment, no injustice, and no corruption. There will be fair play, respect for the Rule of Law, meritocracy, patriotism, respect of constituted authority, youth empowerment, access to equitable, quality inclusive and lifelong education. Workers' salaries will be paid, public officers will be servant leaders and social amenities will be equitably distributed.

Recommendations

- We the people should reinvent accountability and transparency as tools for achieving good governance.
- The States should be platforms for wealth creation and not platforms for wealth sharing.
- Competent and experienced technocrats and administrators should be appointed into public offices to pilot the affairs of the country.
- Nigeria must return to agriculture to provide quality food to the citizens. Soft loans with minimal interest should be provided to farmers to make them more productive.
- Public institutions must be revamped and the right and competent people appointed into positions to drive the development of the nation.
- Industries should be created to provide employment to the people.
- Governments must demonstrate sufficient political will to enable policies to be executed to attain stated

goals and objectives.

References

Achebe, C. (1983). *The trouble with Nigeria.* Enugu: Fourth Dimension Publishing Co. Ltd.

Chidoka, O.B. (2015). Rebuilding the Nigerian dream: Mapping the building blocks. *44th Convocation Lecture,* University of Nigeria, Nsukka.

Ekpunobi, D (2012). *Ogbaru, Anambra East, West LGAs' flood persists.* http://www.igbofocus.co.uk/Anambra_State/Anambra-in-Flood.jpg   Retrieved October 28, 2012.

Ekweremadu, Ike (2014). Key governance issues in Nigeria: My perspectives. *Lecture* delivered at the 54th Founder's Day, University of Nigeria, Nsukka, at Nsukka, Enugu State.

Federal Government of Nigeria (FGN) (1999). Nigerian Constitution. Lagos:

Federal Government of Nigeria (FGN) (2004). National Policy on Education. Abuja: Nigerian Educational Research and Development Council (NERDC). http://www.merriam-webster.com/thesaurus/commitment Retrieved on 7/8/16

Justice, Development and Peace Caritas (JDPC), Catholic Diocese of Nsukka, 2014). Lenten Campaign   2014: Food Insecurity: Hunger in the Midst of Abundance. Nsukka: JDPC.

Kamau, M. & Donoghue, D. (2015). Transforming our world: The 2030 Agenda for Global Action. *Final   Draft of the Outcome Document for the UN Summit to Adopt the Post-2015 Development Agenda.* New YorK: United Nations.

Manyinka, J.,Woetzel, J., Dobbs, R., Remes, J., Labaye, E. & Jordan, A. (2015). Can long-term global growth be saved? *A*

*Report:*McKinsey Global Institute.

Najt, A. B. (2011). Essentials of great leadership: Commitment.
https://4ekselans.net/File/View/5802ce0a-2284-4de2-bf66-e3de3c6ccfbd Retrieved 4/8/16

Nduka, O. (2016). The Valedictory Message of a Nonagenarian to the Nigerian Nation. Port   Harcourt: Gitelle Press.

Offorma, G.C. (2013). Nigeria in 2030. London: Commonwealth Education Partnerships.

Olaniyan, O. (2007). Rethinking transparency and accountability in Nigeria's democratic process.
Conflict Tracking Dossier.Quarterly Review of IDASA. 7, 23-29.

Olojuwon, T.& Noah, A.O. (2010). *Youth and Vison 2010.* Lagos: Central Educational Services.

Onah, G.I. (2011). Intellectualism and the development of a people. *Adada Lecture Series,* No. 1. Nsukka: Ephrata Press.

UNESCAP (2009). Good Governance. United Nations
http://www.unescap.org/pdd/prs/projectActivities/ongoing/gg/ governance.asp.
Accessed July 10, 2009.

CHAPTER 13

WE THE PEOPLE:
Building Towards Corruption-Free Nigeria
from Bottom to Top

Gary S. Maxey, PhD

I love this place called Nigeria. There is no other country in the world where I would prefer to be than right here. I tell my natural-born Nigerian friends that I may love this country more than they because many of them would gladly take flight and never come back if they could. But not me. I am here to stay. As I tell one and all: "I go live here and I go die here!"

On March 4, 2016 I began my thirty-fifth year as a resident of Nigeria. The naturalization process my wife and I started four years earlier could have long ago reached a happy conclusion if not for multiple problems with corruption along the way. We are hopeful it will yet have a positive outcome, because we long ago decided that this is where we will remain, in our happily adopted country of Nigeria. While swallowing lots of garri, pounded yam and amala has done nothing to make me look like a Nigerian, I write these words as much as possible as one who loves Nigeria deeply and considers this country my *home*.

I have been fascinated for twenty-five years with the challenge of corruption in Nigeria. I have understood that the corruption around us is a relatively new intruder into Nigerian society that at its core is solidly ethical. As a result, in the early 1990s I began to collaborate with some of the most widely revered Christian moral leaders in Nigeria—from north, south, east and west—to confront the challenge of ridding Nigeria of the scourge of corruption. Together we met for a total of ten times under the umbrella of the Congress on Christian Ethics in Nigeria. The consuming question on our minds was how Nigeria's Sleeping Giant could be awakened. How could we mobilize the Nigerian

Church to take up its responsibilities to effect moral change in this country? We worked hard at it for more than four years.

We started by recognizing that the issue of Nigerian corruption was of such magnitude that it would be necessary to look at it thoroughly from the standpoint of many different social sectors. We therefore established thirteen working groups to examine the issue of corruption within distinct social spheres—ethics in business and industry, in education, in the armed forces, in law and the judiciary, in politics, in law enforcement, in government and civil service, in natural resources, in banking and finance, in journalism, in family life, in medicine, and in traditional leadership. We chose men and women as the leaders of these groups who had achieved much success with proven transparency in these social spheres and who had gained a wide reputation for Christian integrity.

The assignment for each of these ad hoc groups was to draw in other persons of sterling integrity and to address three basic questions: (1) What are the peculiar ethical issues that we confront here in Nigeria within our particular social sphere? (2) What are the Bible principles that might relate to these issues? And (3) where should Nigerian Christians take their moral stand within this particular social sphere? These committees continued to meet in various venues throughout the country over a two-year period.

Second, we were convicted that we could not proceed toward the final goal of COCEN without first launching an intensive national prayer campaign that would encompass all thirty states and the Federal Capital Territory. We specifically called for prayers of repentance, praying always in the first person (using the pronouns "I" and "we," rather than "they"). We were acknowledging like the Old Testament prophets Daniel and Ezekiel that it is "we" who have sinned morally and ethically here in Nigeria, always resisting the temptation to put the blame on others. We called it *identificational* repentance: "I and my people have sinned and done wrong" (e.g., Daniel 9:5). These prayers of repentance culminated in 1995 with COCEN prayer conferences sponsored in twenty-nine of the then thirty Nigerian state capitals, plus Abuja.

Finally, in November 1997 more than 1,500 delegates came together at the International Conference Centre in Abuja for four action-packed and rewarding days. During those days the thirteen committees were expanded into workshops. They continued to discuss the three questions noted above and also deliberated on how each group could make a contribution toward a central covenant to which all could pledge allegiance. Accordingly, on the final day of the congress the *Nigeria Covenant* was completed. In a public ceremony televised around the country it was signed by all of the delegates.

The November 1997 Abuja congress was understood as the *beginning* of a drive to root out corruption in Nigeria. The foundation in prayer was highly important. The hammering out of key ethical issues was strategic. The signing of the *Nigeria Covenant* was an effective means to pledge loyalty to God and to each other. However, the tragedy of COCEN was that in the months after the 1997 congress the considerable momentum that had been gained gradually dissipated. Before this united group could begin to go forward in a step-by-step process to face the task of dismantling corruption it was allowed to die through lack of decisive leadership. One of the sad realities of the 1990s in Nigeria was that COCEN was allowed to quietly dissolve into inaction.

Now we are twenty years further down the road. Where do we stand as a nation vis-à-vis the question of corruption? As we look back we can see a number of other efforts to root out corruption in Nigeria, some of them imposed by government and others rising from below. Yet NONE of them has produced significant and lasting results and it is arguable that corruption today in Nigeria is more entrenched than at any time in the past. Today we are therefore facing two realities—we have continued to fight a progressively losing battle against rampant and systemic corruption in Nigeria, and no one appears to have a handle on how to turn things around. We talk about fighting or resisting corruption, but there are no significant signs of sustained progress. It is not a beautiful or hopeful picture.

Despite that dismal assessment, however, I remain deeply convinced that Nigeria has within its people all of the necessary ingredients to wipe out at least 95% of its corruption over a relatively short space of time—and certainly less than five years. Facing down corruption in my beloved Nigeria is not an impossible task.

Four Impediments

But why is this not happening? What is holding us back? I believe there are four major impediments that will continue to thwart the realization of the Nigeria of our dreams unless and until they are decisively dealt with and rejected.

Misplaced expectations

Our single biggest mistake in confronting the monster of corruption is our expectation that the solution will come from the top. If one looks widely in the Nigerian media and listens to the daily conversation among average Nigerians it is quite clear that virtually everyone alternatively lodges complaints of corruption against the civil government yet ironically at the same time looks to civil government to show us the way out. The belief is that if we could only get the right people in national leadership they would solve these problems. Even when it is clear that corruption is emanating from somewhere down below it is over and over again expected that the solution will come when *government* springs into effective action. I strongly believe this thinking is both illogical and delusional.

My thesis in this chapter is quite simple: *Corruption in Nigeria will never be solved from the top down. To the contrary, corruption in Nigeria could rather quickly and easily be solved from the bottom up.*

It is common knowledge that the Nigerian political system is shot through with corruption. We know that it is virtually impossible for people of deep integrity to gain positions of significant political power in the country—at virtually all levels. Even in the rare cases where people of integrity achieve positions of power they uniformly discover that there are hundreds of ways their influence for good is emasculated and silenced. In many cases they are blackmailed into complicity with the corrupt system, or they simply throw up their hands in defeat and ride out the storm. In view of this, why Nigerians continue to look to their civil government to solve the malaise of national corruption is one of the major mysteries of modern times. It is not going to happen; full stop!

I well remember the War Against Indiscipline (WAI) launched in 1983 by President Buhari and Vice President Idiagbon. They were out to stamp out corruption and indiscipline in the society. Largely by dint of military force they did achieve a number of visible results. Yet in the end those efforts were short-lived and within five years or less they were all but forgotten.

Thirty years later, after President Buhari's return to power in 2015 he eventually announced his #istandwithbuhari campaign. This was an even broader effort to stamp out corruption than what he championed in the 1980s. Through this campaign President Buhari is attempting to wipe out corruption in a top-to-bottom array of measures. He will predictably be able to make another dent in the overall problem, and perhaps go even farther than he did in the 1980s. Yet for reasons I will explain below his efforts are doomed to ultimate failure even before they are launched. The sad reality is that Nigerian corruption will never be successfully dismantled moving from top to bottom. The probability is that until we understand that reality we will be kept from searching for solutions that can truly succeed.

The Sleeping Giant

In the meantime, the one social or institutional body that would or should have the power and influence to bring about massive moral change in the country is sound asleep. I refer to the Church. There is no other institution in Nigeria that has the capacity to move the masses more than the Church. For that reason alone, if you ask me who is primarily to blame for corruption in Nigeria I will without hesitation pin it primarily on the Nigerian Church. The reason is simple: the Church is not only the single most powerful social institution in Nigeria but its very foundations are all about moral rectitude. Unlike in many other countries around the world, the influence of the Church over Nigerian society is immense. Yet every day this force is woefully squandered because the Church is sound asleep. I charge that its role in stemming the tide of corruption in this country is close to zero.

More than any other social institution, the Nigerian Church has the widespread loyalty of the masses, the *hoi poloi*. Yet regrettably the Nigerian Church long ago abdicated its power and authority to keep the nation on an even moral keel. The consequence is that today it is widely known that the same massive corruption that plagues the business, educational, military, social, legal and political worlds is also abundantly evident within the Church itself. The Church has become a toothless lion when called upon to come to the rescue.

Drunken Stupor

But it is even worse than that; the Church is not just asleep, it is drunk. Over the past forty years very broad sectors of the Nigerian Church have imbibed the poisoned Kool-Aid of the so-called Prosperity Gospel. It is worshiping the Golden Calf. Starting with neo-Pentecostal churches in the mid-1970s, the mania for money has been sanctioned as a gospel right and has spread to virtually all sectors of Nigerian Christianity. No one appears to be immune—from the Roman Catholic Church to the other mission-founded churches (Anglican, Methodist, Baptist, Presbyterian, ECWA, COCIN, etc.) to the Aladura or OAIC churches to the Pentecostals. It is stunning and sad to observe how the importation of this false teaching from America has mesmerized virtually all sectors of the

Church. The result is that the majority of the masses of Nigerian Christians have adopted a very anthropocentric attitude in which everything revolves around self—*my* prosperity, *my* health, *my* wealth, and *my* long life. The mad rush for money has been accompanied by silence on the bigger issues of national, regional and individual integrity. Corruption is not only overlooked, but also at times warmly embraced. Personal ostentation on the part of church leaders and the building of large cathedrals continue to rise as monuments to personal greed, and often funded with blood money from the growing national coffers of corruption.

Getting the Cart before the Horse

The fourth impediment that is stopping us from a solution to corruption is that many of the new-generation churches rising within the country have touted strong kingdom theology without first adequately addressing the deeper issues of their own personal and institutional integrity. They have laudably aspired to influence government with Christian values, but without first thoroughly adequately addressing the basic issues of righteousness and of corruption within their own ranks. These churches have seen many of the issues of corruption within the society and they at times have an honest desire to take a stand against corrupt governments. They are also in many cases making commendable efforts to ameliorate social conditions around them. They share a desire to get more of their own people into positions of political power. Yet they have not stopped long enough to clean house within their own ranks. The mixed multitude among them is still in very hand-in-glove engagement with the massive corruption all around us.

Three Powerful Secrets

As serious as these impediments may be, however, I remain deeply convinced that there is great hope. The truly good news is that Nigeria has all of the necessary ingredients to solve 95 per cent of its corruption problems within a period of less than five years. I believe we can all live to see a corruption-free Nigeria—not only within our lifetimes, but VERY SOON. The reason I say this is that we have three very powerful resources that if mobilized can get the job done.

Nigerians Are a Deeply Religious People with Unequaled Respect for Their Church Leaders

I have already alluded to the fact that the influence wielded by the Nigerian Church is hardly surpassed elsewhere in the world. Church involvement and church loyalty is unusually high. Church attendance is exceptionally strong. For an amazing number of Nigerians their churches command their attention and respect virtually seven days a week. There is hardly anywhere else in the world where one can see such massive engagement with crowds of tens of thousands, hundreds of thousands and even at times millions gathering for extended periods of time organized by churches.

Top church leaders in Nigeria are held in deep respect and even awe by their followers. They are given the kind of loyalty that was known in North American churches only one hundred or more years ago. The result is that whether they realize it or not these church leaders have the capacity to move their followers toward united action along whatever lines they choose. In many cases mere wishes of the leaders become instant commands to be obeyed. The bottom line is that these church leaders have more capacity to move the masses than any other leaders within the society. They are the ones who hold the keys to a massive bottom-up ethical tsunami in this country. It is quite true that virtually 100 percent of these leaders are looking inward to their constituency and do not yet appear to have seen the potential of united action across denominational lines. But once that reality is discovered and the burden for united action is awakened I believe this country will be on the road to ethical recovery.

Theological and Moral Foundations of Nigerian Christianity

Though the Nigerian Church experienced very slow growth until the 1970s its numbers have skyrocketed over the past forty-plus years. At independence in 1960 Christians constituted 30 percent of the Nigerian population. By contrast, nowadays Christians make up more than 50 percent of the country. While there is sometimes a huge disconnect between the blithe bantering of the Prosperity Gospel and the realities of the real world, the truth remains that the Nigerian Church in its origins was established on solid theological and moral foundations. The Holy Bible has had an immense impact on this country, and is more avidly read and cherished than in most other countries around the world. More than 100 years of influence from the Scripture Union has paid huge dividends in convincing the average Nigerian Christian of the truths of scripture, just to cite one potent influence. The result is that even amidst ethical and moral confusion brought on by insipient corruption there remains a strong underlying influence of morality that has not yet been wiped away. That allegiance to the scriptures and to basic Christian theology gives me great hope.

Positive Morality Within Islam and African Traditional Religion

Nigeria is a pluralistic society and clearly so with respect to religion. Islam and African Traditional Religion play important roles in the society. It is quite clear that basic morality and rejection of corruption are a part of the age-old teachings of Islam and ATR, just as they are of Christianity. The simple truth is that if Christians, Muslims and African Traditional Religionists would all be true to their own moral standards corruption in Nigeria would never survive. I am a Christian, and therefore I know how to address myself and my fellow Christians and to call all of us to be true and faithful to the tenets of our Christian faith. And I would hope that there would likewise be men and women within Islam and African Traditional Religion who would have the courage to do the very same thing. If so, Nigeria would be a nation all of us would be proud to own.

Sociological Principles We Can Count On

Despite these three powerful and hopeful factors, however, I am afraid that there is still a pervasive underlying conviction of near helplessness—if not hopelessness—on the part of the average Nigerian citizen. Nigerians are amazingly resilient people. Their passivity and fortitude in the midst of suffering and want is remarkable. There is often a calm resignation, yet ironically at the same time many are quick to express doubt, loss of hope and deep frustration. There is a sense of the nation sitting on the proverbial powder keg waiting for the indescribable blast to bring things to a conclusion. But there are two sociological principles that I believe can help spur us in the right direction.

Corruption in Nigeria can only be Arrested Through a Bottom-up Process

Our experiences over the past decades here in Nigeria have shown us that trying to tackle the monster of corruption from the top down is a hopeless approach. There are a myriad of reasons why that is true. There are not enough armaments in the country to force morality at gunpoint. While we shoot at corruption in one corner it will break out in two or three other places. Moreover, government actions that do not deal with underlying issues of character are doomed to be ineffective and short-lived. Morality cannot be legislated, but must come from the heart.

On the other hand, movements that start at the grassroots and grow and move upward have the power to utterly change a society. To cite a recent historical example (though an admittedly very negative one) think about the homosexual lobby in America. The cry for so-called "gay rights" started very quietly at the grassroots level with a very tiny minority of American citizens—far less than one percent. It may surprise some to know that even today the actual number of practicing homosexuals in America is well below five percent. Yet that tiny minority organized themselves and began making social and political noise until today the entire nation is trying to hold both themselves and other nations around the world to ransom over the demand for recognition of homosexuality and even "gay marriage." It is an amazing demonstration of the power of bottom-up movements.

It Only Takes a Small Minority

There appears to be a conviction on the part of many in Nigeria that the problem of corruption is just too overwhelming to confront. I have spoken to many highly ethical Nigerian Christians—people who would rather suffer heavy loss than to do wrong—who nonetheless believe that facing down corruption in this country is all but impossible. They believe they have a responsibility to be personally ethical, but they also believe that their voice cannot make a significant difference in such a large nation. In a country of 170 million people the impression is that the odds are stacked against those who want to do right.

However, it is important to see that scripturally, historically, and sociologically it never requires a majority to turn a society around. Rather, all it requires is a tiny minority, provided they are properly organized and effectively galvanized into action. In the scriptures one of the constant themes with the Old Testament prophets was that of *the holy remnant*. Though the entire nation might seem to be going to hell, God always preserved a righteous remnant and it was through them that salvation came. When the prophet Elijah was at his deepest point of discouragement, believing that all was lost and that perhaps he alone was faithful to God, his eyes were miraculously opened. God showed him that there were yet seven thousand others in Israel who had not bowed down to false gods.

Great movements in Church history were often sparked off by individuals or tiny minorities—all the way from Martin Luther and the Protestant Reformation to William Carey and the birth of modern missions. Social theorists assure us that in order for a given society to be thoroughly changed all that is needed is for as few as *two percent* of the population to initiate action. Only *two percent*! So my question is, do we have two percent here in Nigeria who would rather suffer serious loss than do what is ethically wrong?

My answer is a very resounding YES. Many of the most ethical people I have known in my life are among my fellow Nigerians. Nigeria may be corrupt to the core, but there are still the proverbial seven thousand who have not bowed their knees to Baal. Out of 170 million people in this nation I am sure we have at least *five percent* – and maybe even *ten percent* – who are ready to stand for an ethically pure nation without compromise, no matter what. That reality gives me enormous hope for this country.

Let me be more explicit. The renowned anthropologist Margaret Mead once said, "Never doubt that a small group of thoughtful, committed citizens can change the world. Indeed, it's the only thing that has ever happened." Over and over again in history, transformation comes as one individual, one church, and one community is changed. And it was exactly in this vein that sociologist Everett Rogers developed his Diffusion of Innovation theory in indisputably demonstrating that for an entire society to turn around or to be won to a particular perspective, behavior or life change all that was required at the outset is the activation of a mere 2%, and often less. Rogers labeled that 2% the True Innovators.

Looking at the broader picture, Rogers demonstrated that there are four types of people in normal societies— Innovators, making up 15 percent of the population (these are the people who bring new ideas and changes into societies); Early Adopters, making up 35 percent (these are the people who once an idea of change has been introduced by the Innovators will not hesitate long to get on board and adopt it); Late Adopters, making up another 35 percent (these are the people who will buy into the ideas and changes, but at a much slower and more reluctant pace), and finally Laggards, making up 15 percent (these are the people who will either adopt change very late or often never). In the first group, as I have indicated—the 15 percent who are Early Adopters, a mere 2 percent is necessary to catalyze a movement that will eventually change the entire group.

The Way Forward

So where do we go from here? How can this actually work? I suggest five important steps we can take.

STEP ONE: Identificational Repentance—Stop the Blame shifting

The pathway that we started down in the 1990s focusing on identificational repentance must be reintroduced and reinforced at the grassroots level. In many sectors of the Nigerian Church prayer over this past generation has turned much more inward and has become far too self-focused. Too often we view prayer as a formula for persuading God to give us something, even sometimes in a manipulative manner. That is not the kind of prayer that will bring us out of our ethical quagmire. We need to once again go on our knees as the prophets of old to say from the depths of our being, "We have sinned."

Nigeria has become too often obsessed with titillating stories of individual and group corruption. It is not uncommon to open our newspapers or turn on the television and learn of new charges and counter charges of embezzlement running into the billions and sometimes, even trillions of Naira. Those issues are surely tragic and no doubt should be pursued by courts competent to mete out justice. But as a people we must continue to go low before God and plead for his mercy on behalf of all of us, as a nation.

STEP TWO: Embrace the WE THE PEOPLE movement

WE THE PEOPLE is a national movement of Nigerian grassroots, engineered by committed Nigerian intellectuals and professionals of every tribe and religion, inside and outside Nigeria. This book, WE THE PEOPLE, is a teaching tool written to present the truths to all Nigerians to convince us on a new way of life that will save Nigeria. Through personal repentance and commitment to a new corrupt-free Nigeria, the group seeks to grow a new breed of WE THE PEOPLE, one person at a time, in a potent bottom-to-top movement that will wipe out corruption in Nigeria. The group firmly believes that it takes a clean bottom to change the top. Therefore the group is bent on cleaning the bottom of society as a prelude to cleaning the top. The movement is both a personal pledge to morality along the lines of ethical issues that are the most salient within our Nigerian society, and it is also a pledge to stand with others from every tribe and religion in Nigeria who have taken the same pledge. Nigeria needs a huge phalanx of attorneys who are prepared to defend anyone pro bono who stands up for justice and ethics in this country and suffers because of their stand. Many have already made such a commitment, and others can be brought in as a part of a united stand at the grassroots level.

STEP THREE: Develop a Thorough Bottom-up Strategy

Corruption in this country can only be dismantled through a step-by-step process. The development of a sane, convincing and comprehensive *strategy* for facing down corruption in Nigeria is one of the most crucial and difficult requirements in this process. Let's face it – we are talking about war, a war against corruption. It is impossible to fight a winning war without a carefully crafted strategy. Military commanders spend years studying war strategies and analyzing the famous battles of history. They know that before one engages an enemy it is absolutely essential to thoroughly understand the enemy. They must know the numerical strength of the enemy, the weapons and ammunition at their disposal, their strongholds, their characteristic tactics, their typical weaknesses and blind spots, etc. To go into battle unprepared and without knowing the enemy is foolhardy. The same thing applies to our war against corruption in this country.

A similar analogy is that of the famous African-American neurosurgeon, Dr. Ben Carson. Over his professional lifetime Dr. Carson has operated on thousands of children, including successfully separating Siamese twins conjoined at the head. In several instances he has successfully removed huge killer tumors wrapped around the spinal cord of a child. So think of the analogy of Dr. Carson facing this type of challenge – how can he remove a killer tumor entwined all around the spinal cord of a helpless child?

The only way he can succeed is through an absolutely expert strategy. It would be totally foolish for Dr. Carson to walk into the operating room without preparation and start cutting open the neck of the child, slicing here and there with his scalpel. To the contrary, he must first spend long hours studying x-rays and MRIs and looking at the tumor from all angles until he understands all of its intricacies with its hundreds of blood vessels and nerves wrapped around that threatened spinal cord. Only after he has understood the "enemy" very well will he then know how to plan his strategy including where to start the surgery and what the many steps thereafter will be. He knows he has only a few hours in which he must complete the task, and once he starts he is steadily carrying out his strategy – from start to finish.

That is precisely what we need in our battle against corruption in this country. Corruption in Nigeria is a formidable enemy. It has entwined itself around every aspect of our society. It is sucking our lifeblood out of us. But it can be dismantled, especially if we are willing to patiently develop a strategy and then to use the overwhelming power of a united grassroots movement to bring it about. We need dedicated men and women of God who understand this monster well enough to map out a step-by-step process, in every case using the power of the masses. Corruption cannot be vanquished in a single day. It must be defeated in a staged process. And with the united strength of the moral backbone of the country it can and will be done. But until we develop a careful Strategy Manual for defeating corruption we will not have a clear picture of how the battle will begin and progress and eventually conclude.

In this bottom-up movement where do we start? That is what our master strategists will have to tell us. I have mentioned thirteen social spheres that were examined in the 1990s in our Congress on Christian Ethics' efforts. Do we begin sector-by-sector – starting, e.g., with ethics in education, or ethics in business? Or do we start locally before moving nationally? Our strategy plan will tell us.

STEP FOUR: Find at Least Ten Absolutely Fearless and Selfless Religious Leaders

The development of a national strategy for confronting and dismantling corruption nationally as a grassroots movement is only likely to happen when strategic religious leaders of all

312

faiths unite to rally their people behind the movement. These must be individual leaders who fear God and who are bold enough to lead their people into this war. Here is where the power of the Nigerian Church will go on display. Regrettably, Nigerians as a whole do not have enough faith in their political leaders to follow their lead in a mass grassroots movement toward ethical behavior, yet there is an organization that can do just that—the Nigerian Church. To be candid, when I see the deep respect that is commanded by many of Nigeria's church leaders I often scratch my head in wonderment as to why they have not gotten together long before now to take a united stand against corruption.

Let me add parenthetically that I am not talking here about engaging any kind of leadership from the Christian Association of Nigeria (CAN). I am definitely not an enemy of CAN in any conceivable way, but CAN is a toothless lion in Nigeria. CAN as a body is more often than not a lowest-common-denominator political force that has never waged this kind of warfare and never will. Rather, this is a war for highly courageous leaders who can rally the masses without caring whose ox is gored.

I understand that taking a stand against corruption in the broadest sense is almost meaningless, because it is such a multifarious enemy and one does not know where to begin. But I am also deeply convinced that if church leaders would agree together in line with a very convincing step-by-step strategy that on a particular day and time they would launch an all-out war in their churches specifically against examination malpractice, or against police bribery, or against motor park touts – particularly with clear education ahead of time – these issues one-by-one could be quickly brought to a standstill. The war against police bribery, for example, would also require a united stand against depriving police of their legitimate pay.

STEP FIVE: Implement a Three-Year National Movement of WE THE PEOPLE

Fighting a war is a costly engagement. But uniting to get it done will be well worth all of the efforts it takes. When citizens right from the bottom begin by personal pledges of integrity and then begin uniting together to wipe out corruption step-by-step the war can be won.

I am fully aware that many who read my words will consider this vision as naïve and impractical. They will quickly assure us that this is a hopeless dream. That will not surprise me. They remind me of the Western Union internal memo in 1876, shortly after the invention of the telephone by Alexander Graham Bell, that said, "This 'telephone' has too many shortcomings to be seriously considered as a means of communication. The device is inherently of no value to us." But for those of us who can be brave enough to see the potential of Nigeria's single greatest resource – our massive population – I believe there is room for lots of hope. And I continue to believe that one day I will live to see a very largely corruption-free Nigeria.

CHAPTER 14

The Role of the Nigerian Youth in Building a New Nigeria through WE THE PEOPLE Movement

Gabriel Nwanze, BSc

Jemila Ibrahim, BSc

The Nigerian youth can be rightly considered as an endangered group.

Not that the world would one day wake up to discover that the Nigerian youths are no more physically present on planet earth, but indeed to be conservative, the Nigerian youths are on the verge of extinction from the scheme of things in Nigeria – socially, politically and economically. The Nigerian youth is virtually irrelevant in piloting the affairs of the country. With this trend, danger lies ahead.

Some interesting data have prompted deep thinking and reflection on the direction which Nigeria is being piloted. The country had an estimated population of 167 million people in 2012, with half of this figure - 82.5 million people – comprising youths aged between 15 and 34 years of age. Of course, the age bracket that defines youth could very well be expanded to include people slightly below the age 15 years, and those above the age 34 years, onward into the forties bracket. When this is done, the population of people classified as youths in Nigeria easily exceeds the 100 million mark. This implies that about 70 percent of Nigeria's population is severely disenfranchised socially, politically and to a very large extent, economically.

The fact that over 80 percent of Nigerians live below the poverty line, is consistent with the stark bankruptcy of economic opportunities facing the Nigerian youths.

The big question is: what are the Nigerian youths doing about this? How is the most vibrant group of people in the country responding to these challenges, abject neglect, and injustices?

It is common to get inspired, act on the spur of the moment, go out and get some things started and follow up with action. It is also common for such missions to be short-lived, creating greater disillusionment, discouragement and depression. However, failure has never been the hallmark of those who succeed.

In a world that advances at incredibly fast pace, the Nigerian youth must reinvent itself as a potent group that must participate in piloting the affairs of the country.

The time for that decision-making is NOW!

CHALLENGES

The Nigerian youth is faced with challenges that hitherto seemed superficial and harmless, but with time and constant practice (destructive indulgence), have become innate in the country, and as some believe, irredeemable, though this belief is wrong. Central challenges occur in physical, environmental and psychological dimensions, and include:

Poor Access to Economic Opportunities

Nigerian youths often tout themselves as being naturally gifted and endowed with intelligence, spirit of hard work and other virtues. Alas, proponents of this belief almost always end their high appraisals with lamentations of lack of access to opportunities that will enable the effective deployment of these gifts. Proponents are also unanimous in their conclusion about the cause of scarce opportunities. The 'culprit' is all too familiar – government.

The Nigerian youth is shut-out in national affairs, and prevented from determining their own future - their collective destiny. Frustration is heightened with the belief that the shut-out and utter neglect is deliberate, and strongly hinged on the selfishness, greed and avarice of the older members of the generation.

Poorly Equipped for Global Competitiveness

The wider impact of lack of access to opportunities within the country is the sidetracking of the Nigerian youth in global affairs. Without proper grooming and training to become relevant even locally, how can one become useful internationally? The average Nigerian youth thus, sees himself or herself from a Lilliputian perspective, relative to his/her peers in the international community. This institutionalized form of inferiority complex holds the Nigerian youth bondage from onset, and it is no surprise when Nigerians are very zealous about dismissing themselves in comparism to advanced countries, and denigrating even their most commendable efforts or those of their countrymen, choosing to find blemish in noteworthy accomplishments.

Decimated Educational System

The bedrock of intellectual development has been rapidly depleted beyond imagination. The once revered educational system that molded legendary leaders with indelible, shinning records is now a relic. In its place, is a make-shift system with great reputation for leaving students with negative memories such as victimization, sexual exploitation, commercialization of exam performance and academic degrees, cultism, incessant strikes and sit-at-home orders by school staff, low quality tutelage from ill-prepared lecturers clutching lecture notes that are laden with plagiarism, excruciating pain through lack of basic amenities within the school, very unhygienic environment and facilities that breed diseases in students, and many other bad memories.

Monetized Religious, Traditional and Social Practices

The last hope of society seems not to have been spared from the blizzard. Religious institutions that should have provided solace to a morally bankrupt and disillusioned society are themselves, struggling under the dilemma of truly defining materialism and clearly demarcating spiritual actions from mundane issues. The integrity of religious leaders has never been under greater trial and attack as at this time. Large inflow of funds, with majority of these donated by unscrupulously dirty citizens, politicians and public office holders, are welcomed with praise and enthusiasm by religious leaders, while the tainted donors are revered. The traditional institutions have not fared any better, failing to act as a storehouse for the preservation of values and customs. With the pivotal, intangible spheres of life being monetized, social practices follow suit, with the poor, being relegated to the grotesque background.

Absence of Mentorship

Mentors have played a huge but somewhat under-celebrated role in shaping the destinies of others. Several success stories portray the people at the centre, and only very few remember to backtrack a little bit, to the days of 'no beginning,' prior to the emergence of a mentor who waved the magic wand. Despite this low publicity for mentors, their irreplaceable influence can never be over-stated.

Mentorship is a key element of success by transmission, which the Nigerian youth has been so deprived of, that when a mentor does appear, he or she is seen more as a demi-god, than a simple, benevolent person trying to bring out the best in another person. It is so bad that even the mentors are sometimes scared away by the overt response and seeming over-desperation of youths, who, knowing that such an opportunity may most likely never come again, scramble for as much as they can get, before, as they fear, the mentor disappears. Such fear is natural, based on the utter lack of mentor-mentee relationships in Nigeria.

Political Instability

Unnoticed, the impact of endangering generations unborn, has taken effect in Nigeria. Much of the present-day youths had not been born when the first military coup took place in the country. Sustained struggle for leadership, bastardization of the polity and jeopardizing life itself became the order of the day, despite numerous warnings that generations unborn would pay dearly for these despicable acts of sabotage. Now, many still wonder where it all went wrong, how the nation "suddenly" found itself in quagmire, and why the present generation of Nigerian youths is suffering very much.

Failure does not occur in one fell swoop. In steady installments, callous irresponsible leaders and politicians have nibbled the wealth of Nigeria away.

The Revenge Mentality

Many Nigerian youths have shown worrisome tendencies to be much more corrupt and inefficient than the very leaders they criticize. I have heard many youths say things like: "Don't worry, it will soon be our turn," or defend those looting the national treasury, on the grounds that God placed the culprits there and would one day, place them too in similar or even better positions, where they would outdo past thievery and out-steal others in record style. There is no need to debunk such erring mindsets in this piece, for such mundane thoughts are self-judgmental. The unfortunate reality is that the vicious cycle of what can be termed as "revenge-corruption" has been deeply etched in the minds of many Nigerian youths, who now see the occupation of leadership positions as answers to prayer for delivery from poverty and rapid elevation to endless wealth.

Sadly, the very impressive display of intelligence, energy, zeal and supposed vision may in the end, be a means to a selfish end; one that seeks to place the fighter and famed future hope at the apex of affairs, not for selfless service to the people as promised, but as personally ordained reward for well orchestrated deceit.

Absence of Structured Youth Leadership

The Nigerian youth cannot shove all the blame to others. The youth have equally fallen short in areas that they should not. An example is the clear absence of a central, dynamic, all-encompassing organizational structure that EFFECTIVELY addresses the social, political and economic fate of the youths in Nigeria.

The youths who should be at the fore front of establishing this very tasking but very profitable structure, are immersed in strengthening the establishment that undermines their destinies, by flocking around corrupt social and political leaders, seeking their attention and offering their unsolicited services to act as servants to the very people they despise and cry against.

Some youths are quick to justify this immorality and unholy alliance by claiming that they must first eat to stay alive and then fight the good fight, while others claim they are engaged in such acts based on the misguided assurance that one does not fight a battle by remaining outside the battlefield, and the illusion that they are going to eventually get what belongs to them. While the battlefield hypothesis appears logical, the motivation is simply self-aggrandizement and a sickening desire to secure selfish space and get the fabled slice of the national cake, for purely personal selfish motives. Many youths have therefore become traitors to their objectives.

IMPACT

These daunting challenges have had profound impact on the Nigerian youth, and mitigated positivity and progress. Core effects are presented:

Altered Focus

A remarkably growing number of Nigerian youths live for the day, because they have been gently nudged away from the right path, little by little, by seemingly good alternatives to their goals and dreams, on the basis that such alternatives were only temporary or 'in the meantime,' while 'focus' is maintained on the primary goal. With time, temporary measures become permanent alternatives, and the youths are urged to thank God for whatever situation they find themselves in, with comparison drawn from less fortunate youths in poor countries who are supposedly wallowing in worse conditions. The youths continue to wave goodbye to their destined paths in this subtle manner, jumping ship with regards to their original objectives, and clustering the career paths of others, in the process, over-populating sectors they have no business in, and distracting others from their own vision. In this way, the youths experience constant change in their vision and mission, as they reinvent themselves whenever the occasion calls, or are advised to "tighten their belts" or to "shape up or ship out."

Have you compared the professional career outlook of specific youths over a period of time? Have you observed that their focus is hardly ever constant? The youths have been compelled by the system, to take what is available at any given point in time. In other words, the system echoes to their sub-conscious, the words, "Be wise: take the money and run!"

Day dreaming

Day dreaming often seems harmless, but in the light of national emergencies, the impact could be colossal. The mind and creativity of the dreamer is held captive by surreal ideas and innovations. The Nigerian youth takes consolation in his strong mental and psychological soothing balm, and destroys the ability to envision with realistic boundaries.

The precious power to envision has been replaced with a make-belief compartment that has over-shadowed productive imagination. Professional and career visioning are replaced with day dreaming and building very impressive castles in the air.

Low Selfesteem

Disillusionment, self-doubt and feelings of inadequacy set in. The youths begin to see nothing good in Nigeria, and consider all other citizens of the world better than they are, in some way. To make up for these, various "defense mechanisms" are adopted, such as illusionary lifestyles and the copy-cat mentality, whereby, Nigerian youths erode their culture and imitate lifestyles and ideologies of residents of other countries that they consider more prosperous, and in some cases, even those that the world has generally acknowledged to be far less prosperous than Nigeria. It is often sad to hear things like: "At least, they have light (stable power supply)," "they have good roads, unlike us," etc, and other denigrating comments like: "Why not? They are human beings, unlike us." Unfavorable impressions of the national image have dragged the self-image so low that psychological escape routes from reality are invented.

Distorted Aspirations

Some years ago, the saying: "if you don't get what you want, then want what you get," dominated the media and mindset of Nigerians within the country. This poisonous saying was happily propagated by several *bad-leaders*, because it was tailor-made for their purposes. What else could very easily console the increasingly disillusioned populace, and reorient them to think around themselves and forget about the shared national wealth?

Like magic, this mentality trickled down rapidly to virtually every facet of life in the country. For instance, the education system boosted this notion, with well qualified students being offered admission to study courses they never heard of in some cases, effectively derailing them from their destined paths in life.

Lack of Confidence in the Elders

The youths readily assert that they are in a battle, not with strangers, but with people in the older generation. With the battle line drawn between the older generation (elders) and the younger generation (youths) in Nigeria, trust and confidence in the traditional roles to be played by elders have naturally disappeared.

Loss of Values

With no one to pass on the time-tested moral teachings of old, due to the raging war declared by the youths on the elders, values diminish, and morality exits through the back door. The youths feel they have been left to survive on their own, so are answerable to no one, and listen to nothing said by the elders. As a result, the good ones among the elders are ignored and so are their teachings. No institution is spared – the traditional, religious and social institutions are all declared as enemies of progress. The youths are forced into unguided rebellion and ultimately, self-destruction. With the current state of youths, Nigeria is sitting on a ticking time bomb.

The New You, The New Nigeria

The challenges are not insurmountable. Individuals like you and I are what constitute the life and soul of Nigeria. We have the power to determine our collective destiny. If Nigeria must actualize its potential, then the citizens must guide the nation through this path. YOU are the Nigeria that you so often hear about.

Self Realization

You were born for a purpose. Your journey to earth was not commissioned in error; neither is your sojourn a mistake. God does not make mistakes.
The questions you must now ask yourself are:
"Who am I?"
"What is my mission on Earth?"
"What did I come to this world to accomplish?"

"What things must I achieve in life?"
"How do I achieve these things?"
"When will I achieve these things?"
"Why must I achieve these things?"

You must have a clear picture of who you are and where you want to be in order for the right sense of purpose to be established in you. Your objectives must be very clear and very precise. Narrow down your self-search in the following way:
"Who can I work with to achieve my mission on earth?"
"How can I start this from my homeland, Nigeria?"

These soul-searching questions are reminiscent of a potentially great leader.
You must realize who you are and what your potentials are, before replicating this in a wider setting, where you will inspire and guide others. Every journey has a starting point, and the journey to a successful "you" starts with "you!" Likewise, the journey to a successful Nigeria starts with "you!" You must know yourself and the unchangeable laws of success, so you can experience success and lead others aright. Self-realization is a critical first step that the Nigerian youth has lacked, or probably not generally aware of. It is not enough to say conventional things such as Nigerian youths are hardworking, intelligent, determined, and all the good virtues that come alongside. For positive change to occur, character should be narrowed down along specific, individual lines, in order to produce a homogenous thought-process in the bid to attain a paradigm shift.

Clear Objectives and Unbroken Focus

A studied outlay of yourself and your objectives will inspire you to focus on the things you need to do in order to achieve those objectives. Objectives can be categorized as short-term, medium term and long-term. Short term objectives are concerned with present and near-future targets, medium term objectives focus more on fairly longer periods for goal attainment, while long term objectives focus on distant time periods. For you to strengthen your present focus, you need to specify your short-term objectives. For you to *significantly* strengthen your present focus, you need to understand your medium term objectives. For you to *fully* strengthen your short-term focus, you need to understand your long term objectives.

Long term objectives are very futuristic and sometimes spanning through life; objectives that you achieve and continue to expand and to build upon, all through your life. The level at which you maintain your focus on present activities determine how strong your focus will be on future activities. Once you are able to maintain an appreciable level of focus from onset, the greater tendency is for you to increase such level of focus, so long as you abide by all the factors required to keep you focused. Factors such as knowledge of your intents and your desired career destination increase your motivation towards success.

Be firm and forthright in your self-assessment. Know what you are drawn strongest to, and begin to map out strategies to actualize you goals. You may or may not go straight away to become active in your "missionary field" or in other words, in the specific task which you have come to earth to accomplish. Chances are that you will begin life just like everybody else and go through the academic system, get a job or start business and have a financial foothold in life before you venture into your chosen mission.

It is important to define your goals. Don't let feelings or emotions determine your decisions, neither should pleasure, fun or excitement be your yardstick. Your hobby may or may not be your destined field. Questions abound, but the crucially important first step is to identify who you are, what you and where you were meant to be on the planet in order to contribute your much-awaited quota to the advancement of humanity.

Build Positive Self Esteem

Low self-esteem propels feelings of unworthiness, inner wretchedness and inadequacy, among several negative traits. Once you arrive at this low point, it becomes easy for you to fall under the negative control of other people, because you believe that such association will provide the supposedly much needed climb and boost in social circles, or in public opinion about you. In this situation, you are drawn towards those who you have considered to be among the most acceptable people in society, who everyone loves, admires and in some cases, are afraid of, with the hope that when people see you in their company, they will naturally spread same love, admiration and reverence to you also. This is hardly ever the case.

People are assessed and judged by their individual qualities, and not based on the qualities of others. If a new person, who has never known or seen you before, comes across you and your group of friends, it will not take much time for the person to spot the differences in each individual in the group. The umbrella impression does not last long. In due time, each person's character, talent, ability and mind-set will be differentiated. This is why it is essential for you to develop your unique character and personality, because you already have a unique character and personality different from any other person on earth. Personalities can be similar, but never exactly the same.

Dedicate your thoughts and energy to something more purposeful, something along the line of discovering more of your good qualities and developing such qualities, and then working with a group that will provide the platform for you to unleash your potential on the world to positively transform society.

Take Steps Towards Self-Actualization

Having undergone the priceless experience of self-realization, and caught the precious glimpse of your future manifestation, you must now take the next step and enumerate your goals with reference to the positive development of Nigeria. Write them down and store them in your file, or in your email folder, so that you do not lose them. Your goals must be brief, clear and precise. In addition to your goals, write down your mission statement and your vision.

After stating your goals, your mission and your vision, proceed to write down how each of these goals can be accomplished, to the best of your knowledge. After this, write down things you know that prevent you from attaining these goals, and write down why you think these things will prevent you from attaining your goals. Afterwards, proceed to write down the antidotes to the problems you have specified.

Tackle these problems within you, and proffer solutions to the problems. If you need to speak to higher sources, then do not hesitate to do so as a matter of life and future happiness, and of success or failure. Do not take this lightly. Do not regard it as an ordinary exercise, or as something you are doing for the fun of it. This is serious business, because the decisions you make today will definitely affect many lives in the future. The issue is, "will such lives be affected positively or negatively after they have encountered you?"

Your influence in society is inescapable. This being the case, such influence must be deliberately structured to be positive, as extensive as possible, and importantly, enduring.

Proceed to the next step, by enumerating the central challenges in Nigeria. Take note of the word "central" because problems could in many instances, be innumerable. Central problems thus, encase sub-problems, and provide ease of unified solutions. After this, outline the solutions to each of the central challenges that Nigeria is facing. Finally, define the roles that you will play in making these solutions a reality.

Outline the Good and the Bad

What are the major influences in your life? Let's start with the human being, because this is the central source of influence. Human beings are indeed, a very wide field to select from, when considering the entirety of humans and the existence of billions scattered all over the world. To enhance efficacy, narrow down the spotlight on humans to the people all around you, and to the people who you have come across in life, and to those who you know that very soon, you will come across. We have already created three categories: the first category comprises the people you have met in the past. The second category is those you are presently associating with, and the third, the people you will meet in the future. These are the three categories of people that form your human influence circle all through your life on earth.

Quickly expanding this circle of influence, we delimit the human encounters from people you have physically met, are meeting or will meet, to include people who you have met, are meeting or will meet through virtual means. More than anything, technology has enhanced this: the people you have met on television and other audiovisual means, the people, you have met through their words in form of music, sermons, speeches and messages, the people you have met through every medium in life, have all affected you in different ways and in different degrees, no matter how minimal. All these physical and virtual people you have met are the major influences which have produced who you are today; who you see when you look at the mirror, and whose voice you hear when you meditate. With this awesomely, overwhelming influence of humans upon your life and entire existence on earth, will it be an overstatement to say that humans are important in shaping your life and your destiny? Rather than being an overstatement, this is rather a gross understatement.

Name Game

Practical steps are unavoidable in the quest for self-reconstruction and self-development. Writing and/or typing is invaluable at this point. Write down the names of the top twenty people who you are closely associating with, and proceed to classify each one of them under specified categories of influence types which they have on you.

Think hard and think deep. Get all the names written down, both for people close to you and those who are not really that close, but who you meet regularly.

Match Those Names

All the names you have written down and categorized have to be screened by no other person but you. Match the names of each of the people you have written down, with the effects they have had on you. Beside each name, write the capital letter "G" for "good", for those who have had good influence and impact on you; "B" for "bad", for those who have had bad influence and impact on you and "SW" for "Still Watching", if you are not yet through with analyzing a particular person, character or personality, and the subject's degree of influence on you, assuming you are just getting to know the person, or else, there is no way someone can really be active in your affairs for a considerable period of time without you honestly and accurately assessing the person's impact on you.

Weights and Measures

For the ones marked "G", turn over to a fresh sheet of paper and write out the heading "Good Influence" at the top section of the paper, and then write the names marked "G" on the sheet of paper. After writing out the names, proceed to rate each of the persons involved, on a scale of 1 to 10. The scale should be such that 1 is the lowest score and 9 the highest possible score. 1 will be the lowest score rather than zero, because it is not possible for someone to have zero impact on you. The level of impact can be extremely minimal, but cannot be non-existent. This is why 1 is the lowest possible score in this impact assessment, as it has to do with human personality and character, and not on an abstract, non-living thing for which the impact occurrence of zero is possible. 9 will be the highest possible score, because we are assessing human beings who are imperfect. There is no way someone can have perfectly good impact on you, because where such is the perception, disappointment can be devastating. No human being is perfect, and so, no one's impact upon you can receive maximum marks, because you are a different person from such a nice individual.

After allocating scores to each of the names on your "Good Influence" category, do the same allocation of scores on another fresh sheet of paper, for the names graded as "B." For the names graded as "SW", give yourself two weeks to scrutinize such persons and transfer their names either to the "G" category or to the "B" category after this time period.

Decision Day

Things have now reached crunch time. It is not going to be easy deciding to make drastic changes in your life, but it is very necessary to do this if you want to succeed in life. The decisions are simple and straight-forward, as there are mainly two decisions to make:

1. Who will you continue to associate with, and who will you discontinue association with?
2. What kind of people will you look out for in your future associations with an intention of getting closer to them, and what kind of people will you avoid?

You must be firm and resolute in your decision-making, and most of all, you must be thoroughly sincere and truthful to yourself about what is good and bad for the goals you have set in life.

Do not mix these decisions with emotions. Use frank and totally honest yardsticks for determining who to hang out with, stick with, be friends with, converse with and be close to. Do not let bias or sentiment becloud your sense of judgment, neither must preference for one person be the main influence over another, based on frivolities and things that have little gain but perhaps, much pleasure, fun and enjoyment. If you take the right decisions, you will most likely be happy for the rest of your life, after going through initial pain as a price and as a natural process towards attaining high standards. No pain, no gain, remember?

High standards are the only way out through the doors of failure and into the doors of success. It is really a choice about remaining happy at the moment and sad for the rest of your life, or remaining "sad" at the moment and remaining happy for the rest of your life. The "sadness" is of course, not sadness that destroys and brings down, but rather sadness that builds and uplifts. In the real sense, this sadness is not really sadness in its actual sense, because you are going through training. If you choose to enjoy the experience, then what is the place of sadness in this? It may very well be stocking up a great and rewarding payday for yourself while having fun in the process.

Do Not Compromise

Be firm in your resolve to become the best you ought to be and to lift others, who will join you in lifting Nigeria. Refusing to compromise means not going back on your word and decision, and not, after a little while, going back to get involved with the very same people you separated yourself from, and doing the very same things you decided not to do anymore. What is the need stirring the hornet's nest when you do not intend to maintain change? An old saying goes thus: "Never start what you can't finish." You have made a decision and you are not going back. Those who wish you well are not going to let you go back, starting from yourself.

YOU are not going to let YOU go back. Yes, the real you is on the inside and the real you wants you to move forward. What you see in the physical world is not the real you, because you are a spirit being. Strengthen your inner self; your true self, and prepare to change the world for the better, starting with your country.

Forget what you see and what you feel, and what you think you're missing. Forget what little loss you may have suffered, or what little isolation or hostility you may be facing and what mockery or teasing that may be thrown your way. All these will not last. All these do not have the stamina and the staying power which your resolve and your decisions have. Hold on; stay on; do not waver; do not look back. You are on a new track and cannot be detracted by detractors. Instead, be motivated by motivators and not be demotivated by demotivators.

Be firm and steadfast. Develop that inner stamina and mental toughness. Be resolute in spirit and do not let mockery, jeers or negative calls deter you from your path, or skid you off from the road towards attaining glory in the future. Those same people, who laughed at you in the past, or are mocking you in the present, will struggle to kiss your feet in the future.

Success is not by birth but by fruitful training. Prior to the training, conscious effort must be made to absorb and apply all the lessons learnt, or the training will not be worthwhile, neither will it be fruitful. Going through a process is not enough; the process must also go through you. Do not lose sight of the big picture and you will always be grateful you stayed strong and remained focused.

Firm, enduring decisions begin in the heart. Resolve to be who you are, or who you want to be. Envision the temptations that will come your way and decide in advance, how you will respond to these.

Live out your words. Practice what you preach. Be a stayer and doer. Nigeria can never be great without each person doing the right thing in his or her own little way.

Believe

Do you believe in the assertion that Nigeria can become the best it ought to be?
Do you believe that you will play a role in actualizing the great objectives of Nigeria's founding fathers? Do you believe in yourself, strong enough to be at the fore in extracting the potentials of Nigeria, Africa's giant and the gem of the Black world, even though the country has been so mismanaged that it has lost grasp of its calling and leadership role in the

comity of nations?

NIGERIA NEEDS YOU

Do not turn your back on your country. Work with others to salvage this great country and restore its destiny.

Join The Right Movement

WE THE PEOPLE is a movement of serious minded Nigerians who want to create a new Nigeria by growing a new breed of grassroots in Nigeria who can clean up Nigeria from the bottom to top, one person at a time. The movement cuts across every boundary—tribal, religious, sex, age, language, culture, political party, and economic status. WE THE PEOPLE have come to the conclusion that none of the existing political parties - PDP, APC, and others has the will, moral convictions, selflessness, and capacity to save Nigeria from its current decadence. Unfortunately, the present day grassroots in Nigeria are corrupt, and divided by tribal, religious, and political party differences and affiliations. This is a major part of the problem of perpetuation of decadence in Nigeria. The WE THE PEOPLE movement has set out to find and grow a new breed of patriotic Nigerian grassroots who will put national pride in a new corrupt-free Nigeria above all tribal, religious, and political party differences. As long as the unfortunate and primitive mindset of tribal, religious, and political party affiliations persists in Nigeria, WE THE PEOPLE of Nigeria will continue to suffer a great handicap, and will never be able to come together to rid Nigeria of all the bad eggs who are destroying Nigeria. Imagine for one minute a Nigeria in which 50 million new breed of WE THE PEOPLE bond together, without any tribal, religious, political party affiliations or considerations. Their only goal and purpose is a new, corrupt-free Nigeria. They are united, and they speak and act with one voice. Through their vote, they can decide who the next president, the governors of every state, members of the national assembly will be; they will flush out all the bad eggs in government, and create a new, corrupt-free Nigeria. The fundamental requirement to become a member of the new WE THE PEOPLE movement is to first commit as a person to shun corruption in your life, become law abiding, remove tribal, religious, political party considerations totally away from your mind. Genuinely resolve to embrace all members of the new WE THE PEOPLE movement as your brothers and sisters. Nigeria needs you through the new WE THE PEOPLE movement. Details of how to sign-up and become a member of the new WE THE PEOPLE is provided at the end of this book. Talk to your friends and family members about joining the new breed of WE THE PEOPLE, but you must emphasize the personal commitments and discipline required to become a member. One person at a time, the goal is to grow a new breed of WE THE PEOPLE who will work together to clean up Nigeria from bottom to top.

The Nigerian youth has a very important role to play in this movement. Rather than worry about corrupt Governors, national assembly members, and other leaders and politicians, make the required necessary commitments to become a member of the new breed of WE THE PEOPLE, and work with them to flush out all the bad eggs through the vote of WE THE PEOPLE. Do not worry about the evil deeds of the corrupt politicians anymore, instead, join the national movement of the new breed of WE THE PEOPLE to flush out all corrupt politicians everywhere. With a population of 100 million youths in Nigeria, if one out of every two Nigerian youths will join this important movement, Nigerian youths alone will provide the 50 million people needed in the new WE THE PEOPLE movement to change Nigeria into a new, corrupt-free, vibrant, and just nation. But we need a clean bottom to clean the top permanently. Will you be a part of that clean bottom? How many of your friends and family members can you convince to be part of the clean bottom? Nigerian youths have the required numbers and power to clean up Nigeria through the WE THE PEOPLE movement. We can have a new Nigeria that makes sense, a new Nigeria where the youths can participate in government, a new

Nigeria where social justice, rule of law, opportunities for unlimited youth development, economic growth, security, functional utilities and infrastructure will be abundant part of daily normal life.

CHAPTER 15

The New Breed of WE THE PEOPLE: Cultivating the Spirit and Mindset of Excellence in the Nigerian Youths/Grassroots

Prof. Peter U. Nwangwu Pharm.D PhD FACCP FASCP

Introduction

We all have one life to live. There is no such thing as reincarnation, which has never been documented or proven. Rather, we know clearly and with great certainty from scientific evidence that the DNA content of each person that has ever lived is unique and characteristic of that person. So if no two people have shared the same DNA content since human life started on planet earth, then no two people are the same from reincarnation. You have only one life, one chance, one opportunity. If you blow away your life, that is it. No repeat performance. Our life is a precious gift from God; what we make of it is a gift to our society and fellow humans, and an expression of gratitude to God who invests gifts and talents in humans for the purpose of blessing the human race with our gifts and talents.

What you make out of your life depends on what you put into your life to develop it and enrich it with skills, knowledge, wisdom, and professional competence. The development of a life is like the building of a house. In building a house you need an architectural plan, a solid foundation, good building materials, and fine finishing details. Let us consider these four elements of building a house, as illustration of what is needed in the development of the mindset and spirit of excellence in the new breed of WE THE PEOPLE, in a new democratic and progressive Nigeria.

Architectural Plan:

Anybody building a good house today needs an architectural plan. The more thoughtful and detailed the plan, the better the outcome of the finished product. You cannot build a house by chance or guess work. Similarly, the new Nigerian youth must have a development plan. If the development of any life is by guesswork or accident, the quality of the finished human product is often undesirable.

Parents have enormous responsibilities to help their children have a good development plan. A father must provide the needed leadership for his family, and create the proper opportunities to help their children give proper thought and planning for the development of their lives. When a father does not have enough awareness to provide this leadership in the home, a mother must take control and help their children give proper thought and plans to the development of their lives. One of the great drawbacks to the new women movement, either in politics or whatever other roles they choose to pursue is that the children may be abandoned like sheep without shepherd. The adverse cost to the family unit, and to society at large is tremendous and most unfortunate. The new Nigerian youth, regardless of the orientation and sense of duty of father and mother, has ultimate responsibility to have a thoughtful and carefully developed plan for the building of his or her life. Perhaps a responsible teacher, or a mentor, can help you think through things and guide you. Such plans must include proper education plans, development of good culture and manners, social and professional skills, patriotism, sense of duty, self-control, discipline, and responsibility, entrepreneurial skills, love of God and fellow humans. Development plans are usually dynamic, and can change in the light of new information and goals.

Solid Foundation

Nobody builds a good house on the sand. Any good building requires a good, solid foundation. The more solid the foundation, the more the building lasts. The new Nigerian youth cannot build his or her life on sand. All that glitters are not gold. The new Nigerian youth must go beyond the glitter, and find real gold for his or her life. You have one life to live. You must build it properly on the solid foundations of life, or it will collapse when the winds of life blow. The winds of life will most certainly blow at different stages of your life. How solid is your foundation to withstand those winds of life when they blow?

Good Building Materials

Any thoughtful builder is very concerned about the quality of the building materials they use in building their house. A good builder wants original materials, not fake materials. Fake materials such as plastic plumbing materials expire and crumble in the course of time, creating a great nightmare of plumbing havocs in the finished building in the course of time. The new Nigerian youth cannot build his or her life with fake materials. There are many fake materials and fake people out there in the world. Stay away from fake materials and fake people as you build your life. As they say in America, "Garbage in, Garbage out". If you build your life with garbage, you will become Mr. Garbage or Miss Garbage, unfit for society and useless to your fellow humans.

Fine Finishing Details

The quality and appeal of a finished house includes the choice of fine finishing details. Remember that fine finishing details is a matter of choice; but it shows. The new Nigerian youth must have the appetite for good choice of fine finishing details in the development of his or her life. If you are a fine polished gentleman or lady, it shows. You become delightful, thoughtful, pleasant to be around, with impeccable character, excellent mindset, and attractive and adorable disposition.

SOME PRACTICAL STEPS TOWARDS THE GOAL

1. *Never stop learning.* The moment you ever feel that you have arrived, that you now know it all, perhaps because you got your Ph.D., you have failed. Be teachable—always. There is so much to learn in life, and from life. Expand your horizon, and learn new things daily. Some of the best things you learn in life about life may come from unexpected people and places. It was the scientist Galileo who once said, "I have never met a man so ignorant that I could not learn something from him."

2. *Have an educated mindset.* Make informed and educated decisions and choices. Do not be gullible, fetish, superstitious, vain or irrational in what you think or believe. Act based on facts and truths, not gossips or speculations. Hate tribal and religious bigotry and prejudice. Many tribal and religious problems in Nigeria today stem from bigotry, prejudice, and uneducated mindset, without truth or fact. Such bigotry and prejudice are like potent poisons that destroy human lives and relationships. The new Nigerian must have an educated mindset, and must always act based on established truth and facts, not on tribal or religious bigotry and prejudice.

3. *Develop simple appetites in life, and shun a life of ostentation.* Nigerians are notorious for a life of ostentation, to show off their wealth, most of the time ill-gotten and stolen wealth. Such life is vain and empty; refuse to be part of it. Several years ago, I was on a business trip to Luxemburg, a small country near France. The following morning, I went downstairs to the hotel restaurant to have breakfast. I was at a table eating when a young business lady from Austria, with her breakfast, approached my table and asked if she could join me at the table. "Certainly", I responded. We were in conversation, and then she asked me, "Where are you from?" I answered, "Nigeria". Then she said, "ooooh, Nigeria, those people who buy

television before they get electricity!" Inside me, I felt like asking, "how did you know?" But I didn't. I simply muttered with a fake serious face, "don't insult my country!" But let me ask you the reader, is it not true in Nigeria that some people buy television before they get electricity, only so they can show off their television as a sign of wealth?

4. *Learn and exercise the discipline of delayed gratification, as a daily habit in life.* Everything comes to him who waits. You do not do things, or buy things, merely because the opportunity to do them is there, or because the desire to do them is there. Certain pleasures in life should wait for the right time and the right circumstances in the view of God's plan for man, as taught by responsible godly religious leaders, and advocated through the opinion of informed decent men and women of integrity in society. Respect your informed conscience and your educated personal convictions, regardless of what the crowd is doing. Sometimes in life, less is more; the discipline of delayed gratification will carry you far in life, and will bless and reward your life abundantly.

5. *Humility is better than pride and arrogance;* therefore, embrace humility.
   Humility is a virtue, pride is a vice, a terrible vice that literally makes your life stink. The manufacturer of a popular shoe polish in America branded it, "Pride— the self-polishing wax". Self-polishing in Nigeria has advanced to incredible heights, and will be found in men and women of all ages and socio-economic class. The art of self-polishing originates from a state of psychological insecurity. Those who are sure of themselves and at peace with themselves do not self-polish. Only in Nigeria have I seen people introduce themselves as pharmacist Garuba, engineer Ademola, surveyor Edet, or veterinary surgeon Egodinma. What is wrong with, "my name is Peter Nwangwu"?

6. *Be reliable, trustworthy, honorable, honest and dependable as a personal tradition and life style.* Let

your yes be YES, and let your no be NO. Put your whole cards on the table always, and play your cards with open hands. Consistently uphold your integrity, even at a personal cost. Do not break the trust of another human who trusted in you. "Sorry" works when a mistake is made, but not when trust is broken. So in life, make mistakes but never break trust, because forgiving may be easy, but forgetting and trusting again is often impossible.

7. *Have a personal identity and strength of character that defines you, and learn to love yourself.* It was Maxwell Maliz who said, "if you make friends with yourself, you will never be alone". And Sheila Murray Bethei said, "One of the most courageous things you can do is identify yourself, know who you are, what you believe in, and where you want to go". Mark Twain advised, "Whenever you find yourself on the side of the majority, it is time to pause and reflect". Sometimes leaders must stand alone, and make difficult and honest informed decisions based on doing the right thing from the true convictions of their heart. A man who wants to lead and conduct the orchestra must turn his back on the crowd.

8. *Develop healthy life styles.* Work hard to maintain healthy eating habits, that includes balanced meals and fruits. Avoid fast foods and fatty greasy meals. Have good exercise and relaxation programs, including consistent regular work out schedule. Invest in a few good friends who are trustworthy. In the words of Pachaudhari, "two things define you in life: your patience when you have nothing, and your attitude when you have everything".

9. *In your job, become indispensable through hard work, honesty, creative initiatives, and going beyond the call of duty to advance and propel your company.* The man who does more than he is paid, will soon be paid for more than he does. In the words of George Halas, "Nobody who ever gave his best regretted it".

10. *Be an entrepreneur if you can.* Several years ago, the

professor in a business class at an American university asked the students to write a proposal on a new good business idea. One of the students thought it will be good to have a courier company who can do next day mail delivery. The professor described his proposal as dumb, and gave him a very poor grade on that course. The student was offended, and eventually went on to establish Federal Express, the first courier next day mail delivery service. He became a multimillionaire, while his professor was still at the university earning about $60,000 a year. In the words of the U.S army general, Collin Powell, "There are no secrets to success. It is the result of preparation, hard work, and learning from failures". Milton Berle once said, "if opportunity doesn't knock, build a door". And Conrad Adenauer stated, "We didn't have a single chance, but we used it". As an entrepreneur, if it is to be, it is up to you. You make it happen, through preparation, hard work and learning from failures. As part of your professional development plans, you may consider getting an advanced degree to facilitate your career development. Perhaps you should consider academic environments outside Nigeria as one option if possible, to propel your academic and professional development.

11. *All that glitters are not gold.* Learn how to separate noise from the real thing. There is a lot of noise and glitter around you. The world around you, and people in the world will lie to you every day. Will you be a victim of the lies, noise and glitter, or can you read in-between the line, and control your destiny?

CONCLUSION

As the saying goes, "As you make your bed, so must you lie on it". You have one life to live. Make it a beautiful and productive life. Have a good plan for building your life, build your life on a solid foundation, use good building materials, not fake materials, and choose fine finishing details to enrich the appeal of your life. Nigeria badly needs a new breed of WE THE PEOPLE, men and women of integrity who will clean Nigeria from bottom-to-top, one person at a time in the important work of building a new breed of fine, honest, and corrupt-free Nigerians. May God bless Nigeria through the gracefulness of a new breed of WE THE PEOPLE.

CHAPTER 16

Transforming the Nigerian Educational System for a More Prosperous and Progressive Nigeria

Prof Peter U. Nwangwu, MSc Pharm.D PhD FACCP FASCP

Introduction

A senior lawyer asked a junior lawyer in his chambers why an assignment he gave him was not executed. The junior lawyer replied, "I forgotted." This is a true story and it is not an isolated event. Data from the Nigerian Universities Commission (NUC) shows that only about 23% of students who enter Nigerian Universities have a credit pass in English language and Mathematics. With very poor foundation from the secondary schools nationwide, most of our university students are poorly equipped for focused and productive intellectual academic pursuits. Many buy passing grades from unscrupulous lecturers with money and sex. Therefore, many university graduates in present day Nigeria are just like the junior lawyer who "forgotted" to do the assignment that was given to him.

But our problems as a nation are even worse. Apart from an overwhelming number of adult illiterates numbered at over 40 million, 90.8 percent of eligible early childhood students, 30 percent of primary school children, 65 percent of Junior Secondary School children and 61 percent of senIor Secondary School children are out of school, deprived of the benefits of education in a country where the Constitution demands free and compulsory basic education as a mandatory law of the land.

An illiterate population is a fertile breeding ground for terrorists, tribalists, and dangerous gullible, volatile superstitious miscreants in society who can be manipulated by disgruntled elements to ferment and ignite great havoc in society. Nigeria therefore direly needs to educate her citizens throughout the country as a matter of great priority. A revised education curriculum that includes the study of the Nigerian Constitution at all levels of education will be a potent tool for nation building. Great national values such as Democracy, Social Justice, Equality, Non-tribalism, Human Dignity, Accountability, Rule of Law, Respect for Diversity and Tolerance, can be taught as part of the educational curriculum and brought to life in the classroom in a manner that will transform each student into a valuable and decent citizen, permanently.

Specific problems and road blocks in our current educational system have been highlighted and discussed briefly in this chapter. A number of these problems and issues can be dissolved over the next four years to bring true sanity to our educational system, and to our national life and polity.

Some Specific Problems with the Nigeria Educational System

1. *The Problem of Mass Failure in WAEC*

The following data from the West African Examination Council (WAEC) on the performance of students nationwide in WASSCE over a six-year period revealed that the percentage of students with five credits including English and Mathematics ranged from 27.53 percent in 2005 to 13.76 percent (2008).

Performance in WASSCE, 2005-2010 (Source: WAEC)

Year	No. of Cndidates	% with 5 Credits including English & Mathematics
2005	1,091,676	27.53
2006	1,184,348	15.56
2007	1,275,330	25.54
2008	1,369,142	13.76
2009	1,373,009	25.99
2010	1,351,557	24.94

The NUC and WAEC reported percentages nationwide include data from private and exceptional schools where students generally do well. If you isolate private school excellent result from the above data, it should not be difficult to understand the tragedy in our public schools where most Nigerian students receive their education.

Education in Nigeria is structured in three tiers: Basic Education, Secondary School education, and Tertiary education. Traditional Basic education offered to children between ages 3 and 14 in Nigeria consist of 3 years of early child care and development education, 6 years of primary education and three years of Junior Secondary education. Non-traditional Basic education includes educational outreach to nomadic and migrant children, Almajirais and mass literacy intervention. Traditional Basic education is followed by 3 years of Senior Secondary School and then Tertiary education.

Solution to the Problem of Mass Failure in WAEC

The problem that shows up as mass failure in WAEC every year is only a symptom of a bad disease that was there all along which could have been diagnosed and treated by standardized and nationwide exam from Junior Secondary school (JS1). Academic weakness of the students will be detected earlier. Poor performing teachers whose students do poorly on the standardized exam will be warned and assisted to do better; but if the teacher continues to perform poorly, s/he will be replaced. There will be no more automatic promotion. The performance of each student on the standardized national exam or a local repeat exam after remedial studies will be a factor in promotion to the next class. If, at every level of their educational experience, both teachers and students put in the same level of effort that they expend every year in preparing for both Junior and Senior WASSCE, the outcome of their learning experience will be remarkably different. By the time a student gets to SS3 under this structure and discipline, the performance will be better and WAEC mass failure will be history. We will still work on teacher motivation and commitment, improvement of facilities and infrastructure where possible and necessary.

2. Problem of Accessability and Enrollment in Schools

The Nigerian Constitution states that "government shall strive to eradicate illiteracy, and to this end, government shall, as and when practicable, provide

> a. Free, compulsory and universal primary education
> b. Free secondary education
> c. Free university education
> d. Free adult literacy programme

In spite of the constitutional mandate to eradicate illiteracy through free and compulsory education, the education ministry in Nigeria has not applied imaginative initiative to enforce free and compulsory Universal Primary Education. Recent data from a 2009 report by the ministry show that of 22 million children expected in early childhood schools, only 2.2 million are enrolled, leaving a short fall of 19.98 million out of school. For primary school, out of expected enrollment of 34.92 million, actual enrollment was only 24.42 million, leaving a short fall of 10.5 million children at home. For Junior Secondary school, expected enrollment was 9.27 million; actual enrollment was 3.27 million, leaving a shortfall of 6 million children out of school. For non-formal adult education out of 40 million illiterate adults, only 500,000 were enrolled, leaving a shortfall of 39.5 million. The problem of accessibility and non-enrollment is even more severe in Senior Secondary schools. Out of a potential enrollment population of 7.2 million, only 2.8 million (28%) were actually enrolled. At the university level, it is reported that only 6% of students who want university education are admitted nationwide.

Solution to the Problem of Accessibility and Enrollment

The Nigerian Constitution has prescribed a free, compulsory primary education. This is an unequivocal law of the land that must be obeyed without exception. For many reasons, it is in the best interest of Nigeria as a nation that we eradiate illiteracy.

In America, education through the completion of secondary school is free and compulsory for all. If a child misses school, or is not enrolled in school, the parents or guardians will be contacted immediately by the school authorities. If it continues, the matter is reported to the local government who immediately contacts the local court. The court will issue a summons for the parents or guardian to appear in court to face the Judge, a warrant for their arrest will be issued. A parent can be put in jail for violating the law of the land, and could remain in jail until the child resumes attending school. But in most cases, most of these parents would plead ignorance of their child's behavior and promise to make sure the child is always in school. Can we implement this in Nigeria? Certainly yes, with proper sensitization, media campaign and carrying all stake holders along, especially the National Assembly and Federal Executive Council. Will Nigeria benefit from such measure? I believe it can, by significantly reducing the many evils of illiteracy in the society.

3. Problem with Teaching Methodology and Unmotivated Teachers

The report of a dialogue between a researcher and a group of teachers at an education workshop illustrates the problem with teaching methodology and unmotivated teachers in Nigerian schools. It was at the end of one of the three-hour workshops with educators. The group had started the workshop reticent, each explaining why they would have to leave early. By the end of the workshop, everyone was still participating and extending the workshop with further questions. The workshop facilitator asked the teachers about their approach toward critical thinking skills among the student learners. The teachers did not understand what the facilitator meant by critical thinking skills; they wanted an example. The facilitator said "Ok, let's say that you are explaining something in class, and a learner raises their hand and challenges your way of thinking about that concept. She has another way of thinking about it. How do you respond?" There was quietness, dead silence. An otherwise animated and at ease group of teachers stared at their hands. The facilitator waited patiently. Finally, one teacher hesitantly spoke: "I can't remember the last time a student asked a question in my class." The facilitator was unclear. He said, "Do you mean you can't remember when a child asked a critical question in your class?" The teacher responded, "No, any question". The facilitator asked, "You mean if you are teaching something – let's say long division – learners do not even ask a question for clarity?" "No", the teacher responded. The rest of the teachers nodded in agreement. "Do all of you have the same experience?" The facilitator asked. They all shook their heads in agreement. "How do you do it then – how do you know learners are listening, let alone learning?" The facilitator asked. Another teacher raised his head, "We know. We know that they are not learning." Another teacher added, "There is one child who listens in my class." She mentions her name. Other teachers shake their heads and agree that yes; she is the one who listens. "So you mean you have the painful task of getting up in the morning, facing the most difficult task of being a teacher, wanting to make a difference in a child's life and knowing that no one is listening?" Slowly others raised their heads, many of them nodding yes. There was silence. One older teacher starts, "You see, we never get to talk like this. The easiest thing is to blame it on the parent – then we don't have to think it is us that fail each day". There was a sense of relief that a long-held secret was not only on the table but shared by other colleagues.

The authority of the teacher is feared in the Nigerian educational system. Teaching methodologies employed do not encourage free thinking and active participation and articulation by the student. In most classrooms in Nigeria, the entire education experience is focused on the teacher, and the class is designed for listening to the teacher, rather than engaging the student in learning. The emphasis is on delivery of the curriculum to a class rather than on learning by the individual student. Very few schools are designed with learning by the individual as the priority of the educational experience. How can we hope for or talk about everyone having the right to basic education in Nigeria when so many teachers do not show up to teach, and so many learners do not show up to learn?

Solution to the Problem of Teaching Methodology and Unmotivated Teachers

We need to retrain our teachers. Teaching and learning is all about the student. Students as individual learners should have the center stage in the classroom. We should motivate and energize our teachers through better pay and performance-based incentives. For example, teachers whose students perform extremely well in national standardized exams will be given a merit award or bonus pay. We should create professional pride in teaching, and use that to motivate and raise the commitment of teachers. Teachers and school administrators will be helped, through dialogue at education seminars, to understand and accept their responsibility in setting examples for students as role models.

One of the most powerful ways children and young adults acquire values is to see individuals they admire and respect exemplify those values in their own being and conduct. Parents and educator or politicians and priests who say one thing and do another send mixed messages to those in their charge who then learn not to trust them. The question of leadership generally, and in the education sphere particularly, is therefore of vital importance. Teachers need to commit to, and uphold the noble calling of their profession to educate and train the learners who will be future leaders of this nation. They must understand that their attitude, dedication, self-discipline, and ideals determine the quality of education.

There was a time when teachers were highly respected members of the society, not just because of their class and educational status, but also because of the nobility of their calling. Once this sense of vocation and professional pride is regained, teachers will once more become respected community leaders.

4. Problem with Understanding the Purpose of Education

In the contemporary Nigerian society, most people believe that the main objective of the education system is to cater to the job market. For many, education is simply a means of social mobility. It is about social status and economic returns. Most parents relentlessly drive their children towards "high achievement" and "excellence", in education, which translated into vernacular, simply means passing exams well. This distortion of the objectives and purpose of education is responsible for many problems in the Nigerian society. The development of our youth into good citizens who are socially sensitive and responsible is often not considered as a major purpose of education. The truth however is that education does not exist simply to serve the job market, but to serve society, which means instilling in pupils and students a broad sense of values that will enrich the individual and society. Inculcating a strong sense of values at school is intended to help young people achieve higher levels of moral judgement, decency and integrity.

John Dewey, a famous American educator and philosopher, draws a very clear distinction between education and schooling. Schooling is a necessary but insufficient component of education. We often talk of education, but in fact focus on schooling. Consider the following distinct characteristics of schooling versus education.

EDUCATION	SCHOOLING
Learning	Teaching
Knowledge	Information
Qualities	Competencies
Humanity	Employability

4.1.1 TEACHING VS LEARNING

In many classrooms, the entire education experience is focused on the teacher, and the class is designed for listening to the teacher, rather than engaging the student in learning. The emphasis is on the delivery of the curriculum to a class - not on learning by the individual student. Few schools are designed with learning by the individual student as the priority of the educational experience.

4.1.2 INFORMATION VS KNOWLEDGE

The lack of proper definition of learning in schools inevitably leads to a focus on the replication of information rather than the creation of knowledge in schools. This is very evident in assessment systems which tend to focus on "right" and "wrong" answers as derived from a curriculum presented by teachers. Even at the university, only very few examples of assessment of students are focused on the creation of knowledge. True education is concerned with the conversion of information to knowledge through a process of reflection, practice and application.

4.1.3 COMPETENCIES VS QUALITIES

The measure of competencies in education inevitably leads to a focus on those aspects of schooling, which can be measured. There is emphasis on the tangible, the pragmatic, the number and the instrumental. The qualities of an educated person, such as a moral sense, engagement with cultural issues and values, the ability to debate and question, are inevitably subordinated to those elements, which are controllable and measurable. Schooling is a necessary but insufficient component of education, but too often the two terms are seen as synonymous.

4.1.4 EMPLOYABILITY VS HUMANITY

For many education systems the fundamental purpose of schooling is to ensure a suitably qualified workforce. However, it is the broad range of human qualities, rather than the narrow and limited view of specific skills that are needed for both employment and coping with complexity of life as responsible and sensitive humans in the society. Such human qualities may include:

- Emotional intelligence
- Commitment to personal growth and learning
- Requisite skills of upholding democracy and pluralism in society
- Perseverance and optimism
- The ability to work and live interdependently
- A clear sense of personal moral values

Additional Comments in Understanding the Purpose of Education

In the official website of the Nigerian Ministry of Education, the mission statement of the Education Ministry is "to reform and restructure the education sector to empower and develop the citizenry to acquire skills and knowledge that would prepare them for the world of work." This is a narrow and defective view of the purpose of education. The National Policy on Education in 2004 described education as an instrument per excellence in effecting national development. It recognized education as a powerful instrument to achieve national objectives, one of which is to make Nigeria a free and democratic society.

Education in Nigeria can be a powerful tool in molding a people from diverse origins, cultural practices, different tribes and languages into one national identity, within a framework democratic in character, that can absorb, accommodate and mediate conflicts and adversarial interests without oppression, injustice or harm, whatsoever. Our educational system, through proper curriculum, should effectively promote qualities such as Equity, Tolerance, Openness, Accountability, Social Honor and Rule of Law, values advocated passionately by the Nigerian Constitution.

Education does not exist simply to serve the market but to serve society by instilling in pupils and students nationwide, good judgement and prime values that will make every educated Nigerian their brothers' keeper.

5. Problem of Disjointed and Dysfunctional Curriculum

The educational curriculum in most Nigerian school systems is disjointed and dysfunctional, unfit for the training of our youth. The education curriculum, the primary means of instilling knowledge, skills and values in young people, cannot be mechanistic and narrow, geared only towards market requirements. An education curriculum does not exist simply to serve market requirements as important as market requirements may be, or for economic growth and material prosperity; the primary purpose of education must be to enrich the individual, and in extension, the broader society.

Being educated for meaningful participation in society means being educated for the market place, as much as for good citizenship. Indeed, productivity and responsibility are interdependent. Accepting that the education sector has a strong role to play in the generation of values, and therefore the exercise of good moral judgement, means accepting that the education curriculum must be designed in a wholesome manner, to educate young people, not only for the market, but for good citizenship. The Constitution of Nigeria should be taught as part of the education curriculum, and brought to life in the classroom as well as applied in all programmes and policy making by educators, administrators and all school officials.

History has essentially been taken out of the Basic and Secondary school education curricula. Teaching history is central to the promotion of all human values, including tolerance. History is one of the many memory systems that shape our values and morality because it studies, records and disseminates knowledge of human failure and achievement over centuries. By studying History, students will not only gain vital understanding of chronology and the dynamics of change over time, but they can also work out and figure out for themselves what is good or bad, what is right or wrong, the power, dynamics and consequences of human decisions.
The many diverse Nigerian arts and cultures, sports and other forms of creative and performing arts should be part of our new educational curriculum.

Solution to the Problem of Disjointed and Dysfunctional Curriculum

Chapter 2 section 23 of the Nigerian Constitution states, "The national ethics shall be Discipline, Integrity, Dignity of Labor, Social Justice, Religious Tolerance, Self-Reliance, and Patriotism." A dynamic outcome-based curriculum must commit us to instilling in learners knowledge, skills and values – the values of a society striving towards social justice, equity and rule of law through the development of creative, critical and problem-solving individuals for the benefit of society. We need education curriculum that will teach all students to abide by the Nigerian Constitution; respect its ideals and institutions, the National Flag, the National Anthem, the National Pledge, and all legitimate authorities. Invariaby, such curriculum will teach all students how to respect the dignity of other citizens and the right and legitimate interests of others, and how to live in unity and harmony, and in the spirit of common brotherhood, as advocated in Chapter 2 section 24 of the Nigerian Constitution. A good and well thought-out curriculum will enable the education system to contribute significantly to the full personal development of each student and to the moral, social, cultural, political, and economic development of the nation at large, including the advancement of democracy, human rights and rule of law. Issues of human rights, tolerance, social justice and inclusivity should be infused throughout the curriculum in a student-centered teaching and learning experience.

Arts and culture empower young people, giving them practical means to express themselves creatively through music, drama, dance, and visual arts, in a manner that spoken language alone cannot. As young people are increasingly bombarded strongly by foreign and international cultures to the detriment and weak support of local arts and culture, learners need a curriculum that will help them understand, recognize and appreciate the value of their own art and culture. Arts and culture can be a specific and examinable learning area within the general education curriculum.

The history of Nigeria, including the Civil War and events that led to the Civil War ensure that we do not as a nation forget the lessons of our painful past. History should be taught in four areas: Local, Nigerian, African and World. The study of History nurtures a spirit of critical inquiry and assists the young learner in the formation of historical consciousness, which plays an essential role in building the dignity of human values within an informed awareness of the past. Three groups of curriculum experts will be assembled immediately to review the above fact and formulate the required curricula for each tier of education in Nigeria. Curricula must be dynamic to meet necessary changes in the needs of a growing and dynamic society; therefore, our groups of curricula experts will meet annually or as needed to keep our curricula from being stale and static.

6. *Problem of Poor Infrastructure and Teacher Shortfalls*

According to the data from the education road map report of 2009 by the Federal Ministry of Education, available classrooms in formal education as at 2006 is 497,871, with a shortfall of 1,152,415 while the existing classrooms for nomadic education is 10,469 with a shortfall of 28,931. Many schools lack the essential infrastructure to enable them function as safe, efficient and effective schools. Majority have no water, sanitation and electricity. The classrooms are very poor, with floors full of holes, broken roofs and ceilings. Windows and doors are often not lockable, so the schools lack security. Few schools have a perimeter fence and enclosures making them open to intruders and vandalism.

The existing shortfall in teachers are 969,078 for early childcare and development education; 388,47 for Primary education; 581 for Junior Secondary education; 1,580,000 for adult literacy; and 12,329 for nomadic education. Poor remuneration, low teacher support, poor motivation and lack of professional pride are significant problems.

The staff strength of Nigerian Universities is 99,464, comprising 27,394 academic staff and 72,070 non-academic staff. Polytechnics and monotechnics have 12,938 academic and 24,892 non-academic staff. College of Education have 11,256 academic staff and 24,621 non-academic staff. The shortfall in academic staff for each sector is 9,548; 17,078; and 14,858 for Universities, Polytechnics, and Colleges of Education respectively.

Solution to the Problem of Poor Infrastructure and Teacher Shortfalls

Some years ago, the then serving President General of my town, Ogidi, in Idemili North Local Government Area of Anambra State, Dr. Obiakor, called me with a request. He stated that of the thirteen elementary schools in Ogidi, none has a toilet. All students, male and female, as well as their teachers, have to go in the bush, with attendant risks such as snake bite. He resolved to call thirteen prominent people from Ogidi and get each of them to donate one toilet to each of the thirteen schools. Each toilet will have three units, one for boys, one for girls and one for teachers. I commended him for his work and not only agreed to donate as requested but pledged to contact the association of Ogidi citizens who live in the United States to work with him in funding other similar projects he may have for the town.

The Federal Government, through the Federal Ministry of Education, should properly articulate a clear vision for the goals of the government in using education as a potent tool for national development and integration. Communities, corporations and individuals should be invited as development partners. The media will be invited to play a significant public relation and mass information role.

Effective administrative teams at the community level will be elected by the people and put in place at town/village, local government, and state levels to properly supervise efficient administration of primary and secondary education in their respective communities. Tertiary level will be supervised by effective governing council, with education experience, and the right passion to serve and contribute to the development of tertiary education. A percent of the federal government allocations for local government will be ear-marked for education. Under a good accountable process, such funds should go directly to the school board who will supervise all spending and account for every penny in a verifiable manner. A similar arrangement can be made with the state for Secondary schools, who will be managed by a local board selected at the community level by members of each community.

The problem of teacher shortfalls is artificial and irresponsible. With the proper will and commitment, we can recruit, train and motivate teachers to teach our children in both Primary and Secondary schools. Many Youth Corp members are posted to schools where they serve meritoriously; then they are thrown away after the one year of free labor. They become unemployed and most of them remain unemployed for years. Yet we say we do not have teachers to teach our children. We have good available teacher manpower to solve our teacher shortfalls, if we want to solve the problem.

As for shortfalls in the Tertiary education system, there are enough qualified Nigerians teaching at universities all over the world who will satisfy all lecturer needs at every Nigerian university. Just before I received my Ph.D. in 1979 in the United States, recruiting teams came from multiple Nigerian universities to interview me in America. Although I turned down the offers they gave me because I had better offers in America, many other Nigerians who were interviewed took the offer and returned to Nigeria.

I came back to Nigeria some years ago after living productively in America for 34 years because a Vice Chancellor in one of the major Nigerian universities knew how to appeal to me to come and help him build the university. Most Nigerians outside Nigeria will come back if they are approached properly with an offer. Unfortunately, Nigerian Universities no longer send teams overseas to go and interview and recruit qualified Nigerians. Furthermore, all students who graduate with First Class Honors in Nigerian Universities should be encouraged to enter a Ph.D. programme immediately as alternative to youth service, for tertiary education academic staff development.

7. Problem of Funding, Resource Mobilization and Prudent Utilization of Resources

There are both real and imaginary funding problems and resource mobilization in the education sector in Nigeria.

There are also significant problems with prudent utilization of resources and lack of creativity and initiative in mobilizing non-governmental funds for the development of the educational sector in Nigeria.

A real problem is that due to financial limitation, government has not been generous in spending adequate money for the development of the education sector. Imaginary funding problems occur when the State Governments fail to access and utilize funds allocated to them by the Federal Government for their schools. By January 2009, a total of 28 state had not accessed their 2007 Universal Basic Education intervention funds totaling N12.513 billion, and 36 states had not accessed their intervention fund for 2008 totaling N29.551 billion. In addition, there is a lot of waste by poor managers in the system, and significant imprudence in the utilization of the resources. Furthermore, the mindset that waits for the government to provide all the money for education development is unfortunate and primitive. There should be significant and compelling creative initiatives to mobilize sizable non-government funds for development of the education sector in Nigeria.

Solution to the Problem of Funding, Resource Mobilization and Prudent Utilization of Resources

Even if the Federal Government was able to spend 26% of the national budget in education as has been advocated as the adequate amount by various groups, it still will not serve the need of education funding in Nigeria. No government anywhere in the world is able to provide 100% of the cost of funding education in the country. Educational development and funding is the collective responsibility of government, the educational schools and institutions, corporate and individual donors in the private sector. The Nigerian government should do more to increase the amount invested on education yearly since education is a very powerful tool for nation building, national integration and national development. All schools in Nigeria at every level must come alive in their responsibility to attract development funds from a variety of sources to support their respective schools. Each Primary and Secondary school should have a fund raising committee drawn from the community and other prominent members of the society will participate. All such funds must be accounted for properly through effective mechanisms established locally for that purpose.

Nigerian Universities have a Deputy Vice Chancellor for Academics and for Administration, but not a Deputy Vice Chancellor for University Development. In America, every university has a Vice President for University Development or its equivalent with supporting staff. This individual and his staff have the responsibility for raising significant funds from non-government sources to fund the university. Some of them raise more money for university than government give to the university. The number one university in the world, Harvard University, does not receive any money from the government. They raise 100% of the money to fund their annual budget, including staff salaries. Harvard university has raised an endowment fund of 36 billion dollars owned by the school. Each year they earn over 6 billion dollars in interest payment from their endowment, which is double their annual budget of about 3 billion dollars. Many American universities raise 50 percent of their annual budget, including staff salaries, by themselves from non-government sources. This culture of financial self-reliance has distinguished American universities from other universities in the world. Every year, in the ranking of the best universities in the world, usually, 18 of the top 20 universities in the world are American universities. Nigerian universities who sit and wait for government funding do not rank within the top 6,000.

8. Problem of Unemployment After Graduation

Annually, only about 10 percent of the 130,000 graduates from Nigerian universities are able to secure a job. This means that each year, approximately 13,000 new graduates are employed in the nation while 117,000 new graduates are added to the unemployment list. Most of the 117,000 new unemployed graduates do not have the right skills or training to secure corporate jobs and do not have the entrepreneurial ability to create new business opportunity and become employers themselves. This inability to get or start a job impacts on the educational system negatively because some young people do not understand why they should go to school at all if graduates they know cannot get jobs after spending so many years in school.

The government has attempted to introduce entrepreneurial studies. The efforts so far have been half-spirited, and the courses half-baked. The educational curricula at the Tertiary education level must include practical and well thought out courses for all levels of students on entrepreneurial studies in every department. Every student must produce and submit a complete Business Plan on a worthy enterprise in the student's area of study in their final year. For those students who have worthy projects and desire to execute such projects as an alternative to youth service, they will be helped through a seed capital from a federal government guaranteed small business loan from a commercial bank. All commercial banks will be required to make such government guaranteed small business loans. Those students who are successful at their business will be assisted with a low interest government guaranteed business expansion loan from commercial banks to support expansion of their profitable business. They will be given a five-year business tax moratorium to assist the development of their business; and also business tax credit for every new employee they hire. The target is to help at least 50 percent of all new graduates to own their profitable business and become significant employers of labor. This will dramatically solve the unemployment problem in Nigeria.

9. The Ultimate problem of Non-Value Based Education in Nigeria

According to the Nwangwu hypothesis, bad and defective educational system in Nigeria is responsible for the psychological insecurity and poor sense of self-worth that relies on materialism, a life style of ostentation, and external psychological props such as vain titles among many Nigerians. The hypothesis further stipulates that most crimes, including bribery, corruption and other evils in the Nigerian society originate from this psychological insecurity and the accompanying lack of proper sense of self-worth. Psychological insecurity breeds greed, irrational behavior, and ostentation. In addition to psychological insecurity, non-education or illiteracy and non-value-based education, is responsible for intolerance, bigotry, human rights violation and abuse, poor sense of equity, social justice and rule of law. Such people lack moral fiber and moral courage; therefore, they can be manipulated easily and used to violate the rights and dignity of their fellow humans. The consequences and costs to Nigeria as a nation are dire and enormous, but they can be contained and managed through proper education and a dynamic and values-oriented education curriculum that includes teaching moral values from the Nigerian Constitution, lessons on patriotism, and pledge of allegiance to Nigeria.

The national madness about money and the quest for money must end. We must begin from early childhood education to lay the proper foundation, and arm our children with proper values that will equip them for sane and responsible life in society. The moral content and character of anyone's life is more valuable than the size of their bank accounts. A value-based education curriculum that will instill such truths in Nigerians at all levels will dissolve this psychological insecurity that is the basis of many crimes and evils in the Nigerian society.

CHAPTER 17

Intellectuals as Nation Builders

Chidi Chike Achebe MD, MPH, MBA

For Chinua Achebe

In the 1960s, Jean Paul Sartre the literary giant and France's leading intellectual at the time, made a series of controversial statements during a public lecture. Incensed by his outburst, a group of French conservatives turned to Charles De Gaul, the French General and President of the 5th Republic, to caution the man of letters. After listening to their complaints, De Gaul responded this way: "I caution Sartre? But Sartre is France..." For De Gaul, Sartre exemplified the highest ideals and aspirations of France - a scholar "par excellence", an intellectual beacon for the world, exercising the fruits of democracy while actively engaged in shaping the destiny of post-World War II France.

The West and other advanced nations did not arrive at this appreciation of intellectuals and intellectual discourse overnight. For centuries, diverse philosophers from around the world grappled with the question of the role of knowledge in society. Al-Kindi, Avicenna, Mullah Sadra and several other Islamic scholars in the Middle East as well as Western philosophers such as Socrates, Aristotle, Descartes, through T.S. Kuhn, to the postmodernists, all tackled this problem. Aristotle believed that 'thinkers' should try to overcome ignorance, and pursue knowledge for its own sake and not merely for its practical utility. Today, there is a comfortable medium that exists between the role of knowledge gathered for the improvement of society and knowledge pursued and accumulated in its purest form.

Nowhere on earth is this example of intellectual balance more vibrant than in the United States of America. (For the purposes of this chapter I will ignore America's grave intellectual incongruities such as slavery, racism, and other constitutional, political, and social hypocrisies). The founders of the "American experiment", Hamilton, Jefferson, Washington, Adams, Jay, Henry, Franklin, and others, were some of the most educated men of their time. Armed with enviable intellectual dexterity, these men fashioned what has become one of the most admired and effective documents in history – The American Constitution. This intellectual record is the foundation of America's much celebrated Democracy, an idea borrowed from the ancient Athenians, defined by Lincoln during his mythical Gettysburg Address as "a government of the people, by the people, and for the people" and emulated around the world.

America's prosperity and global dominance today is not accidental. It was meticulously charted by its constitution, guided by a succession of excellent leaders (for the most part) imbued with world class education and intellect and protected by its democracy. Perhaps the greatest of America's early "Intellectual Presidents" was the 3rd president - Thomas Jefferson. He believed very strongly that America's success could be achieved only through a high-quality educational system for its citizens. Such a system would also depend on teachers -- teachers with the training, authority, and freedom to challenge their students and change their lives as well as lay the foundations of intellectual meritocracy.

Jefferson held that: *"Ignorance and sound self-government could not exist together: the one destroyed the other. A despotic government could restrain its citizens and deprive the people of their liberties only while they were ignorant... Only popular government can safeguard democracy. ... Every government degenerates when trusted to the rulers of the people alone. The people themselves are its only safe depositories. And to render them safe, their minds must be improved to a certain degree...."*[1]

This ancient dedication to educational quality and intellectual foresight has produced America's much envied higher educational system. Its eight Ivy league universities – Harvard, Yale, Princeton, Dartmouth, University of

Pennsylvania, Columbia, Brown and Cornell as well as equally excellent non-Ivy league institutions such as M.I.T, Caltech, Stanford, Chicago, Northwestern, Duke, Johns Hopkins, Michigan, Berkley, Virginia, Georgetown, UCLA etc, have become the global benchmark for educational excellence. Their combined endowment fund of over $150 billion (larger than Morocco's Gross National Product) promises to keep them in this influential position for a long time to come. Harvard, with its $36 billion endowment is easily wealthier than several countries across the globe.

It is little wonder, therefore, that these institutions – the Ivy League in particular- became the honing ground for American leaders for centuries. Every single Supreme Court Justice attended one of the aforementioned institutions. Eight American presidents – John Adams and his son John Quincy Adams, Rutherford Hayes, Theodore Roosevelt and his cousin Franklin Delano Roosevelt, John Fitzgerald Kennedy, George W. Bush and Barack Obama all studied at Harvard. Yale University is the proud intellectual molder for at least four US presidents: The two Bushes, William Taft and William Jefferson Clinton.

The Obama and Bill Clinton presidencies, may very well be the best examples of intellectual leadership at work in recent years. During their two terms, America's economy steadily expanded adding at least 10 million new jobs. The Stock Market hit an all-time high with record profits for individuals and corporations alike. Obama and Clinton achieved this feat, in part, by hiring some of the best and brightest that America had to offer to run the country. Recruiting 'intellectuals' such as Secretary of State Hillary Clinton (2009-2013) and John Kerry; Secretary of Energy Steven Chu – who incidentally, is the first person appointed to the Cabinet after having won a Nobel Prize – are just a few examples.

During the Clinton era intellectuals such as Robert Rubin, one of Wall Street's finest, and Summers (former president of Harvard) in the Treasury department, Robert Reich in the labor department, Brown in the Commerce department, Madeleine M. Kunin former governor of Vermont and

Richard W. Riley in the education department was particularly instrumental in the success of his administration.

The West does not hold a monopoly on economic success buoyed by intellectual ingenuity. On our own continent, the Southern African Nations of Botswana and Namibia, despite having had to fight the catastrophic pandemic of AIDS, are today, some of the fastest growing economies in this hemisphere. Although the legacy of the late South Africa's political and intellectual titan Madiba Nelson Mandela has no peer on the continent, President Mogae tenure as President of Botswana was quite remarkable. His credentials for leadership are impressive - trained as an economist at the Universities of Oxford and Sussex in the UK, he served his country in a number of key positions: He was the Executive Director for Anglophone Africa, International Monetary Fund (1976-80); Governor of the Bank of Botswana (1980-81); Permanent Secretary to the President, Secretary to the Cabinet and Supervisor of Elections (1982-89); and Minister of Finance and Development Planning (1989-92).[2]

This preparation coupled with ethical, moral, and intellectual discipline helped him oversee the fastest growing economy in black Africa with one of the highest GNP per capita incomes. During his presidency, Botswana's economy grew at an average rate of about 9.2%. To place things in context – Botswana's per capita income of $7726 in 2014 is **more than twice that of Nigeria's!**

In Asia, that China is currently poised to join Japan in making the miraculous "leap forward" from underdevelopment to the club of advanced nations in record time, is not surprising to economists or historians. For over twenty years, China's GNP has grown at an annual rate of over 7% per year. By 2015, it had topped $10.9 trillion.[i] China's success was made possible by an uncompromising, concomitant effort to improve her educational system, and to harness the collective intellectual potential of the world's most populous nation. China's recent entry into 'the last frontier-space,' with manned missions, is a testament to how far it has come.

A Nigerian Meritocracy

It is pertinent at this juncture to make a few comments: I am not advocating that Nigerians copy Western culture or civilization. However, I do believe that we should scrutinize more closely, the successes and failures of thriving economies and societies as we lay our path in the world. Very importantly, **I am not** calling for an elitist system or a class structure. Indeed, I am an activist for a meritocracy. It is only under this arrangement that individuals of simple means but with the brightest minds can rise to leadership. Let us not forget that both Barack Obama and William Jefferson Clinton were from simple backgrounds and rose to lead the most powerful country in the world. This could only happen within a structure that actively seeks and celebrates intellectual achievement and merit. In such a system, individuals of privilege can also rise to leadership if they possess the appropriate skills. Some of the most successful of world statesmen – JFK, RFK, FDR, Nehru and his descendants Indira and Rajiv Gandhi are examples. A true meritocracy holds great promise for Nigeria.

The Nigerian Intellectual Conundrum

The dawn of independence in West Africa saw the emergence of leaders in a myriad of fields such as politics, the arts, law, science and medicine, economics and commerce. These giants of men and women from diverse backgrounds were all "intellectuals" and were on a mission to redirect their young nations onto a path of development after years of colonialism. Together, this group brought more recognition and honor to their respective nations than any other set before or since (at least so far).

(In the interest of progressive thinking, I define an "intellectual" as "a thinker or 'visionary' with or without a college education"). What follows is certainly not an exhaustive list but a sample of achievers...

Dr Nnamdi Azikiwe, the father of our country and perhaps

along with Kenneth Onwuka Dike-- the most severely under-celebrated Nigerian, is a quintessential example of such an intellectual. "No National holiday in his honor? Why forever not?" Obafemi Awolowo, Ahmadu Bello, Tafewa Balewa, Aminu Kano, Waziri Ibrahim, Maitama Sule, Ahmed Talib, Judith Attah, Margaret Ekpo, Madam Kuti, Tejumola Alakija, Janet Mokelu, Oyibo Odinamadu, A.A. Nwafor-Orizu, Michael Okpara, K.O. Mbadiwe, S. Akintola, Balarabe Musa, B.Usman, Sa'ad Zungur, Abubakar Rimi, Ado Bayero, Akanu Ibiam, M.T. Mbu, S.G. Ikoku, Francis Ellah, C.C. Onoh, Anthony Enahoro, H.A. Ejuyitchie, Bola Ige, Bisi Onabanjo, Lateef Jakande, John Nwodo, J.M.Johnson, Aja Nwachukwu, R.A. Njoku, O.Akinfosile, Sam I. Mbakwe, S.E. Imoke, Eyo Ita, Melford Okilo,T.O.S. Benson, Ambrose Alli, A. Nwankwo, A.Ogunsanya, Emeka Anyaoku, A. Ekwueme, Senghor and Nkrumah are others that exemplify the best and brightest in politics.

Chinua Achebe, Wole Soyinka, J.P. Clark, Cyprian Ekwensi, Christopher Okigbo, Chukwuemeka Ike, Flora Nwapa, Mabel Segun, Bolanle Awe, Bala Usman, Dr. Tai Solarin, Amos Tutuola, S.J. Cookey, Ola Rotimi, John Munonye, Elechi Amadi, Bruce Onabrakpeya, Ben Enwonwu, Uche Okeke, Ayi Kwe Armah, T.M. Aluko, Ade Ajayi, Emmanuel Obiechina, Kenneth Onwuka Dike, Alvan Ikoku and Senghor are parallel examples from the Arts, Culture and Humanities. Legal luminaries such as Adetokumbo Ademola, Taslim Elias, C.D.Onyeama, Darnley Alexander, T.A.Aguda, G.C.M.Onyiuke, Ben Nwabueze, C.F.O. Anyaegbunam, Rotimi-Williams, Louis Mbanefo, Fani-Kayode, Fatai-Williams, Justices M.L. Uwais, Augustine Nnamani, A. Obaseki, B.O. Kazeem, C.A. Oputa, A.G. Irikefe, Udo Udoma, P.K. Nwokedi and Anthony Aniagolu are examples of intellectuals that stand out from that era.

Legendary economists such as Dr Pius Okigbo, K.I. Kalu and Adebayo Adedeji are further examples of Nigeria's intellectual *crème de la crème*. In Science, we must not forget Drs Okechukwu Ikejiani, M.A. Majekodunmi, Umaru Shehu, Abubakar Imam, Ishaya S. Audu, Jibril Aminu, B.O.

Osuntokun, Tam David-West, F.O. Dosekun, F. Udekwu, L. Ekpechi, Dr J. Ojukwu, T.Agulefo, Chukwuedu Nwokolo, Anezi-Okoro, the second generation Kutis- Olikoye and Beko, T.A.Lambo, Adetokunboh Lucas, O.K. Ogan, F. Adi, P.I. Okolo, Chike Obi, Anya O. Anya and Akin L. Mabogunje (social sciences).

The commercial sector has produced scores of leaders such as Sir Bank Anthony, Sir Odumegwu Ojukwu, and the Dantata/Dangote, Rabiu, and Kontagora families. Others include Musa Dan Fulani, T.A. Odutola, Chris Ogunbanjo, Otunba Balogun, FGN Okoye, A.E. Ilodibe, R.O. Nkwocha, Chief Nnana-Kalu, LN Obioha, Sunny Odogwu, Akintola-Williams and M.N. Ugochukwu. Slightly later, a promising, albeit short lived, trend of educated business chieftains such as Gamaliel Onosode and Alhaji Abdullaziz Ude, A. Modebe, Joe Irukwu, P.O. Nwakoby, the Ibrus, Adekunle Ojora, Earnest Shonekan, Abba Gana, Emmanuel Iwuanyanwu and M.K.O. Abiola emerged.

In *The greatest generation* Tom Brokaw salutes Americans whose sacrifices and work changed the course of American history and put the USA on the path of post-World War II economic expansion and prosperity. We have already shown that West Africa has produced similar individuals. Why then with all this brain power does Nigeria find itself in the "intellectual wilderness?" I hope that we can all agree that our condition today is a consequence of a past of successive military coups, endemic corruption, inept leadership and persistent 'cults of mediocrity'[3] running the affairs of the nation.

It is also important to stress that Nigeria has not developed a culture of celebrating honest, hard-working achievers. Instead we have allowed others to foist upon us a paradoxical anti-intellectual situation in which recognition, indeed the highest National honors, are heaped on former military dictators for, pray tell me, "shooting themselves into power and looting the national treasury?" and their corrupt civilian cohorts who serve these kleptocracies with glee, over "our true heroes". If this was a chapter from Gabriel Garcia Marquez's *Autumn of the Patriarch,* then we could take solace in the fictional nature of this pathetic, comical madness. The fact that this is our reality should make us all pause in horror, ponder deeply, and take action.

It is admirable that most Nigerians possess…. the word 'self-confidence' doesn't quite do it justice, so I term it a *"No be human being wey do am before? I fit do am"* attitude when faced with challenges. This mind set has helped many a Nigerian attain great heights in their respective fields. It has also meant that we have far too often appointed individuals to and/or accepted positions better served by others.

Some may attempt to counter my overall argument by raising the fact that a number of intellectuals have actually served in positions of power and leadership. My rebuttal is this: Even when members of this group such as Ekwueme, Mbu, and Anyaoku etc. have been involved in government, they have far too frequently been given roles under less capable individuals or served for too short a period of time to make the desired impact. Finally, let us not forget that civilians have been in charge of Nigeria's destiny for less than half of our post-independence history.

The failure of the Nigerian educated classes

It is important to point out that some members of Nigeria's educated classes bear their own brunt of pathologies. The historical eagerness of some educated Nigerians to serve under corrupt regimes and accept secondary roles under mediocre leaders, has to be one of the most tragic predicaments of post independent Nigeria. Some believe that this sad situation has been made possible by a systematic, intentional impoverishment of the educated classes – particularly those that lecture in Nigerian universities - under a series of mainly military regimes, creating a group, albeit small, of "pseudo-intellectuals – greedy, petty, scramblers for materialistic accumulation and illicit power."

In the *Wretched of the Earth*, about intellectuals of this ilk, Fanon eloquently posits:

"The unpreparedness of the educated classes, the lack of practical links between them and the mass of the people, their laziness, and, let it be said, their cowardice at the decisive moment of the struggle, will give rise to tragic mishaps." In Nigeria today, we are living witnesses to that tragedy.

The Task before Nigeria

For decades, black people on the African continent and in the Diaspora have looked to Nigeria to provide an example of a nation run by blacks that can attain economic, cultural and political success. Intellectuals from CLR James, Michael Thelwell, Aime Cesaire in the Caribbean to Leon H. Sullivan, James Baldwin, Martin Luther King, Malcolm X, Stokely Carmichael to Toni Morrison, Sonia Sanchez, Johnnetta B. Cole, Cornell West and Julian Bond in the Americas have all at one time or the other, with great anxiety, wondered why Nigeria, with all its human and material blessings seems never to be able to get its act together. One of these great minds recently expressed this concern aloud at a lunch with our own Chinua Achebe this way:

"Are Nigerians not fully aware of what is truly at stake for black people around the world? That her success will mean our success?" These words should give Nigerians "food for thought.

I am not encouraging an intellectual transformation in Nigeria to lead us out of our stupor because others want us to, however romantic and inspiring this might appear, but because indeed so much is at stake and it is absolutely imperative that "we get our act together" in our own self-interest and for posterity.

First: Understanding ourselves and our history

Forty years ago, Chinua Achebe saw the need for an intellectual process that would lead to the empowering "*of peoples who had been knocked silent by the trauma of all* kinds of dispossession" **[4]**. He captures this sentiment succinctly in the following excerpt:

"I would be quite satisfied if my novels (especially the ones set in the past) did no more than teach my readers that their past--with all its imperfections--was not one long night of savagery from which the first Europeans acting on God's behalf delivered them.

This theme--put quite simply--is that African peoples did not hear of culture for the first time from Europeans; that their societies were not mindless but frequently had a philosophy of great depth and value and beauty, that they had poetry and, above all, they had dignity. It is this dignity that many African peoples all but lost in the colonial period, and it is this dignity that they must now regain. The worst thing that can happen to any people is the loss of their dignity and self-respect. The writer's duty is to help them regain it by showing them in human terms what happened to them, what they lost. There is a saying in Igbo that a man who can't tell where the rain began to beat him cannot know where he dried his body. The writer can tell the people where the rain began to beat them. After all the novelist's duty is not to beat this morning's headline in topicality, it is to explore in depth the human condition. In Africa he cannot perform this task unless he has a proper sense of history."[5]

The Oppressive Power of the "Cult of Mediocrity"

Most pundits will agree that the blame for Nigeria's dilemma lies squarely at the feet of the incompetent leadership and mediocrity she has endured over most of the past four decades. First, for the sake of clarity it might be helpful to define mediocrity:

"Ordinariness as a consequence of being average and not outstanding (syn: averageness)"

"A person of second-rate ability; "a team of second-

raters"[xxi]

A nightmare of an 'unending stream' of mediocre leaders, has turned this once burgeoning nation into a 'cesspool of corruption and ineptitude.' Easy access to petrodollars has helped fan skyrocketing corruption, particularly in the public sector. A culture of "kickbacks", government sanctioned bunkering of oil, and the emergence of a corrupt and politically inept leadership, has turned Nigeria into a kleptomaniac's paradise.

Clearly, most Nigerians will accept that a meritocracy within a Democracy will be best for the nation. A true meritocracy transcends ethnicity, class, creed, and gender. It is the only system that will ensure that the best and brightest run the affairs of the nation – a development that will benefit the majority of the population. Can we not put in place a system that constantly seeks excellence, a process that matches the appropriate position with the most qualified applicant; and finally, a culture that asks questions such as "Is this person the best person for the job?"

Meritocracy will also produce a true leadership cadre – based on the tenets of hard work, discipline and excellence. Many that have run the affairs of Nigeria, historically, have often not been part of a true merit based elite. What we have had instead, are individuals and their corrupt cohorts that "shot themselves into power;" "looted and stole themselves into prominence;" or "rigged themselves into office." With such mediocrity, how can we expect that anything will be run correctly?

Many Nigerians look upon their leaders who often rig themselves and their cronies into power with distrust, even disdain. So why have we not seen sustained, peaceful, organized protest? Is it possible that many Nigerians have come to accept the present chaotic, corrupt system they find themselves in? Is it also possible that some strive, often even fight to sustain this present state of affairs, in the delusional hope that if this dysfunctional system persists, somehow they too will have a greater chance of achieving illicit success - emerging as "big men and women" - than in a Democracy that celebrates meritocracy?

Are we blind to a great intellectual's crystal clear perception that "corruption in Nigeria has passed the alarming and entered the fatal stage; and Nigeria will die if we continue to pretend that she is only slightly indisposed?" The ancient Israelites provide profound wisdom for all Nigerians with these words: "It is ill with a people when vicious men are advanced and men of worth are kept under hatches."

Getting Real: How is Nigeria doing?

It is difficult to determine just how badly a country is performing without comparing poverty indices across nations in the world. Here are some indisputable facts: over 70% of Nigeria's 178 million inhabitants live in abject poverty, defined by the *World Bank* as "subsistence on less than $1 a day" – a concept that even a former Nigerian president could not understand!

According to the UN, about $400 billion dollars have been looted from Nigeria's treasury since independence.[xxii] Today, less than 50 per cent of all Nigerians have access to safe water. Nigerians have a life expectancy that is 55 years and infant mortality is over 77 per 1000 births – one of the highest in the world and a figure comparable to that of war torn Afghanistan! So what kind of leaders and followers do we need for a true transformation in Nigeria...?

Servant Leadership and Educated Followership

The concept of the leadership embodying a sacred trust endowed by well- informed followers is an ancient proposition. Historians point to its genesis in ancient Egypt, and later in the Asian civilizations of India and Asian minor. Kautiliya, the renowned strategic thinker from India, published extensively on this subject as far back as the 4th century B.C. [xxiii]. In the treatise, *Arthashastra*, he posits:

"The King (leader) shall consider as good, not what pleases

himself, but what please his subjects (followers)...the king (leader) is a paid servant and enjoys the resources of the state together with the people..."[xxiv]

Most of the world's religions – Islam, Judaism, Buddhism, and Christianity emphasize service and humility in positions of leadership. The teaching of Jesus Christ further expands on this subject: *"You know that those who are regarded as rulers of the Gentiles lord it over them, and their high officials exercise authority over them. Not so with you. Instead, whoever wants to become great among you must be your servant, and whoever wants to be first must be slave of all. For even the Son of Man did not come to be served, but to serve, and to give his life as a ransom for many."* (Mark 10:42-45)[xxv]

Robert Greenleaf is widely considered the modern "father of servant leadership intellectual thought." Greenleaf (1977) described servant leadership in this manner:

"It begins with the natural feeling that one wants to serve, to serve first. Then conscious choice brings one to aspire to lead...The difference manifests itself in the care taken by the servant-first to make sure that other people's highest priority needs are being served. The best test, and difficult to administer, is: do those served grow as persons, do they grow while being served, become healthier, more prosperous, freer, more autonomous, more likely themselves to become servants?"[xxvi]

America's 3rd president - Thomas Jefferson believed very strongly that America's success could be achieved only through a high-quality educational system for its citizens, from whom would emerge world class leaders. He held that: *"Ignorance and sound self-government could not exist together: the one destroyed the other. A despotic government could restrain its citizens and deprive the people of their liberties only while they were ignorant... Only popular government can safeguard democracy. ... Every government degenerates when trusted to the rulers of the people alone. The people themselves are its only safe depositories. And to render them safe, their minds must be improved to a certain degree...."*[xxvii]

In **The Pedagogy of the Oppressed**, Paulo Freire advances the position that education should be used as a means to consciously shape the person and the society through a process he coins *conscientization* - "a more world-mediated, mutual approach to education that considers people incomplete. According to Freire, this 'authentic' approach to education must allow people to be aware of their incompleteness and strive to be more fully human."[xxviii] This process considers education an indispensable right for human development and hence societal advancement.

Some Immediate Suggestions

It is to Nelson Mandela, like Professor Achebe implores in *There was a Country (2012)* "Father of the nation of South Africa, antiapartheid leader, lawyer, writer, intellectual, humanitarian – that present and future African leaders must all go for sustenance and inspiration."

Nigerian leaders can also halt our downward spiral by effectively controlling and restricting access to the nation's wealth, i.e. petrodollars that fuel the corruption in the first place, and directing these resources to develop the nations decaying infrastructure – roads, water, and electricity - and educating the masses.

Putting in place a system of checks and balances that makes "corruption inconvenient" – enforcing jail terms for the guilty; mandating unannounced auditing of private and public organizations, companies, and parastatals, by non-government firms with impeccable reputations; making government earnings public; publishing oil corporation account portfolios - costs, expenditures, salaries, budgets, etc. – can have a profound effect in redirecting Nigeria's downward course and weakening state. The ripple effects of such a transformation would be felt in a myriad of areas. Most profoundly, it would set the stage, at last, for a generation of leaders who adopt public service to "serve the nation and hence the people, and not to get rich."

Nigeria depends on oil for 90-95% of export revenues, and over 90% of foreign exchange earnings. Despite its impressive rally at greater than $100 a barrel in recent years, the recent slump in oil prices should be a precious reminder to all Nigerians that oil is a finite source of energy, and fiscal dependence on the sale of fossil fuels is beset with future financial instability, and does not provide the basis for sound economic planning. At some point, the *Hubbert curve* for world oil will enter the down slope. Extraction will become more expensive and, eventually, this fossil fuel – essential for *transport* throughout the globe -- will disappear."[xxix] It behoves the Nigerian government to begin to seek other sources of energy and diversify the sources of revenue.

In his book *Poverty and Famines: An Essay on Entitlement and Deprivation,* published in 1981, Professor Amartya Kumar Sen argued against the view that a shortage of food was the most important explanation for famines, but suggested the interplay of social and economic factors to elucidate this phenomenon. The Nobel laureate's work has made it clear that several African *Oil exporters* including Nigeria are a collapsed oil market away from famine. Clearly, sustained investment in the manufacturing sector as well as *the Agricultural* sector while the petrodollars are available would be advisable!

The Role of Universities

Nigeria, like India, has an elaborate tertiary educational system. Once upon a time, Nigerians with Indian university degrees faced the embarrassing prospect of being demoted to 'A-level status!' How time has changed... Today, unlike in booming India, however, university graduates of the citadels of higher learning in Nigeria, obtain what a distinguished Nigerian Vice Chancellor has termed "a progressively inferior education," and face dismal job prospects. Compounding this dismal state of affairs, is the explosion of all sorts of new "colleges and universities" in this milieu of mediocrity!

The universities of Ibadan, Nsukka, ABU, Bayero, Lagos, Nnamdi Azikiwe, OAU etc. could become sources of intellectual expertise for a home-grown *High technology industry* that could generate billions of dollars in revenue, if they were to receive appropriate funding from the public and private sectors and attract the immense intellectual capital that exists amongst Nigerians the world over. We must dramatically improve the quality of our educational system from pre-kindergarten to university, if we are to stand a chance at making the "leap forward" from underdevelopment to the club of advanced nations.

The current democratic dispensation provides a novel chance for Nigeria to cultivate a culture of accountability, openness and transparency in government. Empowering the EFCC, will give one much less reason to worry.

Setting an Agenda for Intellectual Re-invigoration and Success

A group of about 10 friends and I representing every corner of our beloved country, went to a local Nigerian owned restaurant for *"isi-ewu"* – variously called *"ngwongwo"* or *"goat-head"*. After this popular delicacy, we spent the next 30 minutes arguing about what best to eat next. One person suggested *'eba',* the other *'amala',* the next *'Tuwo"* and *"dodo and beans'* and so on. We then agreed to order them all and share.

I expose this 'near culinary misadventure' for only one reason: If my Nigerian friends and I can-not agree about what to eat for lunch, I am sure setting a national agenda to rectify the 'intellectual schism' that exists in our society will be akin to pulling teeth without anesthesia. A national sovereign conference as suggested by many may be one platform where the beginnings of such an agenda could take shape.

SOME SUGGESTIONS AND STRATEGIES

1) Improving our Educational system

The first task here would be to pull together the 'best and brightest experienced minds' in education to help us achieve some of the following goals:

A) Revamping our entire educational system. This will require great leadership and financial commitment. There is an important role for government and the Private Sector here. What have the Multinational Oil Corporations done for Nigerians after nearly 50 years of oil profits? Herein lies their opportunity.

B) There needs to be an increased emphasis on excellence, accountability and performance at all levels. Schools that persistently perform poorly should be identified, supported or closed with an appropriate disposition for affected students.

C) Stream lining excessive proliferation of educational institutions without jeopardizing educational opportunity

D) Developing a unified national curriculum at the 3 levels of education that aims for the highest possible standards while taking cultural and religious diversity into account

E) Improving teacher quality through better training and improved salaries and benefits

F) Encouraging and sustaining a reading and book culture. The Nigerian Book Foundation, ANA etc can play a salient role here

G) Finally, starting small and making steady, incremental progress

2) Developing a Culture of Institutional and Intellectual Philanthropy

We should encourage extremely wealthy Nigerians to make a commitment to Nigeria's development by taking part in our intellectual and educational transformation. What's in it for them you may ask? Having their names emblazoned for centuries on buildings, centers, edifices that grace our institutions if they contribute generously to the erection of such structures and the improvement of our institutions. There are other opportunities for permanent connection to intellectual celebrity when these individuals contribute to the endowment of university academic chairs. The money they donate will make it possible for institutions to recruit superstar intellectuals they would ordinarily not be able to afford. In return these superstars of the academic firmament would bear academic titles honoring the benefactors. For instance, Toni Morrison, the Nobel Laureate, a millionaire in her own right, whose career displayed an overwhelming commitment to the intellectual development of America, was for decades the Robert F. Goheen Professor, Council of the Humanities, at Princeton University and Kwame Appiah, the Ghanaian philosopher and aristocrat, at one time was the Laurance S. Rockefeller University Professor of Philosophy at the same institution.

The idea of philanthropy driven intellectual development is as 'old as the hills'. In the 1500s the Medici family of Florence was the chief benefactor of the great Galileo. Howard Hughes, the eccentric American billionaire, left his money after his death to The Howard Hughes Medical Institute in Chevy Chase, MD. According to the institute's website:

"At the end of fiscal year 2015, the Institute had $18.2 billion in diversified net assets, making it America's largest private supporter of academic biomedical research."

Their grants are responsible for cutting edge bio-medical research in Cystic Fibrosis, channel membrane signaling, Muscular Dystrophy, and Juvenile Diabetes. We have already discussed earlier the significance of institutional endowment and the advantages of such investments in the development of the advanced nations. Similar benefits await Nigeria.

3) Addressing immediately potential implosive developments

A recent study focusing on education in Eastern Nigeria showed that Anambra males in particular were dropping out of school at an alarming rate. Most of these young men were opting for business opportunities in the markets. As gloomy as this may seem, I see a silver lining here. We must make education relevant for these individuals. Why don't we institute academic paths for these young men that will lead them to business degrees and probably MBAs?

In advanced nations, every single financial and economic center – New York, Chicago, San Francisco, Philadelphia, Boston, London, Tokyo, Paris etc. -- has an excellent Business School. We already have the Lagos Business School. We must now replicate this idea in Onitsha and Aba, Ibadan, Kano and Kaduna. I am sure we can convince OMATA in Onitsha that an investment to construct a grand and excellent business school and recruit business professors to transform their young men from "traders" to "world class business men" would be in their own self-interest. Our society would reap the rewards of **finally** creating "intellectual business leaders" that would be compatriots in our nation's development as opposed to agents of political and social chaos as we have witnessed in the recent history of Nigerian politics.

4) A role for the Telecommunications/ Information Technology revolution

We are witnessing a steady and rapid revolution in the telecommunications sector in Nigeria. Recent launched satellites, establishment of 500 base stations and news of investment pouring into this sector to the tune of $4 billion over the past several years is encouraging. Better telecommunications will mean increased access to the internet and therefore entrée into the information age that the rest of the world is enjoying. In the 21st century, this access will mean admittance to avenues of commerce, science, the arts and education, and thus intellectual and material power. There is thus a critical part for the IT revolution to play in the envisioned intellectual re-invigoration of Nigeria.

5) The Role of the Press

An American colleague of mine who has visited Nigeria over a dozen times asked me this question recently: "Why do your journalists gravitate towards the most vulgar, corrupt and disdainful Nigerians...reporting their every utterance?" "Surely, they must realize the power they possess to ignore these individuals and help set a national agenda for Nigeria's development?"

Rather than criticize the press, I will only encourage the intellectuals amongst them to help raise the quality of the dialogue surrounding national issues through editorials and articles. It would be refreshing to see more pieces that ask probing questions of our office holders and hold them accountable for mismanagement. Wherever did the practice of exposing government corruption etc. disappear to? I certainly hope it did not die with Dele Giwa.

Celebratory profiles of honest, talented individuals within government would also help to reset national values particularly amongst the youth. My Harvard colleague is right: The Media holds immense power. I am sure they realize it. One can only hope they become allies in this intellectual journey.

6) Democracy as a tool for Intellectual change

Perhaps the most crucial part of this entire process is the involvement of talented, honest "intellectuals" in national politics. There has been a steady and almost pathological apathy amongst the members of this group for years. They have taken the back seat as followers instead of leaders of our potentially great country, watching as we have slipped steadily into near oblivion in the hands of less capable individuals. It is time that we see greater direct political involvement, organization and activism from this group.

WE THE PEOPLE movement is a nationwide movement of the grassroots engineered by Nigerian intellectuals and professionals for a new Nigeria. The goal is to grow a new breed of WE THE PEOPLE in Nigeria who will commit to a corrupt-free Nigeria in their personal lives. Through education and dialogue, the group hopes to transform individual Nigerians, one person at a time, in a national movement that will clean Nigeria up from bottom-to-top. Detailed information about this movement and how to join the movement is presented in the Postface of this book, following the last chapter in the book. The movement hopes to attain the critical mass in numbers required to take back Nigeria, through their votes, from worthless and corrupt leaders and legislatures who have held Nigeria hostage. Through the movement, sound honest intellectuals with character and integrity will be encouraged to run for political office.

Having said that, I must acknowledge the serious difficulties on the ground for most 'honest' Nigerians who do not have the benefit of a 'looted stash of cash from the national treasury' to buy their way into power and influence. One suggestion is to form coalitions among the like-minded to raise funds. Another is to push through a Nigerian version of campaign finance reform in the Senate that limits the amount of money any one individual can spend from his/her private funds for campaign/election purposes. I already foresee difficulties implementing these suggestions, simplistic as some may seem, in present day Nigeria. At least it will be a beginning in an evolving system that aspires to fairness and equality.

7) Borrowing a Leaf (Or Two) From America

The United States of America is without a doubt the world's largest and most successful economy. Like Nigeria, its history has not been perfect. America has had to wrestle with its own demons such as slavery, racism, and other grave constitutional, political, and social, intellectual incongruities. Through it all, however, this country of "conscience," has been able to fashion for itself one of the highest standards of living ever attained in history!

Pundits believe that this success was made possible in part by what has become one of the most admired and effective documents in history – The American Constitution. This intellectual record is the foundation of America's much celebrated Democracy, an idea borrowed from the ancient Athenians, defined by Lincoln during his mythical Gettysburg Address as "a government of the people, by the people, and for the people" and emulated around the world.

America's prosperity and global dominance today is not accidental. It was meticulously charted by its constitution, protected by its democracy, and guided by a succession of above average to excellent leaders, armed with world-class education and imbued (for the most part), with enviable intellectual dexterity. There is much Nigeria's burgeoning democracy can learn from this great country.

References

[1]http://etext.lib.virginia.edu/jefferson/quotations/jeff060 0.htm
[2] United Nations University Public Affairs Unit Lecture Series 2003
[3] Phrase initially used by Chinua Achebe in *The Trouble with Nigeria*: Chinua Achebe, *Trouble with Nigeria,* Fourth Dimension Publishers, Enugu, Nigeria, 1983, p.16.
[4] Excerpt from Chinua Achebe *Home and Exile*. Chinua Achebe *Home and Exile* Oxford University Press, 2000

[5] From the Essay by Chinua Achebe *The Role of the Writer in a New Nation*, Nigeria Magazine, 81, 1964, p157-160

[6] http://www.ccel.org/h/henry/mhc2/MHC21010. HTM.

[i]http://www.cnn.com/2007/US/law/09/20/jena.six/index.html

"Jena's racial tensions were aggravated in August 2006, when three white teens hung the nooses the day after a group of black students received permission from school administrators to sit under the tree -- a place where white students normally congregated.

The guilty students were briefly suspended from classes, despite the principal's recommendation they be expelled, according to Donald Washington, U.S. attorney for the Western District of Louisiana."

"About three months after the nooses were discovered, six teens, dubbed the Jena 6, were accused of beating classmate Justin Barker. The six -- Mychal Bell, Robert Bailey Jr., Carwin Jones, Bryant Purvis, Theo Shaw and Jesse Ray Beard -- were originally charged with attempted second-degree murder and conspiracy, according to LaSalle Parish District Attorney Reed Walters."

"Bell, the only one of the six who remains in jail, was to be sentenced Thursday after convictions for aggravated second-degree battery and conspiracy to do the same, but both charges have been vacated, awaiting further action by the district attorney.

Charges for Bailey, Jones and Shaw also were reduced to battery and conspiracy when they were arraigned, while Purvis still awaits arraignment. The charges for Beard, who was 14 at the time of the alleged crime, are unavailable because he's a juvenile."

[ii] Clarence Page, Chicago Tribune, **_Don't get hung up on nooses in the news_**, _October 17, 2007_

http://www.chicagotribune.com/news/columnists/chi-oped1017pageoct17,1,4103731.column

[iii]Picture from http://www.eac-magazine.com/images/stories/AfricaNigeria/SOMALIA-News.jpg within the text of article _of Africa is not a country_ by Chris Ezeh

[iv] (GDP is defined as the total market value of all the goods and services produced within a country during a specified period, normally one calendar year.)

Also
http://www.economywatch.com/world_economy/china

[v] CIA fact book, 2015

[vi]
http://staff.washington.edu/saki/strategies/101/oppression.htm

These notes give an overview of Pharr's discussion on Oppression in the United States and the systematic and organized way it can be used to keep power in the hands of a dominant few.

[Vii] Deutsch, M. (1973). The resolution of conflict: Constructive and destructive processes. New Haven, Conn.: Yale University Press; Deutsch, M. and Coleman, P.T. (2000). The handbook of conflict resolution: Theory and

Practice. San Francisco: Jossey-Bass; Deutsch, M. and Collins, M.E. (1951). Interracial housing. Minneapolis, MA: University of Minnesota.

[viii]http://en.wikipedia.org/wiki/Pedagogy_of_the_Oppressed

[ix]Ibid

[x]Ibid

[xi]Deutsch, M. (1973). The resolution of conflict: Constructive and destructive processes. New Haven, Conn.: Yale University Press; Deutsch, M. and Coleman, P.T. (2000). The handbook of conflict resolution: Theory and

Practice. San Francisco: Jossey-Bass; Deutsch, M. and Collins, M.E. (1951). Interracial housing. Minneapolis, MA: University of Minnesota.

[xii] Ibid

[xiii] http://staff.washington.edu/saki/strategies/101/oppression.htm

These notes give an overview of Pharr's discussion on Oppression in the United States and the systematic and organized way it can be used to keep power in the hands of a dominant few.

[xiv] Ibid

[xv] Ibid

[xvi] http://staff.washington.edu/saki/strategies/101/oppression.htm

These notes give an overview of Pharr's discussion on Oppression in the United States and the systematic and organized way it can be used to keep power in the hands of a dominant few.

[xvii] Ibid

[xviii]Deutsch, M. (1973). The resolution of conflict:

Constructive and destructive processes. New Haven, Conn.: Yale University Press; Deutsch, M. and Coleman, P.T. (2000). The handbook of conflict resolution: Theory and

Practice. San Francisco: Jossey-Bass; Deutsch, M. and Collins, M.E. (1951). Interracial housing. Minneapolis, MA: University of Minnesota.

[xix] Deutsch, M. (1973). The resolution of conflict: Constructive and destructive processes. New Haven, Conn.: Yale University Press; Deutsch, M. and Coleman, P.T. (2000). The handbook of conflict resolution: Theory and

Practice. San Francisco: Jossey-Bass; Deutsch, M. and Collins, M.E. (1951). Interracial housing. Minneapolis, MA: University of Minnesota.

[xx] Ibid.

[xxi] http://dictionary.reference.com/browse/mediocrity

[xxii] Dulue Mbachu, Nigeria Seeks Domestic Oil Control, Tuesday November 20, 12:05 pm ET, Associated Press.

[xxiii]http://en.wikipedia.org/wiki/Servant_leadership

[xxiv] Ibid

[xxv] Ibid

[xxvi] Ibid

[xxvii]http://etext.lib.virginia.edu/jefferson/quotations/jeff 0600.htm

[xxviii]http://en.wikipedia.org/wiki/Pedagogy_of_the_Opp ressed

[xxix] Paul Roberts, *The End of Oil: On the Edge of a Perilous New World* -- see **http://www.motherjones.com/news/qa/2004/05/pa**

ul_rob_qa.html

And

http://www.amazon.com/exec/obidos/ASIN/0618239774/q
id=1088948208/sr=2-1/ref=sr_2_1/103-4591855-
6171048.)

[xxx] CIA: Unclassified study of the Oil industry in Nigeria,

(Web   site:
http://www.electrifyingtimes.com/deltadawn.html)

[xxxi] Karl Meier, Bloomberg News Agency, June 10, 2004

Also Interviews of former Nigerian and Biafran soldiers,
diplomats and government officials

[xxxi] McCaskie, T. C. 1997. "Nigeria" *Africa South of the
Sahara 1998* London: Europa.

[xxxi] Ibid Nelson, Harold. 1982. *Nigeria: a country study*
Washington: U.S. Government Printing Office.

CHAPTER 18

The A, B, C of How to Transform Nigeria Permanently

Prof. Peter U. Nwangwu, M.Sc Pharm.D PhD FACCP FASCP

Introduction

There are at least eight key problems we must solve to create a new Nigeria. I have used A, B, C to introduce these problems, because it is as easy as A, B, C to understand that these problems are hurting Nigeria and Nigerians direly. The will to solve the problems must be there in Nigerian leaders. Nigeria needs honest leaders with integrity who will focus on these needs as highest needs of the Nigerian people, give energy and impetus to solving them so they can create a new Nigeria for the benefit of WE THE PEOPLE.

- Agriculture and Food Security
- Bribery, corruption, and rule of law
- Crime and Insecurity
- Democracy and National Development
- Economy and Unemployment
- (In)Frastructural Development and Residency Rights
- Genuine Education (Not Schooling) and Youth Development
- Healthcare and Protection of Life

1. Agricultural Development and Food Security

Agricultural economy is strategic to national development, especially in developing countries. Agriculture is not just for providing food, raw materials, employment and income for the citizens. The export of agricultural products brings significant foreign exchange, with positive effect on the country's balance of payment and availability of foreign exchange to support economic development. A stagnant agricultural sector hinders growth of the rest of the economy and limits the resources available to promote development. The agricultural sector is the fundamental breeding ground for industrial and technological growth and technical change. Evidence from the history of national development shows that no country ever achieved significant technological development and productivity improvements without significant growth in agriculture[24]. Agricultural growth and development is indispensable for poverty reduction and equitable national prosperity.

Food is a biological necessity of man. Ensuring food security as a national agenda is good politics. Adequate food consumption fosters the formation of human capital for better quality of labor force, and increased national economic productivity. With hunger, under-nourishment or malnutrition, the national labor force cannot be healthy or perform productively. Adequate food and nutritional security will assure peace, law and order. Rising food prices and hunger have led to angry and violent protests and riots in many parts of the world. A slow growing and comatose agricultural sector can precipitate widespread national inflationary pressures. If national food supply does not keep pace with population growth, food price-induced pressure will reverberate all over the national economy. In many developing countries of the world, including Nigeria, some households spend up to 67 percent of their income on food[25].

---

[24] See Johnston, B.F. & Mellor, J.W. (1961) 'The Role of Agriculture in Economic Development', AMERICAN ECONOMIC REVIEW 51(4): 566-593

[25] See Anita Regmi, M.M. Deepak, James L. Seale Jr. & Jason Bernstein (2001) 'Cross-Country Analysis of Food Consumption Patterns' in Regmi, A. (ed.) CHANGING STRUCTURE OF GLOBAL FOOD CONSUMPTION AND TRADE, Market and Trade Division,

Therefore, even the most modest sudden rise in food prices can deplete their purchasing power, increase economic desperation, lower living standards and lead to acute food insecurity.

At Nigeria's independence in 1960, agriculture attributed to 64 percent of the nation's GDP. In addition, export of agricultural commodities accounted for up to 83 percent of national revenue and foreign exchange income. With the oil boom of the early 1970's crude oil overtook agriculture as the largest contributor of national government revenue and foreign exchange income. By 1970, crude oil share of total exports reached 58 percent, while agriculture share of total exports dropped from 83 percent in 1960 to 30 percent in 1970. By 1974, crude oil share of total exports rose to 92 percent, while agricultural share of total exports dwindled to less than 5 percent. The big surge in crude oil revenue in the early 1970's led to dramatic but inefficient and artificial increase in the economy, fueled by sharp rise in public spending and the attendant waste and phenomenal rise in corruption. Since oil revenues were not efficiently deployed to promote true national development and diversification of national income through non-oil sectors, agricultural growth suffered greatly and lagged behind population growth rate, leading to huge national expenditure on necessary food imports. In addition, the oil boom resulted in overvalued exchange rate, which caused dramatic loss of competitiveness of Nigeria's non-oil exports, especially agriculture. Oil revenues were wrongly used to promote higher levels of public and private consumption, rather than investing in productive and performing assets to assure sustainable increase in national productivity and incomes.

Despite successive and diverse economic blueprints over the years, the Nigerian economy remains undiversified and highly lopsided and skewed, as crude oil still accounts for more than 95 percent of total national export revenues and up to 80 − 85 percent of total government revenues, but

Economic Research Srrvice, U.S Department of Agriculture, Agriculture and Trade Department, (May): 14-22.

contributes less than 4 percent of total employment. Stagnant and neglected agricultural sector contributes above 60 percent of total employment in the nation. Today in Nigeria, agricultural imports far exceed agricultural exports. While agricultural imports amount to over N500 billion annually, agricultural exports are less than N100 billion. Deficient and inefficient fish production has necessitated massive fish importation. While national demand for fish is estimated at about 2.6 million metric tons in 2008, local supply was only about 600,000 metric tons resulting to estimated high annual import of about 700,000 metric tons of fish, at annual import expenditure of over 500 million US dollars on fish alone. Furthermore, whereas Nigeria has potential competitive advantage in many agricultural commodities, including crops and livestock, the unwholesome combination of low yields, high post-harvest losses, and low value addition gave rise to low levels of international competitiveness. For example, Nigeria cassava and rice economies and production efficiency compares very poorly with comparator countries like Malaysia, Indonesia and Thailand. The fact that Nigeria spends above 3 billion US dollars annually on food imports, especially wheat, rice, sugar, vegetable oil and fish, indicates existence of national food deficit from inadequate local agriculture productivity. It is estimated that about 30 percent of livestock slaughtered in Nigeria are imported from neighboring countries.

Meager private sector capital investment, unstable and grossly inadequate public and government expenditure, poor agricultural products to agro-processing and industrial manufacturing activity, grossly inefficient and poorly utilized irrigation systems, low integrity and credibility of government and institutional policies including contradictions, discontinuities, planning without facts and lack of political will, are additional man-made problems that have greatly oppressed the development of the agricultural sector in Nigeria.

Nigerian leaders should engineer a spirited and energetic paradigm shift in our agricultural development from production-oriented to market-led, from farming as a production module to profitable business enterprise module, from sporadic and unstable funding to stable, systematic, sustained funding, from inconsistency and discontinuity in policies, from blind open-ended public subsidies to targeted, focused, object-oriented public subsidy, from import-laden sluggish agricultural exercise to dynamic and potent export-efficient agricultural business enterprise.

Despite the obvious pivotal role of improved technology and equipment and modern inputs and methods in accelerating agricultural productivity, agricultural production in present-day Nigeria is characterized by very low incidence of use of modern inputs such as fertilizer, irrigation, improved seeds and agrochemicals.

Smallholders cultivating less than two hectares of farmland produce more than 90 percent of the total national crop output in Nigeria. Nigerian leaders should create the right economic climate and policy that will stimulate the private sector to engage in very profitable large-scale mechanized farming, and take advantage of the benefit of improved technology and modern inputs in a nationwide agricultural revolution. Nigerian leaders should exercise good governance through sensible and consistent policies and services to the private sector, designed to exercise sovereign responsibilities in setting intelligent rules that will provide for public good, mitigating externalities such as undue competition from imports, and maintaining national law and order. For agricultural development to become effective and sustainable, our national policies and programmes must be based on research insights from our universities and agricultural institutes. We must connect university agricultural research to private sector agricultural enterprise. Large scale mechanized farming in America has made food security in America second to none in the world. American farmers produce so much food that the American government actively pays some of the farmers not to produce any more food. I know we can bring some of these idle farmers to engage in the private sector in Nigeria in highly spirited and efficient large scale mechanized farming. The technology for massive and rapid breeding of cows through artificial insemination is well known and established. Nigerian government should engage the private sector business community in very large scale production of cows by artificial insemination. Fish farming should also be stimulated in abundance in Nigeria. Export of agricultural products as a very significant source of government revenues and high foreign exchange earnings should be restored as in the days before the oil boom.

Nigeria can become a great and beautiful prosperous country. Section 16(1)(a) of chapter 2 of the Nigerian Constituition states, "The State shall, within the context of the ideals and objectives for which provisions are made in this Constitution; (a) harness the resources of the nation and promote national prosperity and an efficient, dynamic and self-reliant economy. Unfortunately, most Nigerian presidents since 1970 have focused on crude oil export as the source of income for the nation, neglecting Agriculture and other resources of the nation. This does not uphold the Constituition of Nigeria, which demands that the government of Nigeria should harness all the resources of the nation, and promote national prosperity and an efficient, dynamic and self-reliant economy.

2. *Bribery, Corruption and Rule of Law*

Bribery, corruption and lawlessness, or selective enforcement of the law, must be dissolved through severe and immediate punishment of all offenders at all levels without exception. We should invest in a potent, adequate and very clean law enforcement command that will restore and maintain sanity and proper respect for law at all levels nationwide. We should stimulate and facilitate integrity, accountability, and transparency as a way of life in Nigeria at all levels, beginning with the President and everyone in his cabinet, as clear examples for the nation. Sometimes the problem with enforcing the law in Nigeria and punishing offenders severely, especially in matters of bribery, corruption and rule of law is that some of our leaders are themselves guilty of bribery, corruption and lawlessness, which renders them impotent in punishing offenders severely. The new Nigeria of our dreams needs a President and cabinet with a very clean and compelling history. The President should have no godfathers, and no debilitating alliances; his total allegiance is to the Nigerian grassroots. There should be nothing to hide and nobody to fear, so he can enforce the law efficiently at all levels.

Bribery, Corruption, and Lawlessness are a tri-pronged potent poison killing Nigeria. The power of this evil over Nigeria is more debilitating than any cancer. It is ruining Nigeria without mercy, and Nigeria may never survive as a nation if it does not get help against the onslaught of the tri-pronged potent poison. Unfortunately, most people in Nigeria do not even understand the great damage the tri-pronged killer of bribery, corruption, and lawlessness is inflicting daily on Nigeria. The eyes of Nigerian citizens are blind in seeing how much destruction Nigeria suffers daily from bribery, corruption and lawlessness. Some Nigerians who have lived in other countries of the world, especially United States of America, and United Kingdom may better understand the level of havoc and destruction the tri-pronged potent poison of bribery, corruption, and lawlessness is inflicting on Nigeria daily. Nigeria can be a good and great country, but bad leadership, and bad followership is destroying the country daily. A book released recently by the senate vice-president, Ike Ekweremadu is titled, "Who will Love my country". This an appropriate question for both leadership and followership in Nigeria. The eyes of both leadership and followership in Nigeria must be opened to see how bribery, corruption, and lawlessness are mercilessly destroying Nigeria daily. When our eyes are opened to the devastation and destruction of Nigeria by the tri-pronged poison, and if we have any love whatsoever for Nigeria, we will pause and reflect on ways to help Nigeria to recover and find freedom from a mortal avenger working hard persistently to destroy Nigeria.

President Buhari attempted to wage a war against corruption. He has focused on high profile cases. Where do you begin, how do you begin? It must feel like a thirsty man trying to drink water from a fire department water hydrant hose. I can tell you that Buhari has not opened up even 0.001% of the cases of abuse of the nation Nigeria by high profile Nigerians. For him, it must sometimes feel like chasing the wind. You do not know where the wind is coming from, or where it is going, but your task is to chase and catch the wind. Now, for every case of abuse of Nigeria by a high profile Nigerian, there must be 10,000 cases of abuse of Nigeria by low profile Nigerians. If we are fighting bribery and corruption to rid the nation of that evil, then we must also fight the cases of abuse of the nation by low profile Nigerians. So given this important fact, do we still believe that it is the job of the president to fight and destroy bribery and corruption in Nigeria? How will he do it? If you were the President, how will you do it, to really fight and end bribery and corruption everywhere and at every level in Nigeria?

This is where the WE THE PEOPLE project comes in. WE THE PEOPLE, the Nigerian grassroots, must save Nigeria from all kinds of abuses it has endured over many years. These are abuses from both leaders and followers. We are looking for and will mobilize a new breed of WE THE PEOPLE, one person at a time, decent and honorable Nigerians who want a new democratic and prosperous Nigeria. We want to do the right thing to help bring about a new and clean Nigeria. The new breed of WE THE PEOPLE in Nigeria will pledge to kill the tri-pronged poison of bribery, corruption, and lawlessness killing Nigeria. Beginning with me, I pledge to love Nigeria and help Nigeria survive the cancer of bribery, corruption, and lawlessness that has been eating Nigeria up mercilessly. In my honor as a new breed of WE THE PEOPLE;

1. I pledge never to demand for a bribe of even one penny from anyone
2. I pledge never to give a bribe to anyone as a condition of gaining a job or contract, etc
3. I pledge never to embezzle or loot public funds committed to my charge, or from anywhere in the public treasury
4. I pledge to be a law-abiding citizen, eschew lawlessness at all

times and at every level

5. I pledge to do the right thing before God and man always to the best of my ability

These five pledges will guide and propel my life and affairs as a new breed of WE THE PEOPLE. I shall endeavor to do for Nigeria the additional duty and act of love by recruiting daily other Nigerians of all tribes and religions who will become a new breed of WE THE PEOPLE, by making the pledges above and joining this national movement of the new breed of WE THE PEOPLE, to love and serve Nigeria. This national mass movement of the new breed of WE THE PEOPLE seeks to clean Nigeria up from bottom-to-top. This movement to clean Nigeria from bottom-to-top is the only realistic hope for Nigeria. We will grow in numbers, one person at a time, Nigerians both at home and in the diaspora. One day, we will attain a critical mass that will ultimately erupt into a national movement of over 50 million people. When we attain to 50 million new breed of WE THE PEOPLE who made the five pledges above, we shall dissolve and neutralize the tri-pronged poison of bribery, corruption, and lawlessness; we will clean Nigeria up from bottom-to-top, Nigeria will be a better place to live. This movement to clean up Nigeria from bottom-to-top is a non-governmental organization (NGO) of decent men and women in Nigeria tired of the current decadence in Nigeria. It is a registered NGO and there will be a directory of members, with their contact information, which shall be protected.

3. Crime and Insecurity

Consider and reflect on the following thoughts and truths regarding crime and insecurity.

- In a dynamic economy where people who want to work are

employed and paid, crime and insecurity will be low.

- Violent conflicts (such as Boko Haram, the Jos crisis, and the Niger Delta militants) have their origins in human insecurity. Generally, insecurity is linked to exclusion and lack of access to resources and power.
- The concept of human security emphasizes the protection of people from grave threats to their lives, safety from harm and violent conflict, and empowerment and adequate control over such social threats as disease, crime and extreme poverty.
- Human security as defined by the United Nations is "freedom from fear and freedom from want."
- Infusing the classroom with the culture of human rights, a sense of equity and inclusion, social justice and equality is fundamental to security in society. How can we speak of or hope for the right to personal security in a society where the school environment is infested with learners and educators who abuse each other verbally, physically and even sexually?
- The virtue and value of debate, discussion and dialogue for security rests on the understanding that a society that knows how to talk and how to listen does
not need to resort to violence
- Psychological insecurity and a poor sense of self-worth which relies on materialism, a lifestyle of ostentation, and external psychological props such as vain titles is the source of most crimes and corruption in Nigeria

We should pursue and implement deliberate aggressive business-friendly government policies that will stimulate private sector business and economic development at a level that will markedly energize private sector job creation and drastically cut down unemployment by 90 – 95 percent. By creating such dynamic economy where people who want to work are employed and paid, crime and insecurity in Nigeria will die a natural death. In addition, an honest and open but focused administration and a leadership style characterized by consensus building, inclusion and accountability shall dissolve and remove all those insecurity and violent conflicts and crime (such as Boko Haram, the Jos crisis, Niger Delta militants, kidnapping) linked to exclusion and lack of access to resources and power. Furthermore, we should teach the nation by good example, the virtue and value of debate, discussion and dialogue because security rests on the understanding that a society that knows how to talk and how to listen does not need to resort to violence.

4. *Democracy and National Development*

A democratic society is characterized by the following:

- Political leaders and representatives selected through elections are completely answerable and accountable to the people
- Individual freedom and personal liberties are guaranteed by the rule of law
- The will of the majority prevails, but minority rights are respected
- The primary function of the government is to protect the safety, wellbeing, economic and human rights of the citizens who elected the government leaders.
- The citizens are able to develop their full capacities in freedom, which respects and encourages individuality and diversity
- A sense of equity, social justice and equality in the mindset and lifestyle of both leaders and citizens is a fundamental requirement for democracy
- Democracy is not a status that is invoked, claimed or talked about, but an experience and way of life that is practiced. It cannot be taught, but must be learned through authentic experience

- Inclusion and consensus building is the pivotal element of a successful democracy
- Democracy is characterized by fair distributive and social justice. If democracy fails to provide for justly distributed socio-economic development, human security is likely to be threatened. The practice of assigning oil blocks belonging to the people of Nigeria to a select few Nigerians does not demonstrate distributive and social justice in Nigeria. All oil blocks rightfully belonging to the people of Nigeria which have been assigned to a select few Nigerians must be revoked and revert back to the Nigerian Federal government for the people of Nigeria. The blocks should be developed by the Federal government on behalf of, and for the benefit of the entire people of Nigeria.
- The quality of the democratic process, including transparent and accountable government, and equality of all before the law, is critical, and should be demonstrated daily in government policies, and the judicial systems.
- Democracy is more than arrangements for the allocation of political power; the emphasis is not on the political system, rather the emphasis is on a democratic society and way of life where all citizens respect the rights of other, and the rule of law is equitably enforced daily nationwide without any exception.
- True democracy is deeply rooted in literate and engaged citizens with human values. Literacy, a sound moral sense through proper education, not schooling, is fundamental to a democratic society. The difference between proper education and schooling is discussed in depth in the chapter on education.

By due reflection on the above truths about democracy, it is obvious that Nigeria is not a democratic society. We talk about democracy but do not live in democracy and have never experienced true democracy as a nation. The grassroots in Nigeria are even denied their fundamental right to elect their own leaders. We witness widespread selection and imposition of candidates in primaries by the leadership of all parties in Nigeria. We witness aspirants, even presidential aspirants, who shamelessly bribe delegates to secure their votes. It is an open secret in society that the vote of the delegates goes to the highest bidder, not necessarily the most qualified person to do the job. A variety of mechanisms are available to party officials to manipulate votes with impunity. Where is the democracy? What do we know of a democratic society? Nigerian presidents should teach the nation through their example the true meaning of democracy. They should allow the nation to experience authentic democracy at all levels as a way of life in society.

- National development is defined as a process of economic, social, political and cultural change engineered in a given society by the efforts of all stakeholders, both internal and external, including the local communities, the governments, the private sector, civil society organizations, NGOs and financial and technical partners, with a view to improving the conditions of life of the entire population of that nation in a sustainable manner.
- National development requires the formation of responsible human capital and social capital, which requires true education, and continuing education, including adult education.
- True national development entails meeting the needs of the present, without compromising the ability of future generations to meet their own needs.
- Lack of recognition of the need to involve civil society, especially grassroots organizations, by giving them a voice in decision-making and the means to participate effectively in society building is one of the major causes of development failure in many African countries. Abuse of human rights, corruption, and social injustice leading to the exclusion of important segments of society is a stumbling block to

economic and social progress and usually paves the way to violent conflicts.

We talk about National Development in Nigeria, but do not appear to understand or respect the fundamental truths that drive true National Development. Nigerian leaders should pursue a broad-based policy of inclusion by involving civil society, especially grassroots organizations, on national development matters. Abuse of human rights, corruption, favoritism and other social injustices leading to the exclusion of any one, or important segments of society, must be dissolved.

5. *Economy and Unemployment*

The economy of Nigeria is dependent mainly on a single product – crude oil. Our past leaders have lacked the creative initiative and energy to diversify our national source of revenue. Before the advent of crude oil, Nigeria did well with being the world's largest supplier of groundnuts. Palm oil, palm kernel, hydes and skin, cocoa, coal and mineral ore were other sources of national revenue that sustained Nigeria. The economy was better, and unemployment was minimal compared with now. With the advent of crude oil our leaders neglected the other economic sources of revenue that sustained us as a nation. With relatively large revenue from crude oil, the greed and propensity to steal and misappropriate money rose astronomically to the point of stupidity with many of our past leaders, their cabinet, and political party. Private sector economic development activity in Nigeria is comatose because of poor infrastructure and utilities, government policies that frustrate business development, very high interest rate for business development loans from commercial banks, lack of creative initiatives and incentives from government to stimulate private sector business development and job creation. Through deliberate aggressive business-friendly government policies, we should drive a potent economic development enterprise everywhere in the nation, expand and diversify sources of national revenue, cause significant economic impact to the community. Our activities should include expansion of industrial output and creation of new industries, with inevitable creation of significant new jobs. Such deliberate aggressive business-friendly government policies should also include significant tax moratorium on all new businesses, tax rebates for new job creation, and government guaranteed single digit interest rates on loans from commercial banks for business expansion. These measures will stimulate the economy remarkably, and drastically reduce unemployment by over 90 percent.

6. (In)Frastructure Development and Residency Rights

Part of the problem with our near primitive infrastructure is that for a long time Nigerian government owned and controlled the business of infrastructural development, including supply of basic utilities such as electricity and water. Even when government eventually realized its errors and decided to privatize, government carried out the privatization in a very corrupt manner. Corrupt unworkable privatization happens when those in government sell the assets of government utility companies to themselves and their friends. Such corrupt privatization exercise is primitive because the large white elephants they sold to themselves are still worthless and inefficient to operate. Infrastructural development projects, including utilities such as electricity and water should be private sector business projects under proper development incentives by government. In addition, it is impossible for one company to supply electricity to a large region. A town like Lagos should have at least 30 different utility companies who generate and supply electricity and compete for the business of Lagosians based on price and efficiency of their service to the people of Lagos. We should create the right conditions and incentives to attract hundreds of infrastructural development companies from all over the world who will come and compete for the business of Nigerians based on competitive pay, efficiency, and quality of services and products. The government will require that Nigerians will be co-owners and shareholders in these infrastructural development companies so that Nigerians will share in the profits of the business of these companies. We know these companies and have the skills to negotiate terms and conditions with them that will benefit Nigeria and Nigerians greatly. In the course of time, the infrastructure will begin to work well in Nigeria as they work well in America. The modern miracle called Dubai is a fine example of a government who had the skill to engage the private sector business community of the world to remarkably transform the infrastructure of an underdeveloped desert country into a modern infrastructural paradise, in our interdependent global village.

On the matter of residency rights, Nigerian law stipulates that all citizens of Nigeria are equal under the law, without discrimination based on sex, religion, or state of origin. This law must be enforced in full to have a fair, just and free Nigeria. Sadly today, Nigerian citizens who live lawfully as legal residents outside their state of origin are denied their basic fundamental rights because they are not indigenes of that state. Residency rights should be developed and enforced in Nigeria, just as it is enforced in America and many nations of the world. State of origin should be replaced with state/place of residence. If youth service outside your state of origin is helpful in creating a more cohesive Nigeria, then a Nigerian who is not discriminated against in any way by virtue of his/her state of origin is more likely to defend the unity of Nigeria vigorously as envisaged in our national pledge. In America and many civilized countries of the world, citizens get employment and run for political office based on their state of residence, not on their state of origin.

7. *Genuine Education (Not Schooling) and Youth Development*

We need a new brand of Nigerian youths who are intelligent, diligent, disciplined, patriotic, selfless, dependable, and committed to a new Nigeria free from bribery, corruption, and lawlessness. Appropriately, the role of the Nigerian youth in building a new Nigeria that we can all be proud of has been robustly presented in Chapter 14 of this book.

Also, because the scope of our needs as a nation in the education and development of our youths is so vast the subject has been extensively discussed in Chapter 16 of this book, "Transforming the Nigerian Educational System for a more Prosperous and Progressive Nigeria".

Thus chapters 14 and 16 have comprehensively addressed the Genuine Education (Not Schooling) and Youth Development needs of Nigeria. If the suggestions and ideas presented in these chapters were taken on board, we would have an education system that would compare favorably with those of the more developed nations and turnout well-rounded youths, who would be ready to play effective roles in the task of building a new Nigeria, free from corruption, lawlessness, indiscipline and all the vices already addressed in this book.

8. *Healthcare and Protection of Life*

In this 21st century, Nigeria does not have even one world-class hospital where equipment, facilities, standard of care and medical practice can be compared favorably with the standard at leading hospitals in the world. Nigerian leaders and affluent Nigerians travel to different parts of the world to receive medical treatment because our leaders have not invested in the development of even one world-class hospital in the country. Unfortunately, over 99 percent of Nigerians cannot afford to fly overseas and pay for medical treatment when they are ill. There should be a law forbidding the Nigerian president and all government officials from going overseas for medical treatment, and definitely not at government expense. If our leaders know that they cannot go overseas to receive medical treatment, then they will be forced to invest in developing a world-class hospital in Nigeria, which will give other Nigerians the benefit of a world-class medical treatment in Nigeria for their own medical conditions.

Apart from development of world-class hospitals in Nigeria, our healthcare policies and priority are defective and feeble. The number one medical research and development need in this country is the development and commercialization of a malaria vaccine, because over one million people die in Nigeria every year from malaria, especially children. The development of any new drug is a very expensive exercise. If malaria was a major problem in America or England, I am certain that multiple malaria vaccines would already be available for commercial distribution. The science and technology for the development of a malaria vaccine is already in place. Nigeria should invest in malaria vaccine production as a priority. Mosquirix is the world's most advanced malaria vaccine in development. It was developed by Glaxo Smith Kline with financial support from the Bill and Melinda Gates Foundation. Mosquirix is in phase II clinical trials involving 16,000 children at 11 trial sites in seven countries. The company had plans to market the product by 2012. Mosquirix uses a recombinant protein that fuses part of the Falciparum circumsporozoite protein (CSP) with hepatitis B surface antigen.

Two other groups in Baltimore, Maryland, USA at John

Hopkins Malaria Research Institute, and Sanaria Corporation have done very interesting advanced work in malaria vaccine development. Sanaria uses an attenuated plasmodium falciparum sporozoite vaccine. The vaccine reported to be 90 percent effective, and is in early clinical trials. Kumar at John Hopkins used genetically modified bacteria to sabotage the life cycle of the malaria parasite. Nigeria cannot sit on the passenger seat with malaria vaccine development, because malaria kills more people in Nigeria every year than the rest of the world combined.

If we are indeed interested in preventative healthcare and protection of life in Nigeria, then we must sanitize Nigerian roads, because more adult lives are lost in unnecessary road accidents each year on Nigerian roads than the combination of the top five adult medical illnesses in Nigeria. There should be speed-limits on Nigerian roads which are vigorously enforced. Driver's license should not be sold on demand to illiterates who know nothing about driving or standard courtesies required of every road user. Driver education and practical driving training is a compelling need in Nigeria for protection of life on Nigerian roads, as an important life-saving preventative health preservation policy in Nigeria.

POSTFACE

The current political and economic landscape in Nigeria is a mess. Peoples' Democratic Party (PDP) had 16 years of incredible opportunity to build Nigeria into a safe, prosperous, progressive nation with social justice, level playing field for all, and entrepreneurial paradise for the many intelligent Nigerian youths. But they did not; they failed woefully. All Progressive Congress (APC), which is largely a group of disgruntled old PDP members promised CHANGE to WE THE PEOPLE. So far APC has not done any better than PDP in respecting the rights and privileges of WE THE PEOPLE as directed by the Constitution of Nigeria. The promised CHANGE has not come.

In spite of several trillion dollars in oil wealth since the early 1970's, Nigeria was a better, safer, more progressive, less corrupt society 60 years ago than now; almost free from the tribal and religious tensions, bigotry and prejudice that has so badly divided the Nigerian nation of today. Sixty years ago, many thousands of people from the Asian country of India flocked into Nigeria in search of the good life. Economic development in Nigeria was at par with or superior to Singapore, Malaysia, South Korea and Dubai. Made in China products were dreaded and avoided like a plague in Nigeria by Nigerians because of the poor quality. Nigeria was the world's largest producer and supplier of several agricultural products. These agricultural products were abandoned for crude oil sales by bad and short-sighted leaders.

Currently, Nigeria depends on crude oil for 80 percent of its national revenue and foreign exchange earnings; the price of oil has fallen from $100 to about $30 per barrel. Furthermore, America, which relied on Nigeria as its second highest supplier of crude oil, discovered massive quantities of oil in America and so decided not to buy crude oil from Nigeria anymore. In effect, it is not just that the price of crude oil, the primary source of income for Nigeria, fell from $100 to $30 per barrel, Nigeria's best customer for crude oil sales no longer needs Nigerian crude and so has stopped buying crude from Nigeria. The consequence is that Nigeria is in a tough economic mess at this time.

If Nigeria had good leaders, Nigeria should have been able to save nearly 50 percent of its national crude oil revenues during several profitable years when the price of crude was $100 and above per barrel. Nigeria did not. Instead Nigeria squandered the income mindlessly. Furthermore, Nigeria should have pursued a balanced economic development plan rather than abandon agriculture. In chapter 18 of this book, "The A, B, C of How to Transform Nigeria permanently, some of these issues were discussed in detail. Today Nigeria is in deep trouble because it is cash poor. This has precipitated government-induced poverty on WE THE PEOPLE of Nigeria. The level of pain and suffering in the country is massive and nationwide.

PDP is quick to blame APC for the current economic nightmare in Nigeria. They want to take back governance in Nigeria because they think they can do better than APC. However, if they cannot do well in Nigeria when the price of oil was $100 per barrel, what can they do for Nigeria now that crude price is $30 per barrel? Furthermore, America, the largest buyer of crude oil from Nigeria, no longer buys Nigerian crude. The massive level of corruption allowed by the PDP government in Nigeria has left deep injuries that Nigeria cannot heal from soon. What will PDP do now in Nigeria that they could not do in 16 years of governance in Nigeria?

WE THE PEOPLE, the grassroots of Nigeria, are sick and tired of corrupt and mindless Nigerian politicians who have abused WE THE PEOPLE continuously. Power belongs to WE THE PEOPLE. Since none of the current political parties can be trusted anymore with power, WE THE PEOPLE shall take back power from all the corrupt and mindless politicians.

WE THE PEOPLE must save Nigeria from further decay and collapse. For WE THE PEOPLE to accomplish this very important task, we need a new breed of WE THE PEOPLE in Nigeria; a new breed of clean, corruption-free, disciplined men and women from every tribe, religion and political persuasion who will solemnly pledge in total commitment to bond strongly as a united group and use their votes in a coordinated manner to elect cerebral intellectuals with integrity, wisdom and foresight to transform Nigeria at all levels.

The WE THE PEOPLE movement is a nationwide movement by a new breed of WE THE PEOPLE, the Nigerian grassroots, engineered by Nigerian intellectuals at home and in the diaspora to save Nigeria from further collapse. The book, WE THE PEOPLE, is an educational tool for the Nigerian people designed to convey the truths about the Nigerian condition and to change the mindset of individual Nigerians, one person at a time; we must have a new breed of clean WE THE PEOPLE at the bottom, the grassroots, to enable us clean up the top. WE are eager to build a strong united force of at least 50 million new breed of WE THE PEOPLE of the Federal Republic of Nigeria, from every tribe, religion, and political party; men and women of every age, economic class and from every ward of every local government in every state and the Federal Capital territory of Nigeria.

The WE THE PEOPLE PLEDGE is presented at the end of this Postface of the book. Please read the pledge carefully. If you can solemnly pledge to fulfill and abide by the stated commitments and thereby become a new breed of WE THE PEOPLE, we shall warmly welcome you into our fold, and will work with you to create a new totally transformed Nigeria. To register as a member of the WE THE PEOPLE movement, please visit: www.wethepeoplenigeria.org.

You know several people who are unhappy about the state of Nigeria today. Give them the opportunity to read the book, WE THE PEOPLE, and help them to become a new breed of WE THE PEOPLE, commit to the WE THE PEOPLE PLEDGE, and register to join the WE THE PEOPLE movement by visiting: www.wethepeoplenigeria.org. WE THE PEOPLE shall transform Nigeria completely for good, permanently. God will bless and renew Nigeria for good.

PROF. PETER U. NWANGWU, MSc Pharm.D PhD FACCP FASCP

WE THE PEOPLE PLEDGE

As a new breed of WE THE PEOPLE of Nigeria, I solemnly pledge to fulfill these commitments, no matter the price, and to support and bond with others who join us in our stand for a corruption-free Nigeria where social justice, liberty, equality for all, and good governance shall be enthroned as a normal way of life.

1. I pledge not to give or receive bribes, or participate in any corrupt practice whatsoever

2. I pledge to respect the dignity of other Nigerian citizens regardless of tribe or religion, to respect the rights and legitimate interests of others, and to live in peace, unity and harmony in the spirit of common brotherhood.

3. I pledge to honor and abide by the national ethics of Nigeria as outlined in the Constitution, which is Discipline, Integrity, Dignity of Labor, Social Justice, Religious Tolerance, Self-Reliance and Patriotism.

4. I pledge to bond with fellow new breed of WE THE PEOPLE of Nigeria, regardless of tribe, religion or political party affiliation; my commitment to WE THE PEOPLE shall override all other tribal, religious or political sectionalism, as we join hands to clean up Nigeria from bottom to top.

5. I pledge to fight corruption and bad governance in Nigeria by fully uniting with WE THE PEOPLE to cast our votes in a coordinated manner that will remove all corrupt and bad leaders and legislators and replace them with clean, capable and honest leaders and legislators with integrity, at every level of leadership and legislature everywhere in Nigeria.

THIS IS MY SOLEMN AND ABIDING PLEDGE, SO HELP ME GOD.

THE PEOPLE'S GRASSROOTS ASSOCIATION FOR A CORRUPTION-FREE NIGERIA

AIMS AND OBJECTIVES

1. To initiate a grassroots movement in the Federal Republic of Nigeria whereby the common man has the capacity and power to change the system for the better, through democratic processes.

2. To advocate for a new nation based on the principles of democracy, equity, and social justice for all regardless of race, religion, ethnicity, or gender.

3. To embark on projects and programs designed to transform Nigeria into a low-crime and prosperous nation for WE THE PEOPLE.

4. To embark on projects and programs designed to bring about a safe, decent, corruption-free, and law-abiding nation where there is a level playing field for all citizens.

5. To be constantly mindful of the voiceless poor of the Federal Republic of Nigeria, to be their abiding advocate, and to work tirelessly for their freedom and emancipation from government-induced poverty, from years of bad governance.

6. To educate WE THE PEOPLE, the grassroots of Nigeria, on accountability and corruption-free

practices as a daily, normal lifestyle.

7. To grow a new breed of WE THE PEOPLE from every tribe and religion in Nigeria who will commit to a clean way of life, and help clean-up Nigeria from bottom-to-top, one changed life at a time.

8. To grow into a strong and potent national association of a new breed of WE THE PEOPLE, with strong patriotic and democratic convictions, who will carefully and properly exercise their voting rights to reject corrupt leaders and legislatures, and support the election of clean men and women of integrity for public office and service throughout Nigeria.

9. To advocate for Governance founded on the Constitution, and deriving all its powers and authority from the Constitution, solely for the benefit and blessings of WE THE PEOPLE.

10. To help build a democratic framework that will serve as a model for Africa.

FOR DETAILS ON HOW TO JOIN THE ASSOCIATION, PLEASE VISIT:

www.wethepeoplenigeria.org.

---

www.ingramcontent.com/pod-product-compliance
Lightning Source LLC
Chambersburg PA
CBHW072004270326
41928CB00009B/1543